Michele Crepaz, Wiebke Marie Junk, Marcel Hanegraaff and Joost Berkhout
Viral Lobbying

Viral Politics

Volume 3

Michele Crepaz, Wiebke Marie Junk,
Marcel Hanegraaff and Joost Berkhout

Viral Lobbying

Strategies, Access and Influence During the
COVID-19 Pandemic

DE GRUYTER

Wiebke Marie Junk acknowledges funding from Tietgenprisen, awarded by the Danish Society for Education and Business (DSEB).
Marcel Hanegraaff acknowledges funding from the Dutch Research Council (NWO), as part of project 'Lobbying in the European Union' with NWO-Veni project number 451-16-016.

DSEB

Developing business since 1880

NWO

ISBN (Paperback) 978-3-11-078390-2
ISBN (Hardcover) 978-3-11-078305-6
e-ISBN (PDF) 978-3-11-078314-8
e-ISBN (EPUB) 978-3-11-079675-9
ISSN 2747-6863
e-ISSN 2747-6871
DOI https://doi.org/10.1515/9783110783148

Library of Congress Control Number: 2022944270

Bibliographic information published by the Deutsche Nationalbibliothek
The Deutsche Nationalbibliothek lists this publication in the Deutsche Nationalbibliografie; detailed bibliographic data are available on the internet at http://dnb.dnb.de.

Cover image: CROCOTHERY / iStock / Getty Images Plus
Printing and binding: CPI books GmbH, Leck

www.degruyter.com

Contents

Figures

Tables

Chapter 1
Viral Lobbying and the Influence Production Process

When the World Health Organisation (WHO) declared the state of *pandemic* on 11th March 2020, the extreme gravity and scope of the COVID-19 crisis became increasingly apparent. 'This is not just a public health crisis, it is a crisis that will touch every sector,' said Dr. Tedros Adhanom Ghebreyesus, WHO director-general, at a press briefing. 'So, every sector and every individual must be involved in the fights' (TIME 2021).

And they did, indeed, become involved: across all sectors and types of social and economic interests, groups mobilised to take part in the political debates about the consequences of COVID-19. In the face of tragically high numbers of human lives at stake, combined with vast economic, social and psychological consequences, a countless number of interest groups took part in suggesting different policy options to limit the spread of the virus, as well as to address the adverse effects of both the disease and the government interventions to fight the pandemic.

The peak association BusinessEurope, for instance, wrote in a position paper on March 16th 2020 that many businesses were 'already facing, or will face, severe financial pressures during the coming months' (BusinessEurope 2021). Moreover, the group urgently called for a set of policy measures 'to help maintain confidence across the business community, protect the business eco-system, and ensure that as many companies as possible survive the present difficulties and are able to help drive the economic recovery when restrictions related to the virus are lifted.' Other groups voiced different concerns, such as the vulnerable position of the elderly and people with pre-existing health conditions, or of children with learning difficulties and their psychological health when subject to social distancing rules.

All these efforts to express the interests of different social and economic groups during the pandemic and, ultimately, attempts to influence resulting policies, are a crucial part of *viral politics* (Chari and Rozas 2021). At the same time, an explicit focus on *interest groups* and *lobbying* is largely absent from recent studies of pandemic politics.[1] Typically, studies of pandemic politics focus on

---

1 Exceptions are a few studies that assess the effects of the pandemic on lobbying positions, biases in lobbying, and political access (Bonafont and Iborra 2021; Eady and Rasmussen 2021; Fuchs and Sack 2021; Junk et al. 2021).

other aspects, such as policy evaluations of and variation in government responses (Altiparmakis et al. 2021; Engler et al. 2021; Chari and Rozas 2021), power imbalances between political institutions (Bolleyer and Salát 2021), authorities' crisis communication (Petersen et al. 2021), and public support or political trust (Devine et al. 2021; Bol et al. 2021; Jørgensen et al. 2021; Lindholt et al. 2021).

Why 'Viral Lobbing'?

In this book, we give centre-stage to another important perspective by studying *viral lobbying*, which we understand as *all attempts by non-state organisations to influence public debates or policies during the COVID-19 pandemic.* This definition includes a diverse set of organisations, which *lobby* i.e. use strategies to pursue their political interests (cf. Baroni et al. 2014), including non-governmental organisations (NGOs), labour unions, associations of professionals, think tanks, business associations and individual firms. We label these non-state organisations engaging in influence attempts, *interest groups.* We are both interested in how these groups pursued their interests with respect to *COVID-19-related policies,* as well as their general ability and practises in *lobbying during the pandemic.*

With this definition of *viral lobbying* in mind, our aim is to contribute in two main ways with our analyses. First, we hope to help analysts, scholars and practitioners interested in pandemic politics to understand the role of interest groups. Input from different social and economic groups is vital for designing policy interventions that take the needs of various actors into account. Therefore, *viral lobbying* has the potential to play a vital and conducive role in designing viral (and other) policies. Yet, it can only do so, if major imbalances in the mobilisation of different interests, as well as in the consultation practices and responsiveness of decision makers can be avoided – despite the severe challenges that the pandemic posed for both interest groups and political gatekeepers. As we show throughout the book, inequalities in the ability to contribute to policies during the pandemic occurred at several stages of what we call the *influence production process.*

Second, we aim to introduce new students of interest group politics to a more broadly applicable framework for understanding lobbying activities and influence on specific (new) policies, based on the case of the pandemic. While the pandemic has been unprecedented and historic on all accounts, it is also a useful example of a highly salient *focussing event* (Kingdon 1984; Birkland 1997), which simultaneously hits existing interest group communities and sets the *in-*

fluence production process in motion on a new set of issues. By analysing viral lobbying after the pandemic hit, we can exemplify the steps involved when interest groups seek to influence new issues, as well as the potential challenges and constraints they face. In this sense, *viral lobbying* can even be interpreted more broadly and denote the situation where a highly salient (set of) issue(s) attracts high levels of lobbying activity (i.e. 'goes viral'), meaning that a large number of interest groups jump on the bandwagon (Baumgartner and Leech 2001; Halpin 2011) and (try to) have a say on the(se) issue(s).

In the rest of this chapter, we unpack the key concepts for our account of viral lobbying that can inform both perspectives: *focussing events* and the *influence production process*. Subsequently, we introduce the structure of the book.

The Spread of COVID-19 as a Focussing Event

In his seminal work on *Agendas, Alternatives and Public Policies*, Kingdon (1984, 94f) describes focussing events as a 'push' that can help 'get the attention of people in and around government'. A focussing event, he continues, is 'a crisis or disaster that comes along to call attention to [a] problem, a powerful symbol that catches on'. In his theory of multiple streams, focussing events can, therefore, help open a *window of opportunity for policy change*. Although Kingdon's theory constitutes a broad 'garbage can' model of the agenda setting process (Kingdon 1984, 86f) and his focus does not lie on interest groups, we deem the 'focussing event' concept useful to study 'viral lobbying' after the outbreak of the pandemic.

Arguably, the outbreak of COVID-19 can be seen as a textbook example of a focussing event that has dominated the political agenda and initiated far-reaching policy change. As Kingdon (1984, 95–100) himself notes, some events, such as those that aggregate harm through a high number of human casualties, are more powerful than others when it comes to attracting attention. Other scholars have added that there is, in fact, a *diverse* set of *potential* focussing events (Birkland 1997; Birkland and DeYoung 2012), meaning only *some* events unfold actual effects on the policy agenda. Moreover, focussing events can vary strongly in their causes (Best 2010): some are non-actor promoted (NAPE), like the spread of COVID-19, whereas others are actor promoted (APE), such as the January 6th Capitol attack. In addition, there are combined cases, sometimes labelled 'triggering events' (van der Brug and Berkhout 2015), where actors such as political parties become important 'issue initiators', that turn an arising problem into a political issue (Cobb and Elder 1983).

All this means that *any* example of a focussing event will share only some features with other events. Furthermore, most *actual* focusing events that fulfil their *potential* in playing a central role in agenda and policy change are likely to seem like outliers, not least because policy (sub)systems tend to be characterised by stability most of the time (Baumgartner and Jones 2010). The spread of COVID-19 surely is an anomaly in this sense: The global spread of the virus and steep increase in serious infections throughout 2020 and 2021 overburdened hospitals and involved over 5 million deaths globally (as reported to WHO 2022). As a result, the pandemic completely dominated the public and media agenda. At the same time, it attracted the full attention of policymakers, policy professionals, experts and interest groups, all trying to come up with potential policy solutions. This means that problem-definition, the search for available policy solutions, and the urgent political will to employ these, coincided. Hence, the spread of COVID-19 marks a 'successful' focusing event that opened windows of opportunity for a number of policies to be introduced, including policies to increase resources in the health sector, to limit personal freedoms, such as the freedom of movement through (international) travel regulations, and policies to pause, but also support, many economic activities. Notably, the pandemic both called attention to *pre-existing* problems, such as understaffed hospitals, as well as causing *completely new* problems, such as turning all physical meetings and interactions into a health hazard.

Yet, despite the uniqueness when it comes to the urgency and agenda-dominance during this pandemic, we see it as a highly fruitful case to study what happens when crises and other events place an issue, or set of issues, on the agenda of interest groups *and* policymakers at the same time. Such an alignment of the agendas allows studying how interest groups attempt to exert influence on the (new) issue(s). In our case, a strong focus lies on COVID-19 related policies, including health and safety measures, sector-specific restrictions and economic rescue packages. Examples of such health and safety measures include regulations regarding the use of masks in public and private settings, social distancing, rules on testing and testing facilities, as well as those introduced in the second phase of the pandemic with vaccination and recovery passes, such as the EU COVID Green Pass. Sector specific measures are regulations, which refer to the definition of essential and non-essential services, as well as all lockdown measures put in place to pause economic activities or allow them to operate at limited capacity. Finally, economic rescue packages entail all stimuli and support mechanisms put in place to counter the negative economic effects of the virus and lockdown measures.

The initiation, design and implementation of these different regulatory and distributive policies has had important consequences for various types of interest groups, which is why they had strong incentives to start or increase their lobbying activities. A (potential) focussing event can, in this sense, trigger the *supply side* of lobbying: interest groups become active and try to affect decisionmaking related to the event. At the same time, a (potential) focussing event can affect the *demand side* of lobbying when an event draws policymakers' attention to a set of policy problems, so that they begin consulting relevant stakeholders in order to gather input for designing policy interventions. While, in Kingdon's terms, such push and pull forces would be reflected in the 'multiple streams', which potentially overlap, we focus instead on the sequence of steps required for the supply and demand side of lobbying to meet after a focussing event. As we will argue in the following, we study this as a chain of strategic decisions and potential outcomes, which we term *the influence production process on (new) policy issues*. The steps in this process cover the attempts by interest groups to influence policies after a focussing event (i.e. the supply side of lobbying), the reactions of political gatekeepers (i.e. the demand side), as well as the potential result of these forces (i.e. lobbying influence).

The Influence Production Process

We build on existing work, which addresses different phases in organising and expressing political interests. Notably, Lowery and Brasher (2004) have used the term influence production process to cover a diverse set of phases including 1) the formation of interest groups, 2) the size and structure of interest group communities, as well as 3) the activities and 4) influence of existing groups (see also: Lowery and Gray 2004). There are some clear advantages to taking such an encompassing view of influence production, which includes the full life-cycle of interest groups and their populations: Other than seeking policy influence, interest groups need to ensure their *survival* as organisations, which means they compete for members and/or funding and need to protect their reputation (Berkhout 2013). These aims are important ends in themselves and intertwined with their attempts at securing influence (Lowery 2007). Put differently, the processes of group formation, organisational maintenance and political influence are not independent from each other, so a mere focus on political influence might underestimate other key motivations for the strategies of interest groups.

At the same time, however, not all phases in such a model of influence production are equally central when we want to understand (viral) lobbying in concrete situations. In March 2020, when the state of the pandemic was announced and governments all over the world were devising complex sets of policy responses to anticipate contingency plans, contain the virus and/or control its spread (Chari and Rozas 2021, 38 ff), a set of complex challenges hit *existing* interest groups and the *existing* group community. Very concretely, existing groups needed to decide how to position themselves on these issues, and what strategies to use to express their interests to relevant decision makers.

Mahoney (2008, 3) describes the 'advocacy process' as a sequence of strategic decisions starting with deciding whether to mobilise on a political debate and ending with potential lobbying success. Our adjusted model of the influence production process builds on her approach: We focus on the decisions and outcomes involved when existing interest groups in the group community try to influence policies on new issues on the political agenda. Although group formation and organisational community dynamics are not focal in our model, we discuss their implications in some of the other stages, given the important links between them (Berkhout 2013; Lowery 2007).

Figure 1 summarises our four-step model of these processes, where a focussing event or other trigger for agenda change kick-starts a sequence of strategic choices among interest groups and leads to potential outcomes in terms of their political access and influence on these issues. Notably, in case of the pandemic, the focussing event can be seen as an *external* shock hitting the community of interest groups (solid arrow in Figure 1.1). In other cases, however, parts of the interest group community might take part in *triggering* agenda change (dotted arrow), for instance in actor-promoted focussing events (Best 2010), such as successful information campaigns, or when groups act as 'policy entrepreneurs' ensuring that the potential symbolic power of a focussing event catches on (Kingdon 1984). Irrespective of these drivers of agenda setting, we argue that once issues are high up on the political agenda, lobbying influence on these issues is a potential outcome of a sequence of steps (1–4).

Issue mobilisation here refers to what is sometimes termed 'second order mobilisation', meaning the question of 'whether organised groups participate in policymaking once formed' (Rasmussen and Gross 2015, 345). An interest group might here face *issue mobilisation problems*, for instance because it lacks resources to prioritise an issue, which means an early halt for the potential influence process (e. g. Fraussen, Halpin, and Nownes 2021). In other situations, the lack of mobilisation might also be a strategic choice, for instance when the issue is contentious and divides members or the public (cf. Bolleyer 2021), so that mobilisation could have negative effects on the reputation, maintenance or even survival of the group (Berkhout 2013; Lowery 2007; Lowery and Brasher 2004). Or else, a group might decide to remain inactive when it knows that its interests will be expressed anyway through other actors. This could be due to 'free-riding' (cf. Olson 1965) or a division of labour with other groups, such as

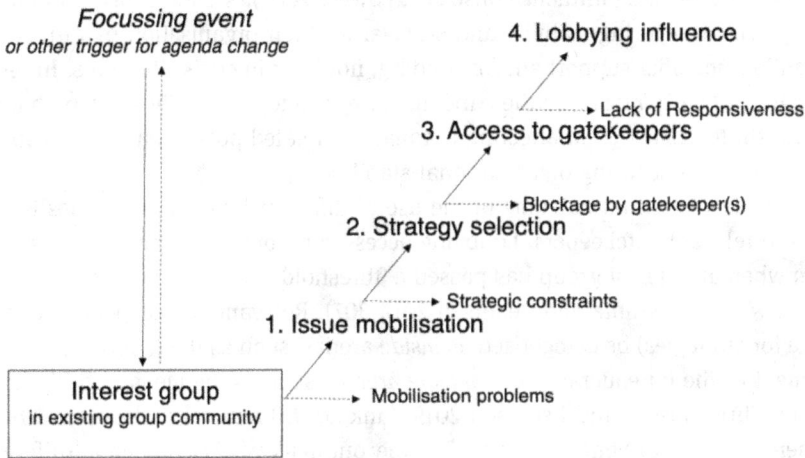

Figure 1.1: Influence production process on a new (set of) policy issue(s).

umbrella organisations, taking on the task of mobilisation (cf. Junk 2019). In case of 'viral lobbying', however, the stakes were so high for all involved actors that mobilising, in one way or the other, on Coronavirus-related issues is likely to have been strategically useful for most if not all groups. This is why we study *issue mobilisation* primarily as the *ability* to mobilise, and to mobilise *early* and *intensely* after the focussing event. Understanding these mobilisation patterns is relevant in and of itself, given that inequalities in the ability to voice different societal interests is undesirable from a normative standpoint that values civil society participation on an equal footing (cf. Habermas 1997; Dahl 1956). Moreover, it is the first step in which eventual biases in political influence might take root.

Second, once an interest group has managed to mobilise on an issue, it faces a number of decisions regarding what *strategies* to employ, while subject to constraints, such as resource shortages. These decisions can include how much to lobby, in which political venues and with what arguments (Mahoney 2008). More broadly speaking, available strategies can be divided into *inside* and *outside* strategies (Dür and Mateo 2016; Hanegraaff, Beyers, and De Bruycker 2016; Junk 2016; Weiler and Brändli 2015), which can be used individually or in combination with each other. *Inside strategies* here mean all tactics employed to interact directly with policymakers with the aim of influencing policy, whereas *outside strategies* target the media and/or public opinion, and thereby potentially also affect policymakers indirectly (Kollman 1998). Yet, as Lowery and Brasher's (2004) model usefully highlights, not all considerations in strategy choice are aimed at seeking influence (also see: Lowery 2007). A main concern of interest groups is securing stability and survival for their organisation by attracting attention, member support and/or funding, not least in crisis situations. In relation to *viral lobbying* during the pandemic, we therefore carefully study both lobbying strategies aimed at affecting Coronavirus-related policies, as well as strategies aimed at securing organisational stability.

Third, a potential outcome of the use of different lobbying strategies is access to relevant gatekeepers. Lobbying access can here be defined as the situation when an interest group has passed a 'threshold controlled by relevant gatekeepers' (Binderkrantz and Pedersen 2017, 307). Relevant gatekeepers can here (like for strategies) be categorised as *inside* arenas, such as the government, parliament or the bureaucracy, and *outside* arenas, such as the media (cf. Binderkrantz, Christiansen, and Pedersen 2015; Junk 2019; Fraussen and Beyers 2016). When it comes to *viral lobbying*, after the outbreak of the pandemic different gatekeepers have faced extreme pressures to act swiftly and effectively, while navigating a situation with extreme uncertainties when it comes to anticipating and controlling (new variants of) the virus (Chari and Rozas 2021). Moreover, some gatekeepers, such as members of parliament, experienced a weakening of their position vis-à-vis the executive (Bolleyer and Salát 2021). In other words, there are different reasons for why access to gatekeepers might be blocked to an interest group: 1) the inability or unwillingness of gatekeepers to consult it and/or 2) the inability of the interest group to contribute, for instance because it faced mobilisation problems, or chose less effective lobbying strategies. In our study, we include these strands of explanations for (un)successful access at the 'demand' and 'supply' side of lobbying.

Fourth and finally, lobbying influence is a *potential* outcome of this sequence of steps: when a group has mobilised and has chosen strategies that have helped it secure access to relevant gatekeepers, decision makers *might be responsive* to the interest group. Lobbying influence can here be seen as the holy grail of interest group scholarship and practice: it is eagerly pursued, but very hard to fathom. Understood causally, it means that a different outcome would have prevailed, had the interest group not become involved (cf. Dahl's (1957) definition of power). This is extremely difficult to ascertain (Dür 2008; Leech 2010; Lowery 2013). We therefore combine three complementary perspectives to the study of lobbying influence to gauge variation in influence of *viral lobbying*. Our underlying assumptions are that influential groups 1) see themselves as impactful throughout the pandemic, potentially even increasingly so over time, 2) attain their policy preferences on Coronavirus-related policies, and 3) are more satisfied with the resulting government policies. In studying different *proxies* for influence at different times, we are especially interested in understanding how patterns in influence vary compared to the other steps in the interest production process, i.e. mobilisation, strategies, and access.

With this framework in mind (Figure 1.1), we trace for each step in the influence production process, whether there are inequalities favouring certain types of groups, such as better resourced organisations, or groups that represent business and other economic interests. In more 'pessimistic' strands of lobbying theory, such biases are a key concern (cf. Schattschneider 1960; Olson 1965). Other, more 'optimistic' theories of lobbying underline the plurality of types of groups that mobilise, get access and potentially influence on public policies (cf. Truman 1951). According to such theories, a key expectation is that the degree to which an organisation is affected by a focusing event should be a driver of lobbying involvement. Throughout the book, we theorise in more detail about these explanatory factors and assess their importance throughout the influence production process. In this way, we hope to provide an empirical assessment of *viral lobbying* that is theoretically rooted and can inform a normative evaluation of the role of interest groups in *viral politics* (see Chapter 8).

Structure of the Book

In sum, throughout the book, we shed light on the elements of our model of the influence production process to explain *viral lobbying* after the outbreak of COVID-19. After presenting our project and the novel data sources we employ to cover lobbying in eight European polities (Chapter 2), the chapters focus on the above stages of the influence production process starting with *issue mobilisation* (Chapter 3), *strategy selection* (Chapter 4), *access to gatekeepers* (Chapter 5), and *lobbying influence* (Chapter 6). In addition, we reflect further on our quantitative findings based on interest groups' *experiences with lobbying during the pandemic*, which they shared in a series of qualitative focus group interviews (Chapter 7). Finally, our concluding chapter sums up our main findings and reflects on the rich evidence provided in the different chapters to help evaluate the workings of *viral lobbying* (Chapter 8).

References

Altiparmakis, A., et al. (2021) 'Pandemic politics: policy evaluations of government responses to COVID-19'. *West European Politics* 44(5–6):1159–79.

Baroni, L., Carroll, B.J., Chalmers, A.W., Marquez, L.M.M., and Rasmussen, A. (2014) 'Defining and classifying interest groups'. *Interest Groups & Advocacy* 3(2):141–59.

Baumgartner, F.R., and Jones, B.D. (2010) *Agendas and instability in American politics*, Chicago: University of Chicago Press.

Baumgartner, F.R., and Leech, B.L. (2001) 'Interest Niches and Policy Bandwagons: Patterns of Interest Group Involvement in National Politics'. *The Journal of Politics* 63(4):1191–213.

Berkhout, J. (2013) 'Why interest organizations do what they do: Assessing the explanatory potential of 'exchange' approaches'. *Interest Groups & Advocacy* 2(2):227–50.

Best, R. (2010) 'Situation or Social Problem: The Influence of Events on Media Coverage of Homelessness'. *Social Problems* 57(1):74–91.

Binderkrantz, A.S., Christiansen, P.M., and Pedersen, H.H. (2015) 'Interest Group Access to the Bureaucracy, Parliament, and the Media'. *Governance* 28(1):95–112.

Binderkrantz, A.S., and Pedersen, H.H. (2017) 'What is access? A discussion of the definition and measurement of interest group access'. *European Political Science* 16(306):306–21.

Birkland, T.A. (1997) *After disaster: Agenda setting, public policy, and focusing events*, Washington, D.C.: Georgetown University Press.

Birkland, T.A., and DeYoung, S.E. (2012) 'Focusing events and policy windows', in E. Araral, S. Fritzen, M. Howlett, and M. Ramesh (Eds.), *Routledge Handbook of Public Policy*, London: Routledge.

Bol, D., Giani, M., Blais, A., and Loewen, P.J. (2021) 'The effect of COVID-19 lockdowns on political support: Some good news for democracy?'. *European Journal of Political Research* 60(2):497–505.

Bolleyer, N. (2021) 'Civil society – Politically engaged or member-serving? A governance perspective'. *European Union Politics* 22(3):495–520.

Bolleyer, N., and Salát, O. (2021) 'Parliaments in times of crisis: COVID-19, populism and executive dominance'. *West European Politics* 44(5–6):1103–28.

Bonafont, L.C. and Iborra, I.M. (2021) 'The representation of business interests during the COVID-19 pandemic in Spain'. *Revista española de ciencia política* 57(1):21–44.

BusinessEurope. (2021) "Responsibility, action and solidarity is urgently required to protect businesses, society and our economy." https://www.businesseurope.eu/publications/re sponsibility-action-and-solidarity-urgently-required-protect-businesses-society-and (accessed June 13, 2022).

Chari, R., and Rozas, I. (2021) *Viruses, Vaccines, and Antivirals: Why Politics Matters*, Berlin: De Gruyter.

Cobb, R.W., and Elder, C.D. (1983) *Participation in American democracy: the dynamics of agenda-building*, Baltimore, Maryland: Johns Hopkins Press.

Dahl, R.A. (1956) *A preface to democratic theory*, Chicago: University of Chicago Press.

Dahl, R.A. (1957) 'The concept of power'. *Behavioral Science* 2(3):201–15.

Devine, D., Gaskell, J., Jennings, W., and Stoker, G. (2021) 'Trust and the Coronavirus Pandemic: What are the Consequences of and for Trust? An Early Review of the Literature'. *Political Studies Review* 19(2):274–85.

Dür, A. (2008) 'Measuring interest group influence in the EU: A note on methodology'. *European Union Politics* 9(4):559–76.

Dür, A., and Mateo, G. (2016) *Insiders versus Outsiders: Interest Group Politics in Multilevel Europe*, Oxford: Oxford University Press.

Eady, G., and Rasmussen, A. (2021) 'The Unequal Effects of the COVID-19 Pandemic on Political Interest Representation', in, *Working paper:* https://www.annerasmussen.eu/wp-content/uploads/2021/06/EadyRasmussen050921.pdf (accessed June 28, 2022)

Engler, S., et al. (2021) 'Democracy in times of the pandemic: explaining the variation of COVID-19 policies across European democracies'. *West European Politics* 44(5 – 6):1077 – 102.

Fraussen, B., and Beyers, J. (2016) 'Who's in and who's out?: Explaining access to policymakers in Belgium'. *Acta Politica* 51(2):214 – 36.

Fraussen, B., Halpin, D.R., and Nownes, A.J. (2021) 'Why do interest groups prioritise some policy issues over others? Explaining variation in the drivers of policy agendas'. *Journal of Public Policy* 41(3):553 – 72.

Fuchs, S., and Sack, D. (2021) 'Corporatism as usual? – Staat und organisierte Wirtschaftsinteressen in der Coronakrise'. *Zeitschrift für Politikwissenschaft*, Online first.

Habermas, J. (1997) *Between Facts and Norms: Contributions to a Discourse Theory of Law and Democracy*, Cambridge: Polity Press.

Halpin, D. (2011) 'Explaining Policy Bandwagons: Organized Interest Mobilization and Cascades of Attention'. *Governance* 24(2):205 – 30.

Hanegraaff, M., Beyers, J., and De Bruycker, I. (2016) 'Balancing inside and outside lobbying: The political strategies of lobbyists at global diplomatic conferences'. *European Journal of Political Research* 55(3):568 – 88.

Junk, W.M. (2016) 'Two logics of NGO advocacy: understanding inside and outside lobbying on EU environmental policies'. *Journal of European Public Policy* 23(2):236 – 54.

Junk, W.M. (2019) 'Representation beyond people: Lobbying access of umbrella associations to legislatures and the media'. *Governance* 32(2):313 – 30.

Junk, W.M., Crepaz, M., Hanegraaff, M., Berkhout, J., and Aizenberg, E. (2021) 'Changes in Interest Group Access in Times of Crisis: No Pain, No (Lobby) Gain'. *Journal of European Public Policy*, Online First.

Jørgensen, F., Bor, A., Lindholt, M.F., and Petersen, M.B. (2021) 'Public support for government responses against COVID-19: assessing levels and predictors in eight Western democracies during 2020'. *West European Politics* 44(5 – 6):1129 – 58.

Kingdon, J. (1984) *Agendas, Alternatives, and Public Policies, Update Edition, with an Epilogue on Health Care: Pearson New International Edition. (2013 reprint of original work published in 1984)*, Harlow, UK: Pearson Education, Limited.

Kollman, K. (1998) *Outside lobbying: Public opinion and interest group strategies*, Princeton: Princeton University Press.

Leech, B.L. (2010) 'Lobbying and Influence', in L.S. Maisel, J.M. Berry, G.C. Edwards and B.L. Leech (Eds.), *The Oxford Handbook of American Political Parties and Interest Groups*, 534 – 52, Oxford: Oxford University Press.

Lindholt, M.F., Jørgensen, F., Bor, A., and Petersen, M.B. (2021) 'Public acceptance of COVID-19 vaccines: cross-national evidence on levels and individual-level predictors using observational data'. *BMJ Open* 11(6):1 – 12.

Lowery, D. (2007) 'Why Do Organized Interests Lobby? A Multi-Goal, Multi-Context Theory of Lobbying'. *Polity* 39(1):29 – 54.

Lowery, D. (2013) 'Lobbying influence: Meaning, measurement and missing'. *Interest Groups & Advocacy* 2(1):1 – 26.

Lowery, D., and Brasher, H. (2004) *Organized interests and American government*, New York: McGraw-Hill.

Lowery, D., and Gray, V. (2004) 'A Neopluralist Perspective on Research on Organized Interests'. *Political Research Quarterly* 57(1):164–75.

Mahoney, C. (2008) *Brussels versus the beltway: Advocacy in the United States and the European Union*, Washington, D.C.: Georgetown University Press.

Olson, M. (1965) *The Logic of Collective Action*, Cambridge: Harvard University Press.

Petersen, M.B., Bor, A., Jørgensen, F., and Lindholt, M.F. (2021) 'Transparent communication about negative features of COVID-19 vaccines decreases acceptance but increases trust'. *Proceedings of the National Academy of Sciences* 118(29):1–8.

Rasmussen, A., and Gross, V. (2015) 'Biased access? Exploring selection to advisory committees'. *European Political Science Review* 7(3):343–72.

Schattschneider, E.E. (1960) *The Semisovereign People: A Realist's View of Democracy in America*, New York: Holt, Rinehart and Winston.

TIME. (2021) "World Health Organization Declares COVID-19 a 'Pandemic.' Here's What That Means." https://time.com/5791661/who-coronavirus-pandemic-declaration/ (accessed June 13, 2022).

Truman, D.B. (1951) *The Governmental Process. Political Interests and Public Opinion*, New York: Alfred A. Knopf.

van der Brug, W., and Berkhout, J. (2015) 'The Effect of Associative Issue Ownership on Parties' Presence in the News Media'. *West European Politics* 38(4):869–87.

Weiler, F., and Brändli, M. (2015) 'Inside versus outside lobbying: How the institutional framework shapes the lobbying behaviour of interest groups'. *European Journal of Political Research* 54(4):745–66.

WHO. (2022) "WHO Coronavirus (COVID-19) Dashboard." https://covid19.who.int/ (accessed June 13, 2022).

Online Appendix

https://www.degruyter.com/document/isbn/9783110783148/html

Chapter 2
The InterCov Project

To trace the influence production process of viral lobbying, we rely on data collected in two surveys we conducted in summer 2020 and summer 2021 in eight
European polities[2]: Austria, Denmark, Germany, Italy, Ireland, the Netherlands,
Sweden and the European Union. As will be discussed in detail in this chapter,
during this period of investigation, *viral politics* dominated day-to-day public
policymaking and interest group activities in these polities.

As the pandemic unfolded, professionals from different backgrounds prob-
ably saw and interpreted what was happening through their specific lens. So
did we as scholars of interest groups and public policy and started the InterCov
project (short for: *Interest Representation during the Coronavirus Crisis*). Although
there were many developments we could not anticipate in the spring of 2020
when the pandemic violently hit Europe, we were certain that the activities of interest groups were going to play a major role in shaping how individuals, organisations and whole countries would cope with the repercussions of the virus. We,
therefore, wanted to document their activities, and shed light on patterns and
potential biases in interest representation during the pandemic. This is why
the project unfolded along with real-world events, in a quicker manner than is
typical for academic research: In April 2020, the initial project idea was developed by Wiebke Junk, and later that month our research team started to draft
the first cross-national survey (*team members: Ellis Aizenberg, Joost Berkhout, Michele Crepaz, Marcel Hanegraaff and Wiebke Junk*). By early June, we were able to
field the first wave of our cross-country survey to capture what European interest
groups were going through at the time (Junk et al. 2020).

As interest group researchers, we were familiar with some of their challenges. We also had several initial ideas about patterns in lobbying after the outbreak
of the pandemic, which we were interested in studying. When designing our first
survey, for example, we expected business associations and firms to lobby for
economic rescue packages to make up for losses in closed sectors due to the pandemic. We also imagined trade unions and associations of professionals mobilising on out-of-work benefits or issues of health and safety standards at work, or

---

2 Survey-based research is a popular and wide-spread approach in interest group research (Dür
and Mateo 2016; Beyers et al. 2016; Binderkrantz, Christiansen, and Pedersen 2020; Allern and
Hansen 2022), and we built on these existing practices to design and field our surveys (Junk et
al. 2020; Junk et al. 2021b). Our approach, however, also differs from standard approaches as it is
tailored to capture the particularities of viral lobbying.

patient organisations advocating for health policy to protect vulnerable people from the spread of the virus. We could, however, not grasp yet how deeply the pandemic would affect interest group mobilisation, their organisational stability, the frequency and modes by which they communicated their concerns and interests to policymakers and the media, and, ultimately, how impactful such communication would be. One year after the first survey, we, hence, followed up with a second survey covering additional angles (Junk et al. 2021b). Its aim was also to help us understand how the role of interest groups had developed since the breakout of COVID-19.

The result of these efforts contribute significantly to the few existing cross-country projects on interest groups in Europe (see: CIG-survey (Beyers et al. 2020), GovLis (Rasmussen, Mäder, and Reher 2018), INTERARENA (Binderkrantz, Christiansen, and Pedersen 2020), PAIRDEM (Allern et al. 2022)). Our first survey in June 2020 was sent to 5,945 interest groups in the eight polities under study here. In June 2021, our second survey was distributed to 5,770 interest groups. A combined overall of roughly 1,500 unique interest groups completed our surveys with a response rate of 22.7 percent in 2020 and 14.3 percent in 2021 in the eight polities. Our analysis of *viral lobbying* relies on these responses. With this data, we complement previous efforts in lobbying research to address a key challenge in interest group scholarship, namely the availability of large-N cross-country data (Dür and Mateo 2016; Beyers et al. 2016; Binderkrantz, Christiansen, and Pedersen 2020; Allern and Hansen 2022). While our data is exceptionally well-suited to address the strategies, access and influence of interest groups during the pandemic, it can also help understand some more general patterns in lobbying (Junk et al. 2021a; Crepaz, Hanegraaff, and Junk 2022).

In what follows, we first provide a brief description of the context conditions in the eight polities under investigation during the 18 months period under study here (March 2020–June 2021). We then describe how we selected the almost 6,000 organisations as potential participants in our surveys, discuss response rates and potential biases in the data collection process. Next, we describe the structure of the survey and its particularities to capture viral lobbying. The chapter then focuses on the three main explanatory variables that we focus on throughout the whole book as determinants in the influence production process: interest group type, lobbying resources and affectedness. We provide descriptive analyses of these factors and discuss these in detail. The following chapters then zoom in on different operationalisations of outcome variables: issue mobilisation (Chapter 3), strategies (Chapter 4), access (Chapter 5) and influence (Chapter 6). These are not discussed here but are explained in each individual chapter.

Background

The COVID-19 Pandemic in Eight European Polities

When the WHO declared the state of pandemic on the 11th of March 2020, COVID-19 was already widespread in Europe. Italy was the most affected of the European countries in the early weeks of the pandemic with an average of 5,200 new daily COVID-19 cases and a shocking daily average of 750 COVID-19 deaths by the end of March. Into the first weeks of April, the virus had propagated in all European countries causing what has been, later that year, called 'the first wave' of COVID-19.

The intensity of this wave varied by country. In Austria and Denmark, for example, infection and death rates never reached the levels found in Italy during this period (WHO 2022). Germany or Ireland, on the contrary, faced a steep rise in daily cases, hospitalisations, and COVID-19 deaths between the end of March and the first weeks of April. Apart from epidemiological reasons, the infection curve 'flattened' thanks to the introduction of policies which all European countries had put in place to prevent the spread of the virus. These fall in the category of *viral policies*, which we discussed in Chapter 1 of this book. These policies include, among other measures, school and workplace closures, cancellation of events, restrictions to movement and public gatherings, restriction to international travel, and the introduction of health and safety measures such as quarantine rules for infected people, social distancing and the use of face coverings and other sanitary equipment.

Of course, the timing of the introduction of such policies as well as their strictness has varied by country. However, scholars have observed levels of uniformity in the range of viral policies European countries have adopted during the first wave (Chari and Rozas 2021; Jahn 2022; Ritchie et al. 2020). For example, while school closures were in place only in Italy, Spain, Greece, Portugal and France as of March 10th, such closures extended to almost all European countries by the 27th of the same month. The same pattern can be observed with the introduction of international travel restrictions, or with viral policies that – instead of preventing the spread of the virus – were put in place to support individuals and businesses affected by such restrictions. Income support measures for people out of work due to the pandemic, for example, fall in this category. These were absent in most European countries in mid-March but were rapidly introduced in all European countries by mid-April and remained in place for long time periods.

This first period of crisis management was followed by a relatively quiet interval, where infection rates dropped, COVID-19 hospitalisations and death rates fell, and lockdown restrictions were to some extent eased (Jahn 2022). This situation was only temporary as in the autumn of 2020 the Alpha and Beta mutations of the SARS-CoV-2 (discovered in the UK and South Africa, respectively) started spreading globally, causing a second wave of COVID-19 in Europe. Scientists labelled these mutations as comparatively more infectious than the previous dominant strain, and this factor facilitated their propagation across the world, including Europe. Similar to what was observed during the first wave, countries across Europe responded with a combination of virus containment policies, such as lockdowns, and distributive policies to buffer their negative effects. In the seven European countries we analyse in this book (in addition to the EU level), approaches to viral policy tended to converge even more as the second wave unfolded. Figure 2.1 displays this trend plotting the COVID-19 Stringency Index, a policy index developed by Ritchie et al. (2020) to measure the strictness of COVID-19 lockdowns and other policies, over time.

As can been seen across all seven countries, an initial rise in policy responses to COVID-19 in the early stages of the pandemic was quickly followed by an easing of such policies during the summer of 2020. This easing was followed by the reintroduction of restrictions in the autumn as soon as infections became rampant again.

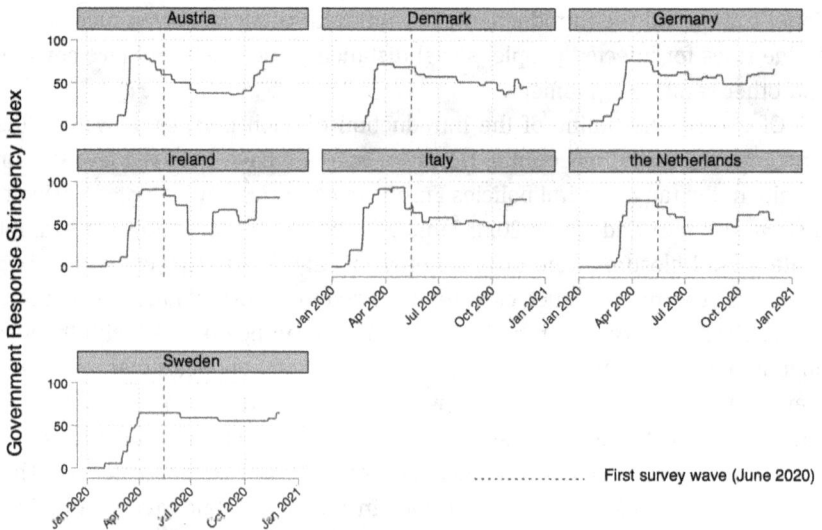

Figure 2.1: Development of COVID-19 restrictions over time for seven countries under investigation. Source: Adapted from Jahn (2022).

Taking both COVID-19 waves into account, however, one can still observe differences between countries. Italy, for example, which had the strictest lockdown in place in March, April and May of 2020, relaxed some of its regulations during the summer. It then introduced strict rules again, this time in line with approaches taken in Germany, the Netherlands, Ireland or Austria between October 2020 and January 2021, when the second wave of COVID-19 hit Europe. Sweden and Denmark took a comparatively looser approach to COVID-19 regulations with the latter scoring lower on the government response stringency index also during the second wave of the virus.

In the first time period, from March to May 2020, the closure of government buildings reduced opportunities for direct face-to-face lobbying. At the same time, the increased need to respond to major public policy decisions was demanding for the internal functioning of interest groups. At later stages, organisations continued to face these challenges but to a different degree or after effective adaptational responses. We account for the stage-wise development of the policy responses by means of the two-wave set-up of our survey (see details below).

In the background of the pandemic, the European Union (EU) played a key role in viral politics as well. Despite its relatively minor involvement in national lockdown policies, the EU has, for instance, provided a framework for the development of rescue packages. By late April 2020, EU member states had in fact already agreed to develop an EU-level recovery fund which was presented on May 27th and had the value of €750 billion. Another key policy at the EU-level concerned travel and movement restrictions. In October 2020, the Council of the EU adopted a recommendation for a coordinated approach to the restriction of free movement of people in response to the COVID-19 pandemic. This decision informs the list of non-EU countries for which travel restrictions were in place, the implementation of passenger locator forms for travel and the creation of the EU Digital COVID certificate for vaccinated or recovered individuals. Finally, the EU has been a key player in vaccination policy. In the summer of 2020, the European Commission conducted talks with pharmaceutical manufacturers to secure future stocks of potential COVID-19 vaccines, which later led to the signing of four contracts with AstraZeneca, Moderna, Pfizer BioNTech and Johnson & Johnson (Janssen), as well as the implementation of a strategy to distribute purchased vaccines across the EU in 2021.

With the role of the EU in viral politics in mind, we include the European Union in our study of viral lobbying, in addition to Austria, Denmark, Germany, Italy, Ireland, the Netherlands and Sweden. These polities were selected foremost based on the availability of comparable lists of interest group populations (Aizenberg and Hanegraaff 2020; Crepaz 2020; Crepaz and Hanegraaff 2020; Binderkrantz, Christiansen, and Pedersen 2014; Binderkrantz, Christiansen, and Pedersen 2020; Naurin and Boräng 2012; Pritoni 2019). Studying them together allows us to provide a relatively comprehensive picture of lobbying during the pandemic in Europe. More generally, this set of countries is relatively similar on a number of relevant political dimensions (e.g. they are all EU member states) which makes it possible for us to study them in a single research design. At the same time, the seven countries under investigation offer a mix of different types of welfare states, types of interest mediation and electoral systems, and different government responses to the crisis. This variation broadens the likely applicability of our findings beyond the countries studied. We argue, therefore, that the sample of polities is well suited to understand the influence production process in western democracies more broadly.

Identifying Interest Groups

We aimed at selecting comparable samples of organisations and firms in the eight polities. To do so, we drew on existing lists of active organisations, such as previous research, lobbying registers, directories of associations and lists of interest group populations. Such mixture of policy-related data sources ('top-down') and society-based data sources ('bottom-up') is recommended (Berkhout et al. 2017) for research questions that cover multiple stages of influence production. When selecting organisations from these lists, we aimed for an equal distribution of different types of interest groups within each polity. We therefore constructed a comparable 'stratified' sample of approximately 150 business associations, 150 profession associations, 150 unions, 150 identity or ideational groups, as well as 150 large firms sourced from lists identifying the firms with the largest revenue in a country (such as fortune 500).

We opted for stratifying the sample by organisation type in order to ensure that we included a high enough number of observations per organisation type, which is important to be able to make inferences about different group types. For this reason, we 'oversampled', for instance, trade unions, given the total number of unions in all countries is low, compared to NGOs or business organisations. Especially considering the potentially prominent role that trade unions and profession groups might have played in representing workers affected by the pandemic, we wanted to include a sufficient number of such organisations in our sample to ensure the statistical leverage needed for modelling group type differences. For each country, our completed stratified sample included approximately 700 interest groups. To cover the large European community of interest groups, we used a larger sample of 1,407 interest groups for the EU.

In total, we identified approximately 6,000 interest groups for which we collected the contact address of the lead political or public affairs specialist or a generalist address when the former was not available. The surveys were developed and sent to potential respondents electronically using the software package *Qualtrics*. The first wave of the survey was in the field from early June to mid-July 2020 and was sent to 5,945 valid addresses. As we sent out the survey, we updated our lists of organisations by replacing non-valid addresses. We ended up with 5,770 addresses for our second survey wave, which was in the field between mid-June and late July 2021. For each wave, we sent three sets of reminders, each at an interval of approximately two weeks.

The overall response rate was 22.7 percent for the first survey and 14.3 percent for the second one (based on surveys completed to the end). Although relatively low in the second wave, such levels of response rates are common in interest group research (Marchetti 2015) and are comparable to other large-N survey-based lobbying projects (Dür and Mateo 2016; Beyers et al. 2020; Binderkrantz, Christiansen, and Pedersen 2020). Importantly, and as seen in Table 2.1, response rates vary considerably between countries.

Table 2.1: Sent surveys and response rates by polity.

	Survey 1			Survey 2		
	Surveys Sent	Completed	Response Rate (%)	Surveys Sent	Completed	Response Rate (%)
DK	730	304	41.6	684	205	30.0
SE	650	225	34.6	600	125	20.8
IE	652	177	27.1	668	90	13.5
NL	700	161	23.0	677	90	13.3
DE	549	97	17.7	495	60	12.1
AT	617	98	15.8	609	86	14.1
EU	1,407	207	14.7	1,386	122	8.8
IT	640	82	12.8	651	46	7.1
Total	5,945	1,351	22.7	5,770	824	14.3

First of all, in Nordic countries we achieved higher response rates compared to other polities, while response rates for Italy, Austria, Germany and the EU remained comparatively low. Ireland and the Netherlands find themselves in the middle of the distribution. Such variation between countries with higher and lower participation in surveys are common, also reported in other interest group studies (e. g. Binderkrantz and Rasmussen 2015; Dür and Mateo 2016; Junk 2019).

An additional interesting observation is the decrease in the response rates (by 8.4 percent based on all responses) when comparing the first and second survey. There are several potential explanations for this. First, this could be due to an increasing COVID-19 *fatigue* after more than a year of pandemic. While our first survey was timed when the pandemic was a (puzzling) *new* reality for organisations, by 2021 organisations were used to it, and it might have been less appealing to answer questions related to the effects of the crisis. Second, the contact lists were newly updated in 2020, and re-used in 2021. In the meanwhile, some people might have moved positions, which meant that our emails were less well-targeted, and could explain part of the drop in the response rate.

In more general terms, a major concern in survey research is non-response bias, which occurs when non-respondents from a sample differ substantially from participants in the survey. This could be introduced by, for example, under-resourced organisations that do not have time to fill out our survey, interest groups that are rarely politically active and have low interest in answering a survey about lobbying, or organisations heavily affected by the pandemic that have other priorities than supporting our research. While we cannot rule out that some organisations have decided to not participate based on these (or other) grounds, we also find much variation among survey respondents in the resources available to organisations, their level of political activity and their perceived affectedness by the pandemic. Therefore, we reason that there are no stark patterns in non-responses related to our main explanatory variables of interest (as the following sections will demonstrate). With this in mind, we believe our data is suitable to offer valuable insights into *viral lobbying* and the influence production process more generally. We move into the description of the survey structure and the data set next.

Structure of the Surveys and Data

Both our surveys consist of approximately 40 questions, which collect information about interest groups' lobbying activities before and during the pandemic, as well as details on each organisation's characteristics and its relationships with membership, supporters and funders. In this section, we give an overview of the questions, and present our focal explanatory variables: interest group type, lobbying resources, and affectedness by the pandemic.

Question Overview

More specifically, the focus of the first survey was on interest group activities during the first months of the pandemic (Junk et al. 2020). We collected information on:

- the intensity and form of disruption caused by the pandemic for interest groups' political activities
- interest groups' perceived affectedness by the pandemic
- the perceived threat to organisational stability caused by the pandemic
- the frequency of using political activities (in general and on viral policies)
- the timing of political activities (that is, week and month of activity)
- the aim of political activity when targeted at viral policies
- the frequency of exchanges between interest groups and policymakers, as well as the media
- the extent to which these exchanges were initiated by policymakers
- the perceived influence of interest groups and their levels of satisfaction with political decisions and viral policies.

In our second survey (Junk et al. 2021b), we followed up on most of these aspects and collected additional information on:

- the frequency of activities aimed at maintaining organisational stability
- the sources of income of interest groups and whether income (from each source) has increased or decreased since the start of the pandemic
- the extent to which interest groups have obtained government funds during the pandemic
- the frequency of contacts initiated by policymakers and journalists.

These foci allowed us to capture the particularities of *viral lobbying* and, as discussed in the following empirical chapters, items for these batteries of questions are used as outcome and explanatory variables to disentangle the influence production process. With over 50 substantive questions related to lobbying practices during the pandemic, it is impossible to cover all items in this book. Hence, we focus on selected elements to trace the influence production process (see Chapter 1). A detailed description of each of the relevant items can be found in the following chapters on issue mobilisation, lobbying strategies, access and influence. The full set of questions can be found in Junk et al. (2020, 2021b).

In addition to the questions, which we tailored to the COVID-19 circumstances, we collected information about organisational characteristics as is common in interest group research. Using these items, we describe the characteristics of respondent organisations based on the three key factors, which throughout this book are treated as potential drivers of *viral lobbying* and explanatory factors in the influence production process.

Interest Group Type

First, we map respondents by interest group type. More specifically, in our survey we asked interest group representatives to identify their organisation as one of seven group types[3]: 1) company or firm; 2) business interest association; 3) association of professionals; 4) labour union; 5) NGO or cause group; 6) citizen membership association; 7) research institute, think tank or semi-public organisation.[4] We excluded other types of organisations in case they were registered in our data sources, most notably public agencies (e.g. municipalities lobbying nationally). We then simplified these seven categories by collapsing them into three: 1) The category of *business groups and firms* covers companies and firms, business interest associations and research institutes, think tanks or semi-public organisations active on economic issues; 2) The category of *profession groups and unions* covers associations of professionals and labour unions; 3) The category of *NGOs and citizen groups* includes NGOs, cause groups, citizen membership association and research institutes, think tanks or semi-public organisations active on social issues.

Using this categorisation of interest groups, we count 470 business groups and firms (34.9%), 448 profession groups and unions (33.2%), and 430 NGOs and citizen groups (31.9%), which have completed our first survey (2020). Among the participants of our second survey (2021), we count 271 business groups and firms (32.1%), 297 profession groups and unions (35.2%) and 277 NGOs and citizen groups (32.8%). In both surveys, this represents a fairly equal distribution whereby each interest group category accounts for approximately one third of the total responses. In Figure 2.2, we display the distribution of these three interest group types by polity, that is, by the polity (i.e. one of the seven countries, or the EU level) in which the organisations are active.

---

3 The number of observations in each category were distributed as follows between these survey respondents (survey 1/survey 2, respectively): 1) Company or firm (13.6%/13.8%), 2) Business interest association: (20.3%/17.4%), 3) association of professionals (21.9%/24.4%), 4) labour unions (11.3%/10.5%), NGOs or cause groups (23.9%/24.3%), citizen membership associations (5.9%/6.0%), research institute, think tank or semi-public organisation (3.3%/3.6%).

4 If respondents chose the latter category, we additionally asked them if their organisation was mostly active on social or economic issues.

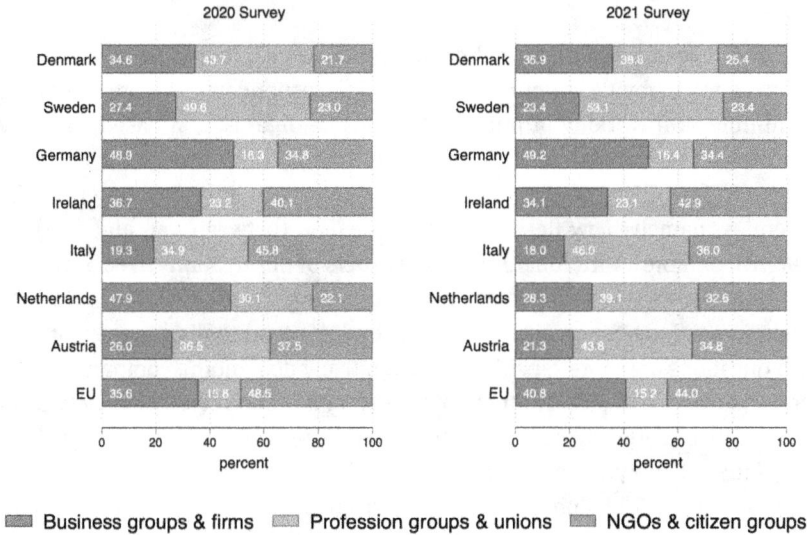

2020 Survey   **2021 Survey**

	2020 Survey		2021 Survey		
Denmark	34.6 / 43.7 / 21.7		Denmark	35.9 / 38.8 / 25.4	
Sweden	27.4 / 49.6 / 23.0		Sweden	23.4 / 53.1 / 23.4	
Germany	48.9 / 16.3 / 34.8		Germany	49.2 / 16.4 / 34.4	
Ireland	36.7 / 23.2 / 40.1		Ireland	34.1 / 23.1 / 42.9	
Italy	19.3 / 34.9 / 45.8		Italy	18.0 / 46.0 / 36.0	
Netherlands	47.9 / 30.1 / 22.1		Netherlands	28.3 / 39.1 / 32.6	
Austria	26.0 / 36.5 / 37.5		Austria	21.3 / 43.8 / 34.8	
EU	35.6 / 15.8 / 48.5		EU	40.8 / 15.2 / 44.0	

▩ Business groups & firms   ▨ Profession groups & unions   ▩ NGOs & citizen groups

Figure 2.2: Distribution of interest group types by polity (both survey waves).

As Figure 2.2 shows, the distribution of group types is not stable across polities, which indicates that the response rates of different group types varied between countries. In Sweden, for example, the proportion of profession groups and unions exceeds that of other group types, while the opposite trend is found in the European Union. Moreover, in both surveys the count of business associations and firms exceeds that of other groups in Germany, while in Ireland NGOs and citizen groups constitute the largest proportion. Overall, distributions are relatively similar between our first and second survey. An exception is the Netherlands, where we see a drop of nearly 20 percent in the responses by business associations and firms to our second survey.[5]

---

5 In general, the response rate among individual firms in the Netherlands is relatively low (Aizenberg 2022). The high response rate during the first wave was therefore an unexpected (but welcome) outcome, while the response rate to the second wave was more in line with previous experiences.

Lobbying Resources

A second relevant organisational characteristic we capture is the availability of resources for lobbying. In our surveys, we ask respondents to note the number of full-time staff working in public affairs in the organisation based on five answer categories: 1) one or less (e. g. one part-time); 2) one to four; 3) five to ten; 4) eleven to fifteen; 5) more than fifteen. Once again, we collapse answers in three categories, namely, *Low* (less than one); *Medium* (between one and four); and *High* (five or more), with roughly equal numbers of observations in each category.

We prefer this approach to asking about an organisation's lobbying budgets, because questions concerning (lobbying) budgets tend to discourage responses. Such questions are more sensitive and cognitively demanding compared to questions regarding staff size. We therefore opted to ask about staff size, now a common practice in (European) lobbying research (e. g. De Bruycker 2019; Flöthe 2019; Junk 2020; Mahoney 2008) and assume that lobbying staff size is a fair proxy of overall lobbying resources employed by an organisation. This allows us to compare interest groups based on their availability of lobbying resources, as summarised in Figure 2.3. More specifically, the figure shows the distribution of the organisations' lobbying resources by polity. Comparatively, figures are quite similar for the 2020 and the 2021 survey. Overall, it can be noted that, in the majority of polities, organisations that fall in the category of low or medium resources are the norm. Exceptions are found in Austria and Germany where a comparatively higher proportion of respondents represent more resourceful interest groups.

An interesting question is whether such lobbying resources tend to be associated with specific organisational types. In Figure 2.4 we therefore show the distribution of group types for organisations with low (public affairs staff <1), medium (1–4) and high (≥5) lobbying resources for both sets of surveys.

The figure partly confirms resource asymmetries described in the literature, but suggests that these are less strong than one might expect. More specifically, in both survey waves, *business associations and firms* tend to exceed other group types in the category of organisations with medium and high lobbying resources. On the contrary, *profession group and unions*, as well *as NGOs and citizen* groups outnumber *business groups and firms* in the category of organisations with low resources. This distribution suggests that business associations and firms tend to be somewhat better-resourced compared to other interest groups. At the same time, we see a considerable share of all types of groups at the different levels of lobbying resources. We therefore reason that both factors merit separate conceptual and empirical treatment in the analytical chapters of our book.

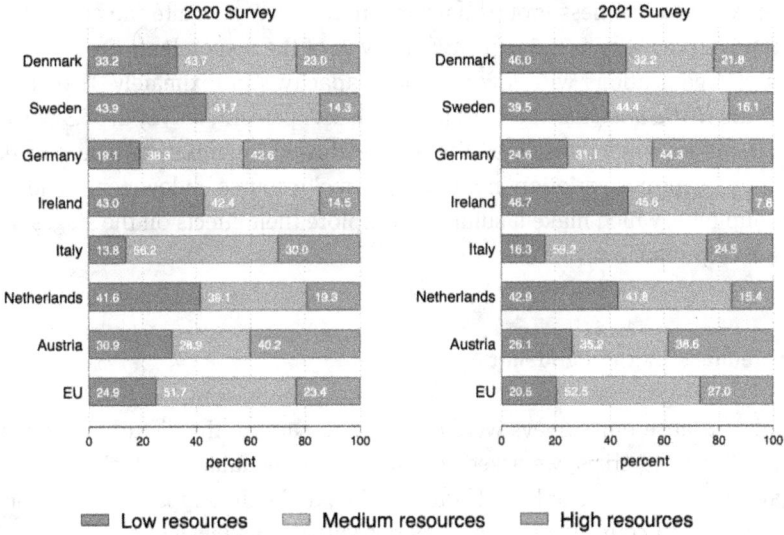

2020 Survey

	Low resources	Medium resources	High resources
Denmark	33.2	43.7	23.0
Sweden	43.9	41.7	14.3
Germany	19.1	38.3	42.6
Ireland	43.0	42.4	14.5
Italy	13.8	56.2	30.0
Netherlands	41.6	39.1	19.3
Austria	30.9	28.9	40.2
EU	24.9	51.7	23.4

2021 Survey

	Low resources	Medium resources	High resources
Denmark	46.0	32.2	21.8
Sweden	39.5	44.4	16.1
Germany	24.6	31.1	44.3
Ireland	46.7	45.6	7.6
Italy	16.3	59.2	24.5
Netherlands	42.9	41.8	15.4
Austria	26.1	35.2	38.6
EU	20.5	52.5	27.0

Figure 2.3: Distribution of lobbying resources by polity (both survey waves).

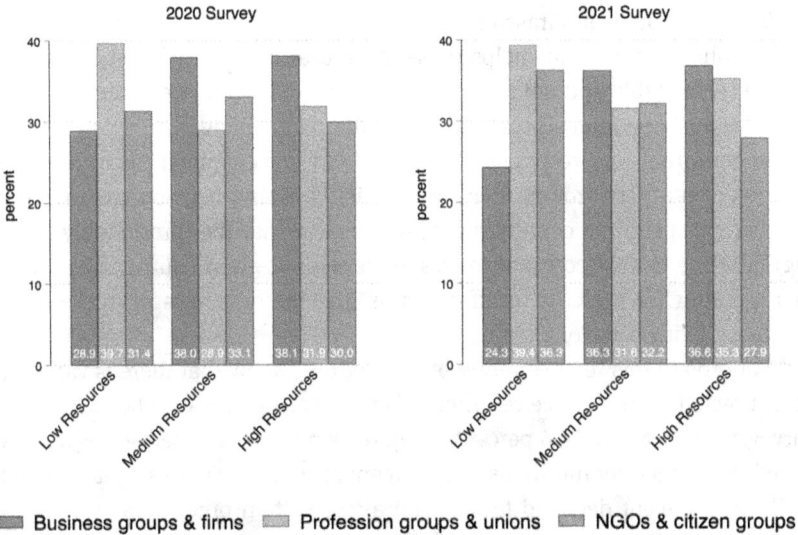

Figure 2.4: Distribution of interest group types by lobbying resources (both survey waves).

At the same time, the distribution of observations documents that not only well-resourced business groups have taken our surveys. Quite the contrary, 33.7 percent (survey 1) and 35.6 percent (survey 2) of the respondents are representatives of organisations with low lobbying capacity. Approximately 33 percent of these are *NGOs and citizen groups* (survey 1: 31.4 percent, survey 2: 36.3 percent), which are generally considered the least endowed organisation type. Our data, therefore, captures variation in interest groups' resource endowment in addition to group type, which make it suitable to explore their effects on the stages of the influence production process.

Affectedness by the Pandemic

Finally, because our surveys were designed to capture the disturbances caused by the COVID-19 crisis, we asked respondents to evaluate to which extent their organisation was more or less affected by the pandemic compared to other stakeholders in their country. Answer categories varied from *much less affected,* to *less affected, equally affected, more affected* and *much more affected.* We asked this question in both surveys with the aim of capturing the extent to which organisations perceived themselves as key stakeholders (relative to others) in viral politics throughout the period of investigation.

The question was phrased in *relative* terms compared to other stakeholders in the polity, because this helps us set a natural baseline for responses, which should be relatable and not too cognitively demanding. As we argued in the previous section, the intensity and timing of the pandemic varied considerably between countries, and respondents are likely to perceive their own affectedness compared to others around them. By explicitly asking respondents to compare to other groups in the country/polity, we ensured that the (presumably underlying) baseline is held constant for respondents in a given country. Our analyses then account for patterns in affectedness and the outcomes of interest within a country (with country fixed effects).

Patterns in this relative rating of affectedness show that there is variation in how affected groups perceived themselves to be, relative to others. In our first survey, we found that 24.6 percent of the respondents saw themselves as less affected than other organisations. 36.2 percent saw themselves as equally affected, while 39.2 percent declared to be more affected than other organisations. This concerns the first three months of the pandemic, during which its salience and sense of urgency was at its highest. This seems to be reflected in a large share of organisations that saw themselves as highly (more than average) affected. Despite the changed circumstances, when we fielded our second survey, a relatively similar pattern still holds, although the share of highly affected organisations decreased. Among respondents to the second survey, 28.8 percent of organisations declared to be less affected, 38.2 percent were equally affected, and 33 percent saw themselves as more affected.

As shown in Figure 2.5, these varying levels of affectedness are also present in the individual polities. A share of between 12.5 percent (Ireland, survey 1) and 36.9 percent (the Netherlands, survey 1) of groups perceived themselves as less (or much) less affected by the pandemic than other interest groups. The share of these organisations is lowest in Ireland and Denmark for both survey waves. Most of organisations at the polity level see themselves either as equally affected or relatively more (to much more) affected than other organisations. The latter category of more affected groups is, however, comparatively larger in Ireland and Austria, where – in both surveys – more than 40 percent of the organisations declared to be at least more affected than other groups. Similar evaluations are found in Denmark in the 2020 survey and in Sweden in the 2021 survey. The opposite is found in the Netherlands, especially in the 2021 survey where only 15.5 percent of the organisations fall in the relatively more affected category.

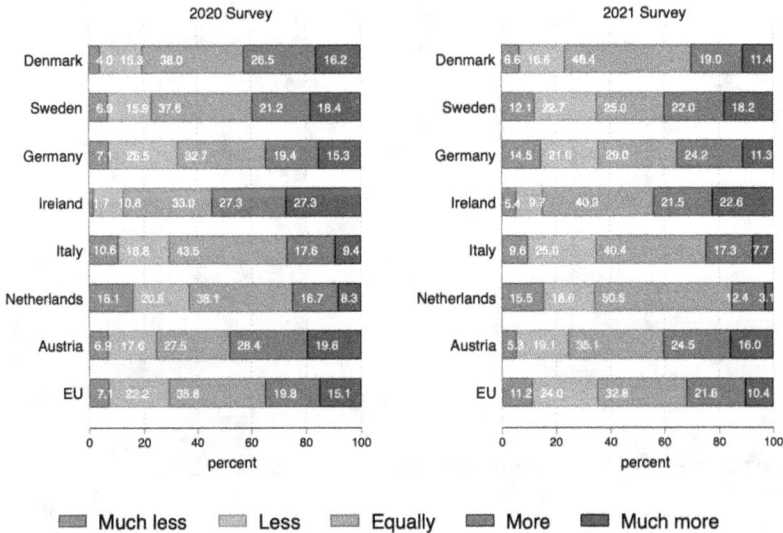

Figure 2.5: Levels of affectedness by polity (both survey waves).

It needs to be noted, that there is a well-documented tendency to over-estimate this kind of assessments among interest representatives. For example, lobbyists are found to often overestimate their impact on public policy (Newmark and Nownes 2017). However, considering that such tendencies are relatively consistent and that our specific measure of affectedness is expressed in *relative* terms to other organisations, we do not believe that – even if present – such a tendency introduces considerable biases in our analysis.

This is further supported by the fact that perceived affectedness does not vary substantially by group type (for both surveys), as Figure 2.6 reveals. In other words, there are no substantial differences in the extent to which *business groups and firms* perceived themselves as more affected by the pandemic compared to *profession groups and unions* or *NGOs and citizen groups*. This also indicates that the COVID-19 crisis, as described in the introduction, has been a system-wide event/shock, which has concerned the entirety of interest group systems.

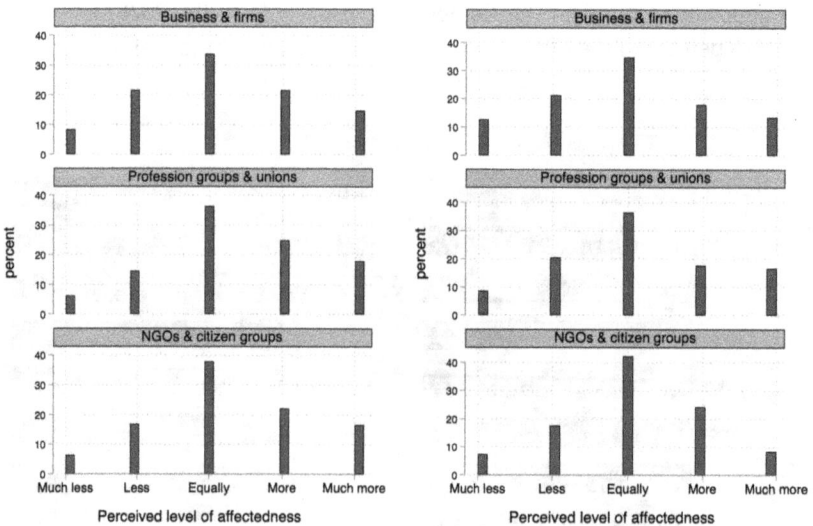

Figure 2.6: Levels of affectedness by group type (both survey waves).

Still, our measure of affectedness has its limitations. As already mentioned, as a subjective and relative measure capturing perceived affectedness, it is subject to potential over- or under estimation. Moreover, some may argue that affectedness strongly varied between sectors. In any case, observations in the same sector are not independent. All organisations in the education sector, for instance, are likely to have been affected by school closures, which makes it likely for educational groups to see themselves as more highly affected[6]. We address this in our econometric analyses by clustering standard errors by 13 sectors in which respondent organisations are active.

In both of our surveys, we asked respondents to identify the main sector of activity of the organisation. For *business groups and firms,* and *profession groups and unions,* this was a filter question listing 18 different sectors of activity[7]. For *NGOs and citizen groups,* the filter question included eleven options[8]. To compare respondents across sectors, we collapsed these categories into 13 different sector categories. Figure 2.7 shows the distribution of respondent organisations by sector for the first survey wave. The distribution is similar for both surveys.

As Figure 2.7 summarises, the highest share of the respondents, approximately 20 percent, are representatives of interest groups active in the *health and social work sector.* One may think that this pattern is heavily influenced by the circumstances of the pandemic. However, as data from national lobbying registers reveal, health and social work is among the most lobbied policy areas in several European countries also in non-pandemic years[9]. At the same time, almost ten percent of the interest representatives in our data work in the *development, aid and human rights sector,* arguably less affected by the pandemic in Europe relative to, for example, health and social work.

With these differences in mind, we acknowledge throughout the analyses that organisations working in specific sectors may have perceived themselves more or less affected by the pandemic. We therefore account for this by clustering standard errors by sector in our statistical analyses. As shown in our other work on lobbying in times of COVID-19, our analyses of trends in lobbying

---

6 Potentially and additionally, interest groups may have evaluated their level of affectedness also relative to other organisations within the same sector of activity, rather than relative to the full population of groups.

7 Agriculture, forestry and fishing; Mining and quarrying; Manufacturing, electricity, gas, steam and air conditioning supply; Water supply; Construction; Wholesale and retail trade; Transportation and storage; Hospitality / Accommodation and food service activities; Information and communication; Financial and insurance activities; Real estate activities; Education; Human health and social work activities; Arts, entertainment and recreation; Other service activities with physical contact, e. g. hairdressers; Other service activities without physical contact, e. g. call centre agency; Other.

8 Environment and animal rights; Development and aid; Human rights; Health care; Consumers; Local development; Social work and care; Education and information; Culture, art, religion and heritage; Sport and leisure; Other.

9 See, for example, lobbying register statistics in Ireland (SPOC n.d.) and France (LHA n.d.). The recently established register in Germany (Bundestag n.d.) lists health in the top five lobbied policy issues (almost 30 % of the declared lobbying activities).

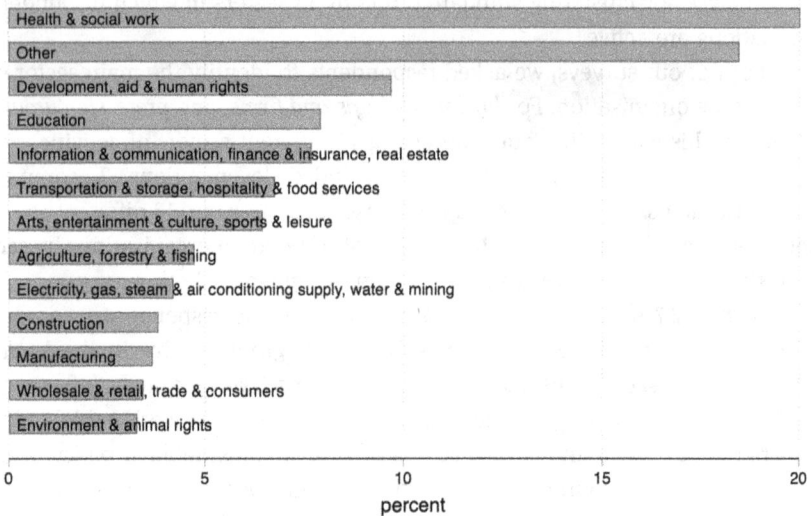

Figure 2.7: Distribution of respondent interest groups by sector (2020 survey).

also hold when further accounting for sector differences (see for example Junk et al. 2021).

Chapter Summary

In our view, there is no doubt that the activities of interest groups have been pivotal during the COVID-19 pandemic. In this chapter, we provided our rationale behind studying *viral lobbying* in seven European countries, namely Austria, Denmark, Germany, Ireland, Italy, the Netherlands, Sweden, plus the European Union. As discussed throughout the chapter, the circumstances of the pandemic in these polities varied, but have also been sufficiently similar to reveal common trends in *viral lobbying*. To capture patterns in lobbying mobilisation activities, strategies, access, and influence (see chapters 3 – 6), we explained how we fielded cross-national large-N surveys in the summer of 2020 and 2021. We designed the surveys to capture the particularities of lobbying during the pandemic. At the same time, they build on measurements of interest group activities that are comparable to lobbying in normal circumstances. In this chapter, we also showed how we stratified samples of business associations, firms, profession associations, unions, citizen groups, NGOs and other organisations in these eight polities. In total, we reached out to almost 6,000 organisations, first in June 2020, and again in June 2021, to capture how interest group had adapted to and 'survived' (in organisational terms) the first wave of COVID-19.

Over two survey waves and eight polities, we collected data from almost 1,500 unique organisations. This data complements existing large-N projects on interest group activities and addresses one of the main challenges in interest group research, namely the availability of cross-country data. Moreover, our data allows comparing lobbying at two moments in time, whereas most existing projects on lobbying do not include variation over time.

In addition to presenting our survey design, this chapter has set the basis for the analyses of the factors which, throughout the book, are identified as drivers of the influence production process. We described our data by *group type, lobbying resources* and levels of *affectedness* by the pandemic. In subsequent chapters, we treat each of these factors as potential explanatory variables in our analyses of issue mobilisation, lobbying strategies, access and, ultimately, influence on public policy. In addition, the chapter provided nuances describing country-level and sectoral differences among our respondents. There is much variation in our data, which we believe allows us to explain viral lobbying throughout the stages of the influence production process.

In the subsequent chapters, we will refer back to the methodological arguments and definitions presented here. The following chapters will also introduce and describe the outcome variables of interest in our analysis. Chapter 3 deals with issue mobilisation, Chapter 4 analyses the use of lobbying strategies, while Chapter 5 and 6 deal with access and influence, respectively. For each chapter, we present the variables' operationalisations in detail, as well as providing a descriptive discussion of their variation.

References

Aizenberg, E. (2022) 'Conflict and salience as drivers of corporate lobbying?'. *Governance*, Online First.

Aizenberg, E., and Hanegraaff, M. (2020) 'Time is of the Essence: A Longitudinal Study on Business Presence in Political News in the United Kingdom and the Netherlands'. *The International Journal of Press/Politics* 25(2):281–300.

Allern, E.H., and Hansen, V.W. (2022) Party-Interest Group Relationships in Contemporary Democracies (PAIRDEM) datasets [Data set]', in. Sikt – Norwegian Agency for Shared Services in Education and Research.

Allern, E.H., Hansen, V.W., Rødland, L., Røed, M., Klüver, H., Le Gall, C., Marshall, D., Otjes, S., Poguntke, T., Rasmussen, A., and Saurugger, S. (2022) 'Introducing the Party-interest group relationships in contemporary democracies datasets'. *Party Politics*, Online First.

Berkhout, J., Beyers, J., Braun, C., Hanegraaff, M., and Lowery, D. (2017) 'Making Inference across Mobilisation and Influence Research: Comparing Top-Down and Bottom-Up Mapping of Interest Systems'. *Political Studies* 66(1):43–62.

Beyers, J., Bernhagen, P., Borang, F., Braun, C., Fink-Hafner, D., Heylen, F., Maloney, W., Naurin, D., Pakull, D. (2016) 'Comparative Interest Group Survey Questionnaire' (Edition: January 2016). *Antwerp: University of Antwerp.*

Beyers, J., Fink-Hafner, D., Maloney, W.A., Novak, M., and Heylen, F. (2020) 'The Comparative Interest Group-survey project: design, practical lessons, and data sets'. *Interest Groups & Advocacy* 9(3):272–89.

Binderkrantz, A.S., Christiansen, P.M., and Pedersen, H.H. (2014) *Organisationer i politik*, Copenhagen: Hans Reitzels Forlag.

Binderkrantz, A.S., Christiansen, P.M., and Pedersen, H.H. (2020) 'Mapping interest group access to politics: a presentation of the INTERARENA research project'. *Interest Groups & Advocacy* 9(3):290–301.

Binderkrantz, A.S., and Rasmussen, A. (2015) 'Comparing the domestic and the EU lobbying context: perceived agenda-setting influence in the multi-level system of the European Union'. *Journal of European Public Policy* 22(4):552–69.

Bundestag. (n.d.) "Lobbyregister: Interessenvertretung gegenüber dem Deutschen Bundestag und der Bundesregierung." https://www.lobbyregister.bundestag.de/startseite (accessed June 14, 2022).

Chari, R., and Rozas, I. (2021) *Viruses, Vaccines, and Antivirals: Why Politics Matters*, Berlin: De Gruyter.

Crepaz, M. (2020) 'To inform, strategise, collaborate, or compete: what use do lobbyists make of lobby registers?'. *European Political Science Review* 12(3):347–69.

Crepaz, M., and Hanegraaff, M. (2020) 'The funding of interest groups in the EU: are the rich getting richer?'. *Journal of European Public Policy* 27(1):102–21.

Crepaz, M., Hanegraaff, M., and Junk, W.M. (2022) 'Is there a first mover advantage in lobbying? A comparative analysis of how the timing of lobbying affects the influence of interest groups in 10 polities'. *Comparative Political Studies*, Online First.

De Bruycker, I. (2019) 'Lobbying: An art and a science—Five golden rules for an evidence-based lobbying strategy'. *Journal of Public Affairs* 19(4):1–4.

Dür, A., and Mateo, G. (2016) *Insiders versus Outsiders: Interest Group Politics in Multilevel Europe*, Oxford: Oxford University Press.

Flöthe, L. (2019) 'The costs of interest representation – a resource perspective on informational lobbying'. *European Political Science Review* 11(2):161–78.

Jahn, D. (2022) 'Politics and corona lockdown regulations in 35 highly advanced democracies: The first wave'. *International Political Science Review*, Online First.

Junk, W.M. (2019) 'When Diversity Works: The Effects of Coalition Composition on the Success of Lobbying Coalitions'. *American Journal of Political Science* 63(3): 660–74.

Junk, W.M. (2020) 'Co-operation as currency: how active coalitions affect lobbying success'. *Journal of European Public Policy* 27(6):873–92.

Junk, W.M., Crepaz, M., Hanegraaff, M., Berkhout, J., and Aizenberg, E. (2020) "InterCov Project: Online Survey on Interest Representation during Covid-19. Edition: June – July 2020." https://www.wiebkejunk.com/_files/ugd/9a0cb4_eb572405723f490f8fd6e464420 f3a33.pdf (accessed June 13, 2022).

Junk, W.M., Crepaz, M., Hanegraaff, M., Berkhout, J., and Aizenberg, E. (2021a) 'Changes in Interest Group Access in Times of Crisis: No Pain, No (Lobby) Gain'. *Journal of European Public Policy*, Online First.

Junk, W.M., Crepaz, M., Hanegraaff, M., Berkhout, J., and Aizenberg, E. (2021b) "InterCov Project: Online Survey on Interest Representation during Covid-19. Second Edition: July – August 2021." https://www.wiebkejunk.com/_files/ugd/9a0cb4_ 7d44f6c80cc84d259983d8bbdfa3a729.pdf (accessed June 13, 2022).

LHA. (n.d.) "Le répertoire (La Haute Autorité)." https://www.hatvp.fr/le-repertoire/ (accessed June 14, 2022).

Mahoney, C. (2008) *Brussels versus the beltway: Advocacy in the United States and the European Union*, Washington D.C.: Georgetown University Press.

Marchetti, K. (2015) 'The use of surveys in interest group research'. *Interest Groups & Advocacy* 4(3):272–82.

Naurin, D., and Boräng, F. (2012) 'Who are the lobbyists?: A population study of interest groups in Sweden'. *Statsvetenskaplig tidskrift* 114(1):95–102.

Newmark, A.J., and Nownes, A.J. (2017) 'It's all relative: Perceptions of interest group influence'. *Interest Groups & Advocacy* 6(1):66–90.

Pritoni, A. (2019) 'Preferring Rome to Brussels: Mapping Interest Group Europeanisation in Italy'. *South European Society and Politics* 24(4):441–62.

Rasmussen, A., Mäder, L.K., and Reher, S. (2018) 'With a Little Help From The People? The Role of Public Opinion in Advocacy Success'. *Comparative Political Studies* 51(2):139–64.

Ritchie, H., et al. (2020) 'Coronavirus pandemic (COVID-19)'. *Our world in data.* available at https://ourworldindata.org/covid-vaccinations?country=OWID_WRL (accessed June 13, 2022) (accessed.

SPOC. (n.d.) "Register of Lobbying, Reports & Statistics (Standards in Public Office Commission)." https://www.lobbying.ie/reports-statistics/ (accessed June 14, 2022).

WHO. (2022) "WHO Coronavirus (COVID-19) Dashboard." https://covid19.who.int/ (accessed June 13, 2022).

Online Appendix

https://www.degruyter.com/document/isbn/9783110783148/html

Chapter 3
Issue Mobilisation

In every modern society, we find large numbers and various types of organisations; large and small commercial corporations, schools, hospitals, NGOs, voluntary associations, labour unions, cause groups, associations of professionals and so on. These organisations have relevant missions and tasks that vary in the degree to which these intersect with public policies. A major multinational airline company, for example, will have a public affairs department, but as proportion of its turnover this might still be small. A chair of a small patient association may occasionally meet hospital directors and politicians, but is likely to spend more time on organising self-help sessions. Even labour unions commonly have more staff working on legal advisory services for members than on public policy monitoring.

While these political activities may be small relative to the core tasks of these organisations, they are substantial in terms of their relevance for the policy process. This became especially apparent at the start of the COVID-19 pandemic when policymakers and interest groups faced severe new policy problems. The design of respective policy interventions depended heavily on input from different social and economic interests that could help policymakers to make more informed choices regarding the complex trade-offs at stake, for example between economic and health-related risks in crisis management.

Yet, organisations vary a great deal in the extent to which they are politically active, and, over time, their political activity also follows the ebbs and flows of the saliency of the policies they are interested in. To the extent to which organisations engage in activities aimed at influencing public policies, they take the role of interest groups in the policy process (see behavioural definition noted in Chapter 1). We label the activation of the public policy function of existing organisations *issue mobilisation*.

The degree and nature of issue mobilisation is important, firstly, because of its empirical and normative implications for all other steps of the lobbying process – i.e. the strategies, access and influence of interest groups. Put differently, the extent to which an organisation mobilises on public policy issues in the first place affects the variety of strategies it may be able to choose from, as well as the variety of policies and policy instruments it can engage with and potentially have a say in. This mattered especially during COVID-19; organisations faced serious challenges maintaining their activities, gaining access and securing a policy voice. This is studied in full detail in the subsequent chapters. Given the stepwise nature of influence production outlined in the introduction, we, however, first assess whether organisations dropped-out completely or were forced to seriously downscale their operations and were, therefore, not able to (effectively) advocate their interests.

Secondly, in normative terms, issue mobilisation potentially creates inequalities between interest groups in the extent to which they voice their concerns (e. g. Lowery et al. 2015). In case interests are not organisationally voiced, public policies will not be informed by plausibly relevant groups – even if access is abundant and interest group participation to policymaking is actively sought by policymakers. Importantly, if we want to assess the capacity of interest group systems to provide a somewhat unbiased voice reflecting concerns in society, we also need to know whether voices persist under more stressful circumstances.

Lastly, issue mobilisation is important in an even broader way. The degree to which organisations in society take responsibility and engage with politics can affect democratic stability, because organisational engagement can act as a counterweight to short-term populism (e. g. Truman 1959) and balance exclusively state-centred power concentrations (e. g. Acemoglu and Robinson 2020). A society without meaningfully diverse organisational political engagement, in other words, is likely to be more sensitive to political instability and concentration of power in the executive. Such society-based counterforces are also, or even especially, important in crisis situations, where other factors such as legal emergency procedures potentially contribute to instability and lack of controls on power. Regarding COVID-19, for instance, parliamentary oppositions were initially characterised by a 'rally around the flag' solidarity, adding positive sentiments to government initiatives, but, as time passed, showed to be adequate criticisers of executives (Louwerse et al. 2021). Interest groups have the potential to play a similar and complementary role.

For these reasons, we aim to assess in this chapter why some interest groups *mobilise* more or less intensely on policy issues than others, when an event potentially triggers their interests. We study issue mobilisation during the pandemic by looking at whether, when, and how intensely groups began to try to influence COVID-related policies. We are especially interested in differences between organisations and think that COVID-related lockdown measures created special circumstances that potentially magnified hypothesised differences between organisations. Earlier studies show several changes in the behaviour of interest groups, suggesting that the pandemic activated interest groups into action (Eady and Rasmussen 2021; Bonafont and Iborra 2021; Junk et al. 2021; Fuchs, Sack, and Spilling 2021; Fuchs and Sack 2021). Yet, these studies have not explicitly addressed issue mobilisation.

In the following, we first theoretically identify three plausible explanations for differences in issue mobilisation. The first explanations follow from theories of initial group mobilisation, and we identify why these may also be relevant in explaining *issue mobilisation*. Specifically, we build upon arguments about social and policy 'disturbances' as triggers of mobilisation (Truman 1951), leading us to hypothesise that more affected organisations by the pandemic should be more intensely politically active on COVID-19 related policies. In addition, we expand on Olson's (1965) argument on collective action to encompass policy activity, which leads us to expect that business interests, as well as more highly re-sourced groups compared to others, are more likely to mobilise more intensely. As a second and alternative explanation, we consider the internal challenges that the COVID-19 crisis produced within organisations, and the extent to which these hampered policy engagement.

After formulating our hypotheses on these relationships, we present our analysis based on three different operationalisations of issue mobilisation, namely as *mobilisation success*, in terms of *speed*, and as varying in *intensity*. On the whole, we find that relatively heavily affected organisations, as well as groups with large numbers of public policy staff were more likely to mobilise, and did so more speedily and intensely. We also find that NGOs and citizen groups were relatively disadvantaged compared to business organisations on two of our three measures of issue mobilisation. We close with reflections on the implications of these findings.

Drivers of Issue Mobilisation in Times of Crisis

Issue mobilisation is distinct from interest, group or member mobilisation. Inter-est mobilisation deals with the formation of collective action organisations and the recruitment of new members or the on-going maintenance of member rela-tions.[10] A plethora of theories and studies deal with interest mobilisation (e. g. Lowery and Brasher 2004). In fact, Baumgartner and Leech (1998) note in their extensive review of interest group research that this is the most saturated subfield, on which few, if any, empirical or theoretical innovation is needed or to be expected. While this may be somewhat of an overstatement, also given new 'digital' modes of mobilisation, we follow their suggestion to assume that a focus on existing, potentially politically active organisations is of greater inter-

---

10 It can also include the establishment and retention of public affairs departments within (semi-public) companies or liaison offices of public agencies.

est to our understanding of interest group politics in COVID-19 times than the problem of initial group mobilisation.

Recent scholarship seems to reflect this assessment, and several studies attend to issue mobilisation (e.g. De Bruycker, Berkhout, and Hanegraaff 2019; Hanegraaff et al. 2015; Rasmussen, Carroll, and Lowery 2014), sometimes labelled, 'second-order' or 'second-stage' mobilisation or *politicisation* (Bolleyer 2021). This focus makes sense, as emphasised by Leech et al. (2005, 26): 'the problems of mobilisation do not end after an organisation is formed. No organisation has unlimited resources, and no organisation wants to expend efforts on a hopeless cause.'

Rasmussen, Carroll, and Lowery (2014, 252) identify the *second stage of mobilisation* as 'the decisions of individual organisations to mobilise on concrete policy issues'. De Bruycker, Berkhout, and Hanegraaff (2019) discuss the link between interest aggregation into organisations and interest articulation in the policy process and note that organisations internally have to 'form' an interest or a policy position in case new circumstances arise, such as in response to new legislative proposals. The relative efficiency of this 'policy positioning', they argue, is part of the collective action process, and may be observed in the speed with which organisations respond to new policy initiatives. Connectedly, Bolleyer (2021, 498) presents an organisational governance perspective on the relative politicisation of civil society organisations consisting of two stages: (1) a decision for or against political engagement and (2) the widening of the variety of political activities on the part of the organisation. Put differently, issue mobilisation varies dichotomously, in the sense that organisations are either politically active or not, but additionally varies in terms of intensity, which may be conceived in several ways: in terms of the variety of political tactics, their frequency of use, but also the speed of mobilisation.

We adopt such a view of issue mobilisation and explore different factors which may explain whether organisations mobilise, how much and how fast. To do so, we first draw on adaptations of regular mobilisation theories and, subsequently, include more proximate, organisational explanations.

Explanations Based on Mobilisation Theories

To some conceptual extent, organisations face similar challenges during their formation and when mobilising on policy issues. These challenges can be associated with the 'optimistic', pluralist argument by Truman (1951) and the more pessimistic arguments by Olson (1965), respectively, and they lead to two expectations regarding the extent to which organisations vary in their levels of issue mobilisation.

To begin with, Truman (1951) notes that organisations will have to identify the exact collective interests that merit aggregation and articulation. In his so called 'pluralist' argument, the source of collective interests lies in a *change* in the relationships among individuals. For instance, when medical knowledge progresses through new research or technology, the relationships among the members of a medical association may change with some doctor-members being more knowledgeable than others. This change must then be addressed to restore stability, for instance by updating the qualification standards in relevant parts of the medical profession. Sometimes the source of change lies in the mobilisation of other interests (e. g. Lowery and Brasher 2004). For instance, when a new 'alternative' subset of the medical profession mobilises, say those specialising in new treatment forms, established medical associations may respond by opening or closing their associations to newcomers. Given the breadth of contemporary policy processes, such changes in the relationships among individuals, labelled 'disturbances' by Truman, commonly have a more proximate source in changes in public policy.

Obviously, the COVID-crisis produced a lot of changes in relations among individuals, especially concerning the work they do. Some sectors, such as hotels and restaurants, completely closed for the time being; other sectors faced heavy losses, and large parts of the population could not engage in their daily pursuits. Existing organisations immediately faced new issues that merited internal formation, prioritisation and attention in the policy process.

This classic argument resonates with more recent studies of interest groups, sometimes labelled as 'neopluralist'. For instance, Halpin, Fraussen, and Nownes (2018) (also: Fraussen, Halpin, and Nownes 2021) identify *internal* drivers of issue prioritisation. More specifically, the extent to which the core constituency or the group's mission is at stake, heavily determines the priority an issue will receive from group leaders. This is especially the case when internal working routines, as addressed below, facilitate responsiveness of leaders to membership concerns.

In the context of COVID-related lockdown restrictions, leaders had to assess the extent to which the pandemic impacted the organisation and its mission. In cases where group leaders considered their organisations' mission more directly affected by COVID-19 compared to others, it is plausible that these leaders invested more heavily in political activities than other organisations. This leads to our first hypothesis, which expects a positive link between the level of affectedness of an organisation during the COVID-19 crisis and their issue mobilisation, in terms of the likelihood to mobilise, mobilisation speed and intensity.

H1 'affectedness hypothesis': the higher the level of affectedness, the more likely is i) issue mobilisation, as well as ii) timely and iii) intense issue mobilisation on Coronavirus-related policies.

Other theories of mobilisation, would, however, expect a different pattern. As famously emphasised by Olson (1965), mobilisation might be hindered because members (or potential beneficiaries) of organisations may want to avoid investing energy in the organisation, plausibly free-riding on the participatory efforts of others (also e. g. Knoke 1986; Rothenberg 1988). Given organisational leaders will need the support of members, such free-riding can have far-reaching consequences.

Among other potential implications, this dynamic is likely to play out differently between business and non-business interests (e. g. Berkhout, Hanegraaff, and Maloney 2021; Hanegraaff 2015). Business associations are more likely to draw upon a closed set and relatively small number of members, plausibly with relatively concentrated interests. This facilitates a relatively easy resolution of collective action problems, because individual benefits are more likely to outweigh the costs of contributing to the common effort. In addition, business organisations are well-placed to offer material selective incentives (e. g. critical market data) or subtle forms of forced riding (e. g. accreditation), that are less available for those mobilising other types of interests. This is consistent with Olson's (1965, 132) 'by-product' argument, where some groups can overcome free-rider problems because lobbying becomes a by-product of other member benefits. Based on this reasoning, leaders of business associations should have more strategic flexibility to attend to the representation of interests in public policy, compared to other groups[11]. Moreover, as noted by Heinz, Laumann, and Nelson (1993), public affairs departments of firms also face 'mobilisation' issues when justifying their political work internally in relation to other departments. While this internal justification will not always be a done deal (e. g. Hart 2004), it is plausibly easier to politically activate a well-prepared and hierarchically controlled public affairs department than to coordinate collective political action in a voluntary association.

These theoretical arguments on group type differences are likely to play out even more heavily during the COVID-19 pandemic. That is, the 'cost' of collective action, also when conceived more broadly, is likely to have increased under COVID, especially disadvantaging those organisations who already had to invest heavily in resolving collective action problems by means of the provision of se-

---

11 Yet, also note more nuanced findings in De Bruycker, Berkhout, and Hanegraaff (2019).

lective incentives. For instance, some of the selective material incentives provided by business interest groups, e. g. data on changes in the market, could still be relatively easily provided, whereas some of the expressive or solidary incentives offered by non-business groups, such as annual membership meetings, events or regular outings with volunteers, were impossible or heavily restricted after the outbreak of the pandemic. Our second hypothesis is, therefore formulated, as follows:

H2 'group type hypothesis': Business organisations are more likely to i) mobilise on Coronavirus-related policies than non-business interest groups, as well as ii) to engage in timely and iii) intense issue mobilisation.

In addition, one can reason based on Olson's argument that resources should be a key predictor of mobilisation. As Olson (1965, 132) puts it 'lobbies are the by-products of organisations that obtain their strength and support because they perform some function in addition to lobbying'. It follows that some organisations will be 'stronger' than other organisations because of the 'other function' they perform, and therefore the scope for the employment of 'by-products' (lobbying) is larger. In simple terms, an organisation with a profitable members-services department will have more slack resources to invest in a large public affairs department (see also: Hanegraaff and van der Ploeg 2020), and this will ease mobilisation on issues that arise. Therefore, we expect that, independent of the type of group, the availability of (staff) resources gives organisational leaders the opportunity to mobilise politically, as our next hypothesis summarises.

H3 'resource hypothesis': The more resources a group has, the more likely is i) issue mobilisation on Coronavirus-related policies, as well as ii) timely and iii) intense issue mobilisation.

Alternative Explanations Based on Internal Organisational Pressures

This application of Olson's long-standing theories of mobilisation can, however, also be challenged. De Bruycker, Berkhout, and Hanegraaff (2019, 308) note that one 'cannot readily conflate first-stage and second-stage collective action problems'. Similarly, Lowery (2015, 12) observes that 'simple' policy- or organisational implications drawn from Olson's logic of collective action are unwarranted, and that one needs 'a richer appreciation of the internal life of interest organisations' in order to assess why, and on what issues, interest groups lobby.

More concretely, after the initial group formation and the resolution of collective action problems is managed sufficiently, organisational challenges shift towards the internal arrangement of the diverse tasks of the organisation. The continuation and further development of core tasks will require a lot of attention from the leaders of organisations. The engagement with public policy, as indicated above, is, or becomes, a 'by-product' or secondary activity of many, if not most, organisations active in politics.

Bolleyer (2021) focusses on this dynamic within civil society organisations and notes that there is a tension between attending to membership services and engaging with politics (also see: Albareda 2018; Schmitter and Streeck 1999). The membership- and policy-oriented activities operate under distinct 'logics of exchange' (Berkhout 2013), and may require different organisational working procedures to perform effectively. For instance, in order to service their membership, a patient organisation might want to recruit and facilitate large numbers of volunteer-run self-help meetings, while public policy engagement would require them to professionalise and move away from volunteering.

The distinct dynamics of such organisational tension may differ across associations, especially between organisations with substantial professional staff working on public policy and volunteer-based or less resourceful organisations. However, what seems to apply across all politically active groups is that organisations with problems in their primary activities will need to focus their attention on those problems and, as a consequence, scale down secondary activities, most notably their policy-oriented (lobbying) activities.

This is especially relevant when COVID-related restrictions created challenges to the primary working processes of organisations. For instance, consider two patient organisations primarily active as 'self-help' communities and that are similar in terms of affectedness and group type, but one of which deals with a disease that does not impact 'digital' engagement, whereas for the other 'digital' engagement is impossible. Under COVID-lockdown, the 'primary' task of the facilitation of communication among the patient community moved online relatively easily in the first case, but was fully discontinued in the second case. This is likely to also have reduced the possible issue mobilisation of this latter organisation, given that strategic attention plausibly fully focused on finding some alternative way to facilitate the primary tasks. This reasoning leads us to expect that internal organisational pressures, such as problems with primary membership activities, are a hindrance to mobilisation, as summarised in our final hypothesis.

H4 'internal problems': The stronger the pressure on primary activities within an interest group, the less likely is i) issue mobilisation on Coronavirus-related policies, as well as ii) timely and iii) intense issue mobilisation.

An underlying assumption for all these hypotheses is that we see the spread of COVID-19 and the following lockdown restrictions as a focussing event (see Chapter 1), and expect this to have impacted organisations' ability to mobilise politically. At the same time, we expect these effects to vary depending on the organisations' level of affectedness, group type, resources and internal organisational problems, as stated in our hypotheses. In the next section, we test these expectations based on data from our cross-national surveys (see Chapter 2).

Analysis: Issue Mobilisation during the Pandemic

In line with the multifaced nature of issue mobilisation, as our dependent factor, we empirically differentiate between three dimensions of issue mobilisation: (1) whether any issue mobilisation occurs, (2) the speed of mobilisation relative to the COVID-19 triggering 'disturbance' and (3) the intensity of mobilisation in terms of the number of times political activities were implemented. These operationalisations are based on several survey items found in the first of our surveys (Junk et al. 2020) and will be explained further below. In what follows, we first present univariate, descriptive figures of different indicators of issue mobilisation and subsequently discuss a number of multivariate regression models to assess the explanatory power of affectedness, group type, resources, and internal organisational problems.

Overview of Mobilisation Patterns

We first present some *descriptive* statistics related to our different mobilisation measures. Our first operationalisation of issue mobilisation, *mobilisation success*, is based on a survey item in the first wave of our data collection effort. We asked the respondents to indicate 'if and when [their organisation's] political activity started to target Coronavirus-related policies'. Organisations that answered that they did not do any Coronavirus-related political work during this time period are considered not to have mobilised (0), whereas all organisations that mobilised *at some point* between March and the end of May 2020 are considered to have mobilised successfully (1). Around 75 percent of our respondents who answered this question $(N=1,567)$[12] conducted Coronavirus-related political work in the months following the first COVID-19 outbreak. Remember that our sample construction aims to include potentially politically active organisations. This suggests that the 25 percent of the organisations for which we do not observe any issue mobilisation are plausibly limited to do so because of the circumstances, potentially combined with the factors identified in our hypotheses (e. g. they may be unaffected by the pandemic or lack the resources to get involved).

Second, as an indicator of the *pace* or speediness of issue mobilisation, we took the numbers of weeks into account that it took organisations to target their political activities at Coronavirus-related policies. This measure is based on the same survey item, where respondents could enter the month and precise week between the beginning of March and the end of May 2020. To construct this variable capturing *mobilisation pace*, we disregard respondents who had indicated that they had not engaged politically, as we consider these as not having mobilised. Figure 3.1 shows the distribution across groups in terms of the *pace of mobilisation*. There is a more or less equal distribution over the five pace categories we identified. The first four categories reflect the respective four weeks in March. That is, organisations with highest pace are those that mobilised during the first week of March; high pace indicates mobilisation during the second week of March, etc. The lowest pace category refers to all organisations mobilising from early April onwards. Some organisations were clearly able to focus on the Coronavirus-policy initiatives quickly (nearly 19.4 percent of active groups doing so in the first week of March), whereas for others adaptation was slower (with 21.6 percent of active groups mobilising from early April onwards).

Furthermore, we derive the *intensity* of issue mobilisation by combining the length of the lobbying period with a question we asked on the frequency with which respondents aimed political activities at influencing Coronavirus related policies during the time they were active (in the weeks between March 2020 to the end of May 2020). Answer categories ranged from 'almost daily' to 'only once' after the respondent started their lobbying activities on COVID-related issues. To proxy the actual number of lobbying instances by the group, we weighted this response by the number of weeks respondents had indicated to be politically active (see Figure 3.1), which should give us a relatively precise indication of their lobbying intensity.

---

12 Note that the number of observations can diverge somewhat from the numbers of fully completed surveys (see Chapter 2), given that we also use observations from surveys that were not completed to the end. In addition, missing observations exist on some variables, when respondents chose not to answer individual questions.

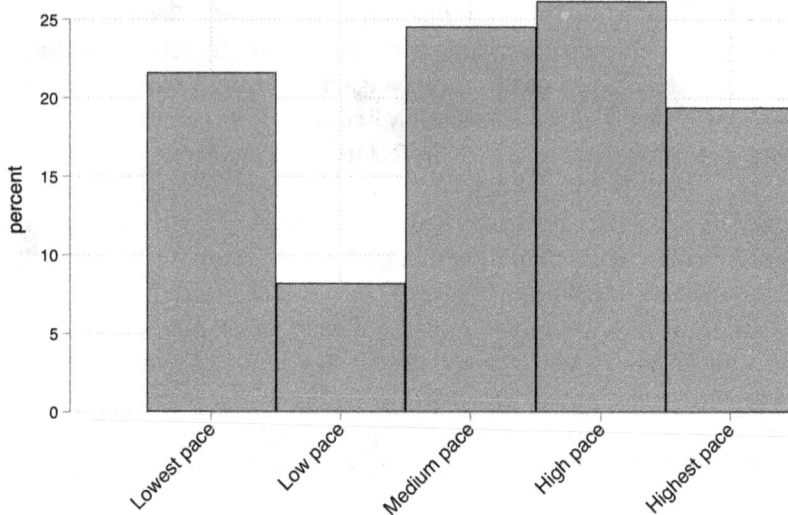

Figure 3.1: Pace of mobilisation (2020) (excludes non-mobilised groups).

Figure 3.2 shows this variable, which combines speediness and frequency of mobilisation into a frequency (count) with which organisations tried to influence Coronavirus-related policies. It is calculated based on the frequency question multiplied by the number of weeks of lobbying activity. As the figure shows, we observe a cluster of organisations that mobilised intensely (50 or more times). These account for approximately twenty percent of organisations and are represented by the bars on the right-hand side of Figure 3.2. On the left-hand side of the figure, we find organisations that mobilised less intensely. This accounts for the majority of organisations.

This skewed type distribution where a minority of interest groups account for a large share of lobbying is commonly found in measures of political activity on issues (Baumgartner and Leech 2001; Binderkrantz, Bonafont, and Halpin 2016; Braun et al. 2020; Hanegraaff, van der Ploeg, and Berkhout 2020). It is routinely attributed to the 'bridge' function particular 'insider' or 'core' organisations have within group systems (LaPira, Thomas, and Baumgartner 2014; Berkhout et al. 2017). The largest proportion of organisations has a medium or intermittent level of issue mobilisation, which is represented in the bars on the left-hand side of the Figure 3.2 (around the 10 mark on the x-axis).

In the next section, we present models to explain the variation in these measures of issue mobilisation.

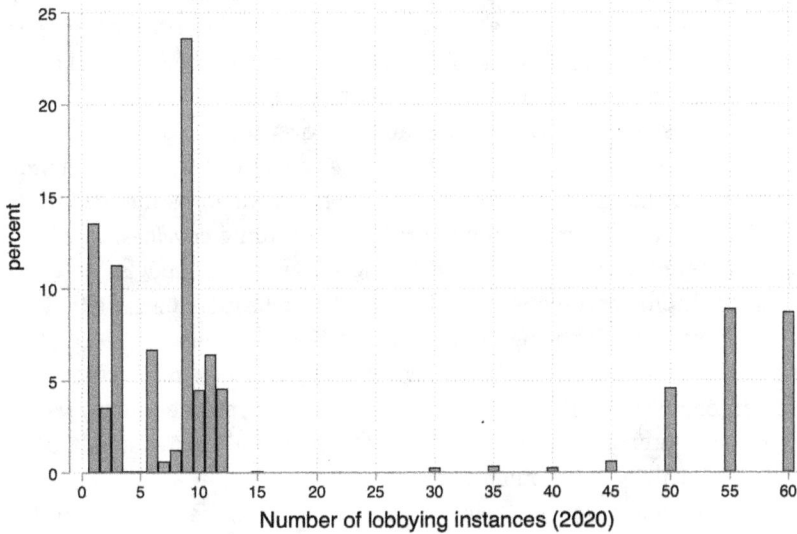

Figure 3.2: Intensity of mobilisation (2020) (excludes non-mobilised groups).

Explanatory Models of Issue Mobilisation

In the following, we present the results from several regression models; each related to one of our dependent variables. In each model, we include all explanatory factors we considered in our hypotheses, as well as a number of control
variables.

To test Hypothesis 1, we use a measure of *affectedness*, which relies on a survey item measuring the extent to which an organisation, according to its own
perception, was 'more or less affected by the Coronavirus crisis, compared to
other stakeholders in [country]'. Answer categories take five values, from
'much less affected' (1) to 'much more affected' (5). For Hypotheses 2 and 3,
we distinguish between *business groups and firms, profession groups and unions,*
as well as *NGOs and citizen groups,* using *business groups and firms* as reference
category. We measure resources for lobbying through an item that captures the
number of staff working on public affairs in the organisations (in full time equivalents). Answers are grouped in three categories of low (<1), medium (1–4) and
high (≥5). These variables are explained in more detail in Chapter 2, which also
summarises their distribution.

Additionally, Hypothesis 4 provided an alternative explanation based on the *internal problems* faced by organisations. To capture these, we asked several questions about the implications of COVID-19 for the membership of the organisation. Respondents could indicate the extent to which members or supporters 'cannot organise day-to-day activities' and are 'over-burdened' with work. Both of these were measured on scales from 0 (strongly disagree) to 10 (strongly agree). We take these as indicators of the internal challenges the organisations faced during the pandemic: internal problems regarding *activities*, and internal problems regarding *workload*. By including these in our models, we can test whether such problems reduce the intensity of mobilisation, because they divert attention away from lobbying, as we hypothesised.

In all analyses, we control for the age of an organisation and for the extent to which an organisation is an umbrella group. We also include dummy variables for countries to explore differences between them, and cluster standard errors by sector of activity of the interest groups.

The full regression output in table form can be found in the Online Appendix to the book (Table A3.1). To ease interpretation for the reader, we have chosen to only display coefficient plots of the key explanatory variables. Figure 3.3 shows such plots based on a series of regressions. Where the confidence intervals (straight lines) of the plotted coefficients (dot in the middle) do not overlap with 0 (the vertical dotted line), we can say with high certainty that there is a significant relationship between the explanatory factor and issue mobilisation.

We use different regression estimation techniques to account for the different nature and distribution of the three dependent variables. More specifically, Figure 3.3 reports estimations derived from logit regression models to explain *issue mobilisation* (top of the figure), ordered logit regression to explain the *pace of mobilisation* (middle) and negative binomial regression to explain the *intensity* of mobilisation (bottom).

Jointly, these models help explain why some groups mobilise more than others. As a general pattern, they suggest that especially organisations with large numbers of public policy staff and those who indicate to be highly affected by the COVID-19 crisis were more likely to engage in issue mobilisation. In all different operationalisations of issue mobilisation, we find significant and substantial effects in the direction that we theoretically expected for these factors: more affected (H1) and better-resourced organisations (H3) are more likely to mobilise, and to do so in a more timely and intense manner.

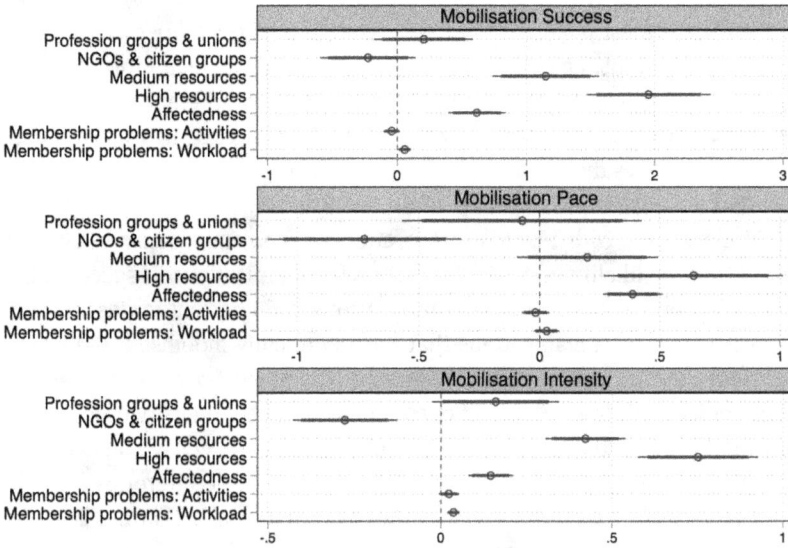

Figure 3.3: Logit regression on issue mobilisation (top chart), ordered logit regression on pace (middle chart) and negative binomial regression on the intensity of mobilisation (bottom chart). Coefficients and 95/90% confidence intervals.

Notes: The figure is based on a series of three regressions, one for each dependent variable (success: logistic regression; pace: ordered logistic regression; intensity: negative binomial). The first includes all organisations, including those that did not mobilise (n=1018), whereas we assess the effect of pace and intensity for those that actually mobilised (n=784 and n=778, respectively). Included controls in all these models were: organisation age, the group's potential status as an umbrella organisation, and fixed effects for the country/polity. In addition, we include the two variables capturing internal organisational problems. Moreover, we clustered standard errors by sector given that mobilisation for groups within a sector is likely to be related. For results in table form see Table A3.1 in the Online Appendix. Measures of goodness of fit (pseudo R-squared) lie at 0.19 (success), pace: 0.06 (pace), and 0.03 (intensity).

Moreover, the size of these effects is substantive. Our models predict[13] that the probability that the *least affected* groups will mobilise successfully is 56 percent. This reaches 94 percent for *most affected* organisations, a substantial difference of 38 percentage points between highest and lowest levels of affectedness. More-

---

13 All predicted probabilities/values are based on the main models (see Figure 3.3) when holding all other variables at means.

over, once they mobilise, the probability that highly affected organisations will do so at the *highest pace* is 25 percent, while this is only 7 percent for least affected organisations. Least affected organisations are, in fact, more likely to mobilise at a *slow* (13 percent) or *slowest pace* (34 percent). Finally, our models suggest that, least affected groups are predicted to engage in approximately 11 lobbying instances during the studied period, while organisations at the highest level of affectedness are expected to do so 20 times.

Similarly, but with regards to the effect of *lobbying resources*, our models predict that the likelihood for better-resourced organisations to successfully mobilise is 93 percent, while this percentage drops to 66 percent for less resourceful groups. Among the organisations that have politically mobilised, the likelihood that highly resourceful groups will do so at the *highest pace* is 20 percent, but only 12 percent for low-resourced ones. In terms of the intensity of mobilisation, our model predicts that resourceful organisations would engage on average in 22 lobbying instances compared to only 11 for less resourceful groups.

This is consistent with earlier studies covering non-crisis time periods, but the strength of the effect suggests that the plausible implications for other parts of the influence production process are likely to be even more substantial than theoretically discussed. This general finding is also consistent with some of the journalistic accounts of lobbying under COVID. For instance, highly affected sectors with well-staffed public affairs departments, such as aviation, seem to have been more successful in voicing their concerns than less affected and less well-staffed interests, such as those of parents' groups relying on (closed) day-cares or students' associations in (online) academic education. In the conclusion, we highlight the, in our view ambivalent, normative implications of these findings.

In contrast to our Hypothesis 2, however, different types of groups are relatively similar in terms of their ability to conduct political activities (*mobilisation success*, on the top of Figure 3.3). This suggests that Olsonian collective action problems do not 'simply' translate into issue mobilisation challenges. Our two other models, however, do indicate relevant differences between group types: *NGOs and citizen groups* mobilised at a significantly slower pace and less intensively compared to *business groups and firms*. For example, our model suggests a significantly higher probability of NGOs and citizen groups mobilising at the *slowest* pace (24 percent) compared to the *highest* pace (10 percent). Conversely, for business groups and firms, as well as for *profession groups and unions*, mobilisation at *highest* pace is more likely (18 and 17 percent predicted probability, respectively) than the *slowest* pace (from 13 and 14 percent). Moreover, our model predicts that, in terms of *intensity of mobilisation*, NGOs and citizen groups will engage in approximately 12 instances of lobbying, while this number is higher for business and firms (16) and profession groups and unions (19).

Concerning Hypothesis 4, Figure 3.3 only provides weak evidence for any effect of internal problems, and, where this exists, it partly runs in the opposite direction than expected. Rather than hampering lobbying, some internal problems may motivate lobbying, as seems to be the case for situations where members are overburdened with work (see models: *mobilisation success* and *mobilisation intensity* in Figure 3.3.). This finding could be explained by similar mechanisms as the effect of affectedness.[14] Regarding internal problems affecting activities, however, coefficients are not consistently significantly different from zero.

Substantially, the effect of internal problems related to members' workload on the likelihood of mobilisation success and more intense mobilisation are relatively small. This equals to a 7 percent increase in the likelihood of mobilisation success when an organisation moves from the lowest to the highest extent of internal workload challenges. In terms of intensity, our model predicts an increase of 5 lobbying instances for the same change in internal workload problems. Contrary to our expectation, this suggests that challenges to primary processes within organisations, such as pressures coming from excessive workload, can *activate* (instead of hinder) interest groups into lobbying. This may relate to the specific circumstances of the pandemic, during which, in many instances, internal organisational challenges overlapped with policy disturbances. For example, imagine associations of professionals drafting internal recommendations for health and safety protocols while, at the same time, lobbying for COVID-19 policy on the issue.

Overall, we found strong support for Hypothesis 1, related to the level of affectedness, and Hypotheses 3, which expects the importance of resources for issue mobilisation. We also found support for Hypothesis 2, which suggests that business groups should have an advantage in issue mobilisation: Those NGOs and citizen groups that did mobilise, mobilised less quickly and less intensely than business groups. Regarding Hypothesis 4 on internal problems affecting an organisation's procedures, however, we found no evidence that these hinder mobilisation.

---

14 This is substantiated by the fact that there is a low but significantly positive correlation between the indicators of affectedness and internal dynamics, ranging from 0.19 to 0.26.

Chapter Summary

Large numbers of societal organisations have the potential to actively engage with public policy. Yet in practice, as we showed in this chapter, issue mobilisation varies substantially between organisations. We considered whether, how fast and how intensely organisations mobilised on COVID-19-related issues after the outbreak of the pandemic. Our findings show that highly affected groups by the pandemic, as well as better-resourced organisations and, to some extent, business groups mobilised significantly more than other groups.

These findings help us evaluate several normatively and theoretically relevant explanations for differences in issue mobilisation. To start, the findings clearly show that relatively heavily affected organisations are more likely to politically voice their interests and issue mobilise compared to organisations that see themselves as less affected than others. This pattern is in line with what earlier and contemporary pluralist theorists expect when they identify 'disturbances' as important triggers of group mobilisation (Truman 1951). Our findings confirm other recent studies (e.g. Halpin and Fraussen 2017) that suggest that disturbances not only affect membership mobilisation by also heavily impact issue mobilisation choices on the part of existing organisations. We consider this a broadly positive phenomenon. Normatively speaking, the interest group system *should* be biased in favour of heavily affected interests after a focussing event. This creates opportunities for citizens and other actors to meaningfully participate in politics. For policymakers, this means a broader range of voices can be included in the initiation and execution of public policy. To illustrate, it is likely that during the pandemic the interests of heavily affected health care professionals have been widely voiced. This is not only beneficial to the professionals themselves, but plausibly contributed to better-informed public policy decisions concerning the health crisis.

Second, our findings also support expectations derived from Olson's famous *Logic of Collective Action*. We find relevant differences across group type, even though these only hold for the intensity and the pace of mobilisation rather than for the general mobilisation success. This finding can qualify how collective action problems translate to issue mobilisation (see also: De Bruycker, Berkhout, and Hanegraaff 2019). It is not the case that diffuse interests (represented by NGOs and citizen groups) fail to mobilise after a focussing event. Yet, they are not as fast, and act less persistently compared to business groups. This still constitutes a form of group type bias, but the picture is less bleak than the pessimistic account presented by Olson.

We also found strong empirical evidence that better staffed organisations were more likely to issue mobilise on COVID-19-related issues and did so faster and more intensely. Arguably, this supports the Olsonian so-called 'by-product' theory, whereby lobbying is a by-product of other functions organisations can fulfil for their members. Better-resourced organisations should have advantages on both accounts. At the same time, this argument is relatively unspecified regarding whether and when leaders decide to direct available resources to the political process. What we showed, however, is that available staff for public affairs strongly affects an organisation's ability to mobilise. Resource inequalities between organisations can, therefore, introduce problematic biases early on in the influence production process, because organisations with low resources may be unable to mobilise (quickly and intensely) on new issues.

In addition, we assessed a potential alternative explanation regarding internal management challenges as important barriers for mobilisation. However, we found no support for this expectation. In fact, our findings that higher internal problems regarding the workload of members actually *increase* mobilisation intensity can provide further support for our hypothesis regarding affectedness as a driver of mobilisation. In the rest of the book, we focus more on this factor.

To conclude, based on our results regarding issue mobilisation on COVID-19 related issues, we are relatively 'optimistic' about the ability of interest group communities in the studied countries to respond to a focussing event. Around 75 percent of groups in our sample mobilised on these issues, and a core of approximately 20 percent of the mobilised groups were quick and highly active, potentially providing a bridging function for a broad range of affected groups.

In the subsequent chapters, we examine whether these patterns are also observed in the strategic choices of interest representatives (Chapter 4), and in the degree to which they gain access (Chapter 5) and potentially influence on policy outcomes during the pandemic (Chapter 6).

References

Acemoglu, D., and Robinson, J.A. (2020) *The narrow corridor: States, societies, and the fate of liberty*, London: Penguin.

Albareda, A. (2018) 'Connecting society and policymakers? Conceptualizing and measuring the capacity of civil society organizations to act as transmission belts'. *VOLUNTAS: International Journal of Voluntary and Nonprofit Organizations* 29(6):1216–32.

Baumgartner, F.R., and Leech, B.L. (1998) *Basic interests: The importance of groups in politics and in political science*, Princeton, New Jersey: Princeton University Press.

Baumgartner, F.R., and Leech, B.L. (2001) 'Interest Niches and Policy Bandwagons: Patterns of Interest Group Involvement in National Politics'. *The Journal of Politics* 63(4):1191–213.

Berkhout, J. (2013) 'Why interest organizations do what they do: Assessing the explanatory potential of 'exchange' approaches'. *Interest Groups & Advocacy* 2(2):227–50.

Berkhout, J., Beyers, J., Braun, C., Hanegraaff, M., and Lowery, D. (2017) 'Making Inference across Mobilisation and Influence Research: Comparing Top-Down and Bottom-Up Mapping of Interest Systems'. *Political Studies* 66(1):43–62.

Berkhout, J., Hanegraaff, M., and Maloney, W.A. (2021) 'Looking for 'Voice' in Business and Citizen Groups: Who's Being Heard?'. *Political Studies*, Online First.

Binderkrantz, A.S., Bonafont, L.C., and Halpin, D.R. (2016) 'Diversity in the News? A Study of Interest Groups in the Media in the UK, Spain and Denmark'. *British Journal of Political Science* 47(2):313–28.

Bolleyer, N. (2021) 'Civil society – Politically engaged or member-serving? A governance perspective'. *European Union Politics* 22(3):495–520.

Bonafont, L.C., and Iborra, I.M. (2021) 'The representation of business interests during the COVID-19 pandemic in Spain'. *Revista española de ciencia política* 57(1):21–44.

Braun, C., Albareda, A., Fraussen, B., and Müller, M. (2020) 'Bandwagons and quiet corners in regulatory governance. On regulation-specific and institutional drivers of stakeholder engagement'. *International Review of Public Policy* 2(2):209–32.

De Bruycker, I., Berkhout, J., and Hanegraaff, M. (2019) 'The paradox of collective action: Linking interest aggregation and interest articulation in EU legislative lobbying'. *Governance* 32(2):295–312.

Eady, G., and Rasmussen, A. (2021) 'The Unequal Effects of the COVID-19 Pandemic on Political Interest Representation', in, *Working paper:* https://www.annerasmussen.eu/wp-content/uploads/2021/06/EadyRasmussen050921.pdf (accessed June 28, 2022)

Fraussen, B., Halpin, D.R., and Nownes, A.J. (2021) 'Why do interest groups prioritise some policy issues over others? Explaining variation in the drivers of policy agendas'. *Journal of Public Policy* 41(3):553–72.

Fuchs, S., and Sack, D. (2021) 'Corporatism as usual? – Staat und organisierte Wirtschaftsinteressen in der Coronakrise'. *Zeitschrift für Politikwissenschaft*, Online First.

Fuchs, S., Sack, D., and Spilling, F. (2021) Working Paper Series 'Comparative Governance' No.5, April 2021, Universität Bielefeld. Available online: https://doi.org/10.4119/unibi/2954321 (accessed June, 15 2022).

Halpin, D.R., and Fraussen, B. (2017) 'Conceptualising the policy engagement of interest groups: Involvement, access and prominence'. *European Journal of Political Research* 56(3):723–32.

Halpin, D.R., Fraussen, B., and Nownes, A.J. (2018) 'The balancing act of establishing a policy agenda: Conceptualizing and measuring drivers of issue prioritization within interest groups'. *Governance* 31(2):215–37.

Hanegraaff, M. (2015) 'Transnational Advocacy over Time: Business and NGO Mobilization at UN Climate Summits'. *Global Environmental Politics* 15(1):83–104.

Hanegraaff, M., Braun, C., De Bièvre, D., and Beyers, J. (2015) 'The Domestic and Global Origins of Transnational Advocacy: Explaining Lobbying Presence During WTO Ministerial Conferences'. *Comparative Political Studies* 48(12):1591–621.

Hanegraaff, M., and van der Ploeg, J. (2020) 'Bringing the middleman back in: EU umbrella organizations and interest group access in the European Union'. *Comparative European Politics* 18(6):963–81.

Hanegraaff, M., van der Ploeg, J., and Berkhout, J. (2020) 'Standing in a Crowded Room: Exploring the Relation between Interest Group System Density and Access to Policymakers'. *Political Research Quarterly* 73(1):51–64.

Hart, D.M. (2004) '"Business" Is Not An Interest Group: On The Study Of Companies In American National Politics'. *Annual Review of Political Science* 7(1):47 – 69.

Heinz, J.P., Laumann, E.O., and Nelson, R.L. (1993) *The hollow core: Private interests in national policy making*, Cambridge: Harvard University Press.

Junk, W.M., Crepaz, M., Hanegraaff, M., Berkhout, J., and Aizenberg, E. (2020) "InterCov Project: Online Survey on Interest Representation during Covid-19. Edition: June – July 2020." https://www.wiebkejunk.com/_files/ugd/9a0cb4_eb572405723f490f8fd6e464420 f3a33.pdf (accessed June 13, 2022).

Junk, W.M., Crepaz, M., Hanegraaff, M., Berkhout, J., and Aizenberg, E. (2021) 'Changes in Interest Group Access in Times of Crisis: No Pain, No (Lobby) Gain'. *Journal of European Public Policy* Online First.

Knoke, D. (1986) 'Associations and Interest Groups'. *Annual Review of Sociology* 12(1):1 – 21.

LaPira, T.M., Thomas, H.F., and Baumgartner, F.R. (2014) 'The two worlds of lobbying: Washington lobbyists in the core and on the periphery'. *Interest Groups & Advocacy* 3(3):219 – 45.

Leech, B.L., Baumgartner, F.R., La Pira, T.M., and Semanko, N.A. (2005) 'Drawing Lobbyists to Washington: Government Activity and the Demand for Advocacy'. *Political Research Quarterly* 58(1):19 – 30.

Louwerse, T., Sieberer, U., Tuttnauer, O., and Andeweg, R.B. (2021) 'Opposition in times of crisis: COVID-19 in parliamentary debates'. *West European Politics* 44(5 – 6):1025 – 51.

Lowery, D. (2015) 'Mancur Olson, the Logic of Collective Action: Public Goods and the Theory of Groups', in S. Balla, M. Lodge and E.C. Page (Eds.) *The Oxford Handbook of Classics in Public Policy and Administration*, Oxford: Oxford University Press.

Lowery, D., Baumgartner, F.R., Berkhout, J., Berry, J.M., Halpin, D., Hojnacki, M., Klüver, H., Kohler-Koch, B., Richardson, J., and Schlozman, K.L. (2015) 'Images of An Unbiased Interest System'. *Journal of European Public Policy* 22(8):1212 – 31.

Lowery, D., and Brasher, H. (2004) *Organized interests and American government*, New York: McGraw-Hill.

Olson, M. (1965) *The Logic of Collective Action*, Cambridge: Harvard University Press.

Rasmussen, A., Carroll, B.J., and Lowery, D. (2014) 'Representatives of the public? Public opinion and interest group activity'. *European Journal of Political Research* 53(2):250 – 68.

Rothenberg, L.S. (1988) 'Organizational Maintenance and the Retention Decision in Groups'. *American Political Science Review* 82(4):1129 – 52.

Schmitter, P.C., and Streeck, W. (1999) 'The organization of business interests: Studying the associative action of business in advanced industrial societies': MPIfG discussion paper No 99/1. Available online: https://www.econstor.eu/bitstream/10419/43739/1/ 268682569.pdf (accessed June 28, 2022)

Truman, D.B. (1951) *The Governmental Process. Political Interests and Public Opinion*, New York: Alfred A. Knopf.

Truman, D.B. (1959) 'The American System in Crisis'. *Political Science Quarterly* 74(4):481 – 97.

Online Appendix

https://www.degruyter.com/document/isbn/9783110783148/html

Chapter 4
Strategy Selection

Once interest groups have decided to engage in political action, the question of strategy selection arises. The existing scholarly literature identifies different strategic options, from which interest groups can choose, and assesses several underlying mechanisms, which help explain variation in the chosen strategies across interest groups (Grant 1978; Walker 1991; Beyers 2004; Weiler and Brändli 2015; Dür and Mateo 2013; Junk 2016; Hall and Reynolds 2012; Hanegraaff 2015; De Bruycker 2014; De Bruycker and Beyers 2019).

Such studies largely assume a degree of 'standard' operating procedures in terms of the political context, agenda change, access to political institutions and organisational mobilisation. To date we know little about how *disruptions* affect such regular patterns of strategic choice, although disruptive *focussing events* (see Chapter 1) and shocks to modern political systems and their economies occur regularly (Chari and Bernhagen 2011). Under such crisis circumstances, strategic choices by interest groups may be different and, at the same time, especially consequential. In this chapter, we therefore explain potential differences among interest groups in their use of lobbying strategies during the COVID-19 crisis as an example of a system-wide focussing event.

There are only few studies which deal with the question of lobbying strategies in such crisis circumstances. Exceptions include Muraleedharan and Bryer (2020), who explore how migrant NGOs used social media platforms to mobilise public support for government intervention during the 2015 refugee crisis. Moreover, Adelino and Dinc (2014) researched firms in corporate distress who lobbied government after the financial crisis to receive stimulus funds. With a focus on financial actors, Blau, Brough, and Thomas (2013) studied banks' political activities on bailout funds (also see: Woll 2013; Kastner 2018; Keller 2018). As a final example, the work by LaPira (2014) after 9/11 underlines the importance of studying lobbying in times of crisis. His research shows that, after the terror attack, two trends emerged in Washington's interest group system: first, established groups *realigned* to the newly salient security issue; second, interest groups at the edge of the representational subsystem were *replaced* by new organisations, which took advantage of new opportunities to have a voice in policymaking. These are significant trends that merit further attention.

While the mentioned studies help understand lobbying in times of crises, a major shortcoming is that they focus mostly on the mobilisation of interest groups whose constituency is primarily affected and disrupted, such as financial stakeholders after the financial crisis. At the system level, studies of the impact of such shocks on the strategic choices of *all* interest groups are very rare (but see: Timoneda and Vallejo Vera 2021). As a global health crisis, which affected different kinds of organisations across sectors in various ways, the COVID-19 pandemic offers the opportunity to provide a birds-eye perspective on the strategic considerations interest groups make after a disruptive focussing event.

In this chapter, we use this unique opportunity and provide two perspectives on strategy selection. First, building on the literature regarding tactics that aim to *influence policy*, we analyse the extent to which different types of interest groups rely on 'inside' or 'outside' lobbying strategies. *Inside strategies* refer to activities seeking contact with policymakers, elected officials or civil servants, whereas *outside strategies* refer to activities targeting the media and the public, for instance aiming to organise media campaigns or public protest (see for example: Beyers 2004; Binderkrantz 2005; De Bruycker and Beyers 2019; Hanegraaff, Beyers, and De Bruycker 2016; Junk 2016; Kollman 1998)[15].

The interest group literature identifies these two routes of 'direct consultation' (inside lobbying) and 'public voice' (outside lobbying) as theoretically distinct (Walker 1991; Maloney, Jordan, and Andrew 1994; Beyers 2004), yet potentially interrelated (Berkhout 2013), given successful outside strategies (e. g. media campaigns) can indirectly affect the inside arena (e. g. legislators). Moreover, there is an acknowledgement of variation within these routes: Media campaigns, for instance, are notably different from protests in their scope and implementation. In this chapter, we build on such theoretical distinctions to understand variation in the use of lobbying strategies during the COVID-19 pandemic and, consistent with the earlier chapter, we explore whether group type, resources, and level of affectedness explain the choice of interest groups to use inside and outside strategies to influence policymakers.

Second, we note that the COVID-19 crisis has been a major threat to the *survival* of interest groups. Recent literature suggests that the survival prospects of interest groups significantly impact their strategic considerations (Hanegraaff and Poletti 2019; Witjas, Hanegraaff, and Vermeulen 2020). However, empirical studies substantiating such claims are still rare. Once again, the pandemic provides an opportunity to study the effect of survival fears on the strategic choices of interest groups, hereby identifying whether such considerations, indeed, drive the strategy selection of interest groups. We therefore test whether interest

---

15 Note that various channels can be used for these activities, for example email, mail, phone and text with the aim of scheduling meetings or accessing the media or formal consultation procedures (see also: Crepaz, Hanegraaff, and Salgado 2021).

groups, which fear for their survival more than others (i. e. higher *mortality anxiety*), prioritise strategies which could alleviate this pressure.

For both analytical foci, we draw on knowledge provided by classical interest group scholarship to identify when to expect similarities and differences in the use of strategies. At the same time, we assume that lobbying strategy selection in times of crisis might deviate from what applies to other circumstances (cf. early studies of lobbying in COVID-19 times: Junk et al. 2021a; Bonafont and Iborra 2021; Eady and Rasmussen 2021; Crepaz, Hanegraaff, and Junk 2022). This means that we tailor our expectations to the circumstances of the pandemic.

In a nutshell, our findings point to three main trends: First, we find that higher *resources* for lobbying and higher *affectedness* by the pandemic are consistently associated with more frequent use of both *outside* and *inside* strategies. Second, we find differences between group types: NGOs and citizen groups use social media (outside) strategies more frequently, compared to business organisations, and strategies of direct communication (inside) less frequently. Finally, while the employment of strategies of organisational stability varies by group type, we confirm that *mortality anxiety* is an important driver of the selection of strategies.

In the next section, we start with a broader introduction to the literature on organisational strategies, in which we make a distinction between policy-oriented strategies and survival-related strategies. Based on this discussion, we formulate hypotheses for both categories of strategic considerations. In the following section, we test our hypotheses, and we end with concluding remarks in the final section.

The 'Logic of Influence' and 'Logic of Survival' in Strategy Choice

We see the global pandemic as potentially pivotal for interest groups, both based on a 'logic of influence' and a 'logic of survival' (cf. Berkhout 2013). In the first logic, groups employ strategies to ensure that they have a say in relevant new policies, whereas, in the latter, strategies aim at securing the continued functioning and existence of an organisation. In the next sections, we explain these two logics potentially underlying strategy choice, each in turn.

Inside and Outside Strategies to Secure Policy Influence

We start with policy-oriented strategies. As argued, existing literature labels the direct route of consultation as 'inside lobbying' (Grant 1978; Walker 1991; Beyers 2004; Weiler and Brändli 2015; Dür and Mateo 2013; Junk 2016; Hall and Reynolds 2012; Hanegraaff 2015; De Bruycker 2014; De Bruycker and Beyers 2019). It is expected that interest groups pursuing such strategies seek to increase or maintain their prominence as part of insider circles of decision-making. Insider strategies are generally associated with the choice of an interest group to engage in 'negotiation' and 'bargaining' directly with policymakers (Beyers 2008).

The activities that aim to affect public policy via the media and by means of public protest are typically labelled as 'outside lobbying' (Kollman 1998; Tresch and Fischer 2015; Thrall 2006; Dellmuth and Tallberg 2017). They include all forms of public political strategies whereby interest groups prioritise 'voice' and 'loud politics' over 'quiet' negotiation, or when used independently of inside-oriented strategies or in combination in an integrated campaign (Beyers 2004; Lipsky 1968; Keller 2018). The selection of these outside strategies follows at least two rationales. First, outside lobbying mobilises membership and public support, potentially making a political issue more salient among the public with the aim of simultaneously creating a favourable membership recruitment environment, as well as improving the political calculus on specific policy battles (De Bruycker and Beyers 2019). In media campaigns and protests, 'communication among societal interests, policymakers and citizens becomes visible to a broader audience', and it is among the campaigners' objectives to attract attention of the broader public (Beyers 2004, 213).

Secondly, even when potential supporters are already exhaustively mobilised, outside lobbying sends cues and indirect messages to policymakers who – like the public – become exposed to public political communication (Maloney, Jordan, and Andrew 1994). The literature agrees that this mode of information transmission differs from what happens with inside strategies, and that public arenas, as opposed to institutional ones, are ill-suited for extensive discussion of technical information and negotiation (Beyers 2004; Junk 2016), but have the potential to increase the salience of an issue or change its framing (Junk and Rasmussen 2019). Individual interest groups, of course, rarely fully control on-going issue discussion, and, therefore, need to strategically coordinate their campaigns in order to 'ride the wave' of potentially favourable movements in media salience or public opinion.

While it is often assumed that interest groups choose between these strategies depending on the goals of political action, more recent literature has paid attention to the factors which *constrain* interest groups in strategy selection.

These constraints arise from the side of the organisation and the interest mobilised (the *supply* side) and from the side of policymakers and the issue at stake (the *demand* side).

From a supply perspective, the constraints relate to, firstly, the nature of the organisation's membership and support and, secondly, its availability of resources to employ in lobbying (Dür and Mateo 2013; Junk 2016; Hanegraaff et al. 2015; Dellmuth and Tallberg 2017). Demand side perspectives put emphasis on the nature of the issue itself (distributive or regulatory: Dür and Mateo 2013; issue with public good character and issue complexity: Junk 2016), and the institutional characteristics which determine policymakers' willingness to engage in consultation (Beyers 2004; Victor 2007; Mahoney 2008; Weiler and Brändli 2015).

These approaches build on the implicit assumption that the choice between inside and outside lobbying is a trade-off, and that groups will chose *either* inside *or* outside strategies. Many existing studies, however, suggest that lobbying strategies should actually be considered as complementary, where a combination of both will make it more likely to impact policy (Baumgartner and Leech 1998; Dür and Mateo 2016; De Bruycker and Beyers 2019; Dellmuth and Tallberg 2017; Pakull, Marshall, and Bernhagen 2020). De Bruycker (2019, 3) explains that a combination of lobbying strategies can be used, as long as 'goals, the communication channels, the message, and the target audience are all in sync'; that is, compatible. This is perhaps why research focussing on the use of outside strategies finds that lobbying the media appears to follow the same resource constrains found for inside strategies (Thrall 2006). Media lobbying and inside lobbying may, therefore, differ to a lesser extent than generally assumed (Tresch and Fischer 2015).

To this approach, recent scholarship adds social media as a (relatively) new arena for political action (Brown 2016; Van der Graaf, Otjes, and Rasmussen 2016). Chalmers and Shotton (2016) conceptualise outside lobbying on social media as part of an organisation's broader media strategy, which helps an interest group in shaping public debate around an issue, as well as the public image of the organisation.

The Selection of Influence Strategies during the Pandemic

In this chapter, we take a supply-side oriented approach to the analysis of the determinants of policy-oriented strategies. This is because we keep the issue context (the COVID-19 pandemic) constant, as well as the policy context (*viral policy:*

lobbying on health and safety regulations, travel and movement restrictions and economic rescue packages).

Based on this context, our first basic assumption is that interest groups have engaged more frequently in outside, compared to inside strategies. This is because we expect the strain of the pandemic and the lockdown restrictions introduced by governments to have, first, made it more difficult for interest groups to reach out to policymakers (Junk et al. 2021a). Secondly, we expect that the pandemic made it more burdensome for interest groups to engage in inside strategies, which tend to be more costly (Maloney, Jordan, and Andrew 1994). Thirdly, the high media salience of pandemic politics made outside lobbying more attractive for organisations aiming to communicate policy preferences and frames in both traditional and social media (Eady and Rasmussen 2021).

In addition to the balance between inside and outside strategies, we are interested in what factors explain the use of each of these strategies. Notably, they could be explained by the same factors, which would suggest that the same organisations *persist* in inside and outside lobbying (cf. Beyers 2004; Klüver 2010). Or these strategies could have *divergent* explanations, which would indicate that different organisations use inside and outside strategies. To explain variation across organisations, we use the same indicators as employed in other chapters, namely group type, resources, and the level of affectedness. We start with *group type*.

The literature generally associates the use of inside strategies with business organisations and that of outside strategies with NGOs and citizen groups, as well as profession groups and unions. This is because the latter rely heavily on public means of communication to maintain, enhance and mobilise their membership and support base (Schlozman and Tierney 1986; Maloney, Jordan, and Andrew 1994; Berkhout 2010; Dür and Mateo 2013). For NGOs and citizen groups, for instance, attention-grabbing campaigns serve the triple function of satisfying the existing membership base, providing 'free' publicity for recruitment of members and supporters, and indirectly influencing public policy. In contrast, the closed membership structures of business associations and the material selective benefits they offer do not rely on media attention. This makes their leaders organisationally less dependent on getting the public's attention.

This is likely to apply also in the context of COVID-19. As we already discussed, the outbreak of the pandemic and the introduction of restrictions have turned working conditions for numerous professions on their head. Certain professions were deemed as essential, for which new protocols of health and safety had to be put in place. Others were relegated to remote and distant working, more indirectly forcing substantial adaptation of working procedures. Regardless of how severely affected, we expect profession associations and unions to have used extensive outside strategies to signal their membership that their interests were given a voice. Similarly, for some NGOs and citizen groups (such as patient groups), the pandemic has made core issues more salient. Other public groups (such as human rights cause groups), in contrast, relied on public reframing of their core policy issues in relation to COVID-policies in order to avoid being marginalised in the political debates. This could, for instance, be seen in the privacy concerns raised by human rights groups on the initiation of contact-tracing applications. All this means that both profession organisations, as well as NGOs and citizen groups had strong incentives to mobilise their supporters through outside strategies to signal political engagement.

For business organisations, on the other hand, we expect inside lobbying to have been a dominantly used strategy. Business associations have strong incentives to provide concentrated benefits to their membership (Berkhout 2010; Dür and Mateo 2013; Hanegraaff, Beyers, and De Bruycker 2016). This is likely to be the case in the context of COVID-19, where business associations may have decided to use inside lobbying to influence COVID-19-related policy, such as health and safety regulations and economic rescue packages for specific sectors and member constituencies. Similarly, we argue that politically active firms engaging directly in lobbying would have had incentives to engage mainly in inside strategies, given they lack a membership they need to reach through outside lobbying[16]. More generally, especially when trying to secure concrete benefits for themselves or their members, such as priority in the re-opening of sectors or larger economic help packages, we expect business organisations (including firms) to have preferred direct consultation (inside lobbying) to public discussions (outside lobbying), given such particularistic benefits might be unpopular with the public.

Based on these arguments, we do not expect that the pandemic has fundamentally overturned the way in which profession organisations and unions, NGOs and citizens groups, and business actors employ inside and outside strategies. If anything, the crisis should have emphasised the propensity of profession organisations, NGOs and citizen groups to rely on outside lobbying, while business organisations (including firms) should have (even more) reasons to rely on inside strategies. We therefore hypothesise:

---

16 One can argue though, that shareholders, ownership or customers might be a media audience firms want to reach when they can foster a good reputation in the media.

H1 'group type hypothesis': Business organisations are more likely to engage in inside strategies and less likely to engage in outside strategies during the pandemic, compared to NGOs and citizen groups, as well as profession associations and unions.

Interest groups also face *resource* constrains in the selection of lobbying strategies. The literature associates inside lobbying with organisations that have higher resources available for public affairs (Grant 1978). Others warn against this simplistic view, since outside strategies, such as media campaigns, street protests and conferences, can be quite costly as well (Kollman 1998; Thrall 2006; Wilson 1961). It is also reasonable that interest groups, if specialised in one route of communication, are more likely to invest available resources in what they are familiar with (Hanegraaff, Beyers, and De Bruycker 2016). That said, it is likely that COVID-19 has strongly affected interest groups' ability to engage in costly outside strategies. That is, many COVID-lockdown measures have made it impossible for organisations to mobilise members through public rallies and protest activities.

Outside lobbying in COVID-19 times is, therefore, most likely oriented towards lobbying the media and social media to communicate frames, shape public debate and send cues to core and potential supporters (cf. Chalmers and Shotton 2016; Brown 2016; Thrall 2006). Lobbying the media (especially social media) is arguably less costly than seeking direct consultation with policymakers. In addition, the high public saliency of pandemic policy has transformed media and social media into more attractive venues for lobbying compared to circumstances where policy issues are less salient (cf. Junk 2016). It is therefore likely that, when faced with resource constrains during the pandemic, interest groups are more likely to use outside lobbying.

In classic works, the outside strategy is conceived of as an instrument of the 'powerless', weak, or challengers of government (Lipsky 1968; Schattschneider 1960). As Lasswell (1950, 235) writes, 'an established elite is usually so well situated in control of the goods, violence, and practices of a community that a challenging elite is constrained to rely chiefly upon symbols'. Thrall (2006), however, suggests that the media venue, despite it being assumed to be a 'weapon' of the weak (also see: Gamson and Wolfsfeld 1993), attracts resourceful organisations as well, or even especially[17]. An increasing number of studies suggest that media strategies are common amongst well-resourced organisations and even corporations and organisations hiring specialised consultants (Aizenberg and

---

17 See also the cumulative hypothesis noted in Binderkrantz, Christiansen, and Pedersen (2015), and the indexing hypothesis by Bennett (1990).

Müller 2020; Huwyler 2020). Building on these findings and taking stock of the high salience of pandemic politics, we therefore formulate the following expectation:

H2 'resources hypothesis': Better resourced organisations are more likely to engage in both inside and outside strategies during the pandemic, compared to less resourced organisations, but the difference is more pronounced for inside lobbying.

Finally, we argue that policy disturbances inform strategy selection. We have documented in the previous chapter that disturbances drive interest group issue mobilisation. Organisations that were more heavily *affected* by the pandemic were more likely to become politically active (controlling for other factors such as resource constrains). This echoes pluralist theory (Truman 1951) applied to issue mobilisation (Rasmussen and Gross 2015), whereby disturbances in the policy environment activate organisations whose interests are affected or under threat.

We also believe this mechanism to be tied to strategy selection. On the one hand, affected organisations can be expected to seek the most direct way to policymakers, and seek to increase their prominence within policy circles. They should, therefore, be likely to use inside strategies. Applied to the case of COVID-19, for example, affected organisations such as business actors in the airline industry, associations of teachers and health care professionals, and patient groups, had high stakes in policy and are likely to have tried to communicate this to policymakers. We expect them, therefore, to seek direct consultation with policymakers and increase their chances of affecting pandemic-policies compared to less affected groups.

On the other hand, a high degree of affectedness may also help frame the position of affected organisations as 'popular' among the public, increasing the strategic attractiveness of outside lobbying (Kollman 1998). In contrast, problems unrelated to the pandemic may have had less 'news value' (Galtung and Ruge 1965), and may, instead, have been less popular among the public, thus decreasing the strategic attractiveness of outside lobbying for less affected groups. To illustrate this better, the concerns regarding restricted opening times of supermarkets, whose profit margins increased substantially during the pandemic, are unlikely to sympathetically resonate among the public on media platforms, given the more precarious and vulnerable position of other stakeholders. We, therefore, expect less affected organisations to have taken a step back from outside communication and not to have mingled too much in public debates.

In sum, we expect that more affected groups are more likely to use both inside and outside channels more frequently during the pandemic, compared to less affected groups, as Hypothesis 3 summarises.

H3 'affectedness hypothesis': More affected organisations are more likely to engage in both inside and outside strategies during the pandemic than less affected organisations.

Strategies to Secure Organisational Survival

While a focus on policy-oriented strategies is widespread in interest group research, the unique circumstances of the COVID-19 crisis allow us to paint a broader picture of the strategies available to interest groups. The crisis has put many organisations under serious strain causing uncertainty and fears about long-term survival. In the literature, these fears are called *mortality anxiety.*

All approaches discussed so far ultimately assume that strategy selection is informed by the 'logic of influence', where interest groups seek to influence policies or public discussions. The additional question we ask in this chapter is whether and how the threats posed by the pandemic to organisations' survival also affect strategic considerations. In other words, were organisations, who feared more about the continuation of their activities, more likely to select survival driven (non-policy oriented) strategies to alleviate such threats compared to organisations, that were less concerned about the sustainability of their activities?

Based on existing theories, we expect to observe variation in the degree to which organisations initiated activities to improve their long-term prospects. Organisation theory and ecological studies of interest groups remind us that interest groups are survival-seeking organisations and that policy-oriented activities are often instrumental, secondary means to the primary goal of organisational maintenance (Gray and Lowery 2000; Lowery 2007; Berkhout 2013; Berkhout et al. 2015). Only few studies of lobbying strategies point towards this nuance. Hanegraaff, Beyers, and De Bruycker (2016), more specifically, observe that organisational maintenance and competition for resources between groups drives the selection of outside strategies in international contexts. Hanegraaff and Poletti (2019) confirm that survival-related calculations and mortality anxiety drive the selection of lobbying strategy also at the national level.

The study of the relationship between mortality anxiety and lobbying strategies remains, however, at its infancy. Usually, it is only included, as we have done in the previous section, as part of the theoretical considerations to identify differences in the strategic repertoire of business and non-business interest groups, rather than explicitly measured. Further specification is needed because, first, nuances regarding the effects of specific forms of mortality anxiety (for instance related to resources, support or influence) have not been explored so far. Secondly, existing studies still conflate policy-driven and survival-driven lobbying strategies, which makes it more difficult for scholars to disentangle trends in strategy selection. Finally, in most existing studies of interest groups, mortality anxiety is only investigated as dependent variable rather than explanatory variable (Gray and Lowery 1997; Halpin and Thomas 2012).

Hanegraaff and Poletti (2019) and Witjas, Hanegraaff, and Vermeulen (2020) try to provide a theoretical spine to link motivations of organisational maintenance to the selection of lobbying strategies. Like Witjas, Hanegraaff, and Vermeulen (2020), we follow Stinchcombe (1965), who conceptualises three *forms of mortality anxiety*, related to *wealth*, *power*, and *legitimacy*. We see all three of these forms of anxiety as potential explanations for different survival-oriented lobbying activities, that is resource-extraction strategies (in relation to wealth), public-oriented strategies (power) and base-oriented strategies (legitimacy). In the following section, we formulate expectations about how they apply during the COVID-19 pandemic.

Mortality Anxiety and Survival Strategies during the Pandemic

The first, *wealth*, concerns material resources without which interest groups cannot survive. It follows that if this dimension is perceived to be under threat, for instance following a loss of income from membership contributions, public funding, sales or capital value, organisations can be expected to mobilise in a way that guarantees sources of income in the future (Witjas, Hanegraaff, and Vermeulen 2020). To avoid organisational death or default, organised interests should, therefore, turn to lobbying for survival, including pressuring governments to intervene with regulatory and distributive tools, typically public funding, grants for organisational maintenance (Salgado 2014), rescue packages after economic shocks (Adelino and Dinc 2014; Keller 2018) and state aid (Chari 2015). In COVID-19 times, the vast shocks produced by the pandemic and the lockdown measures introduced by governments to tackle it, have brought many organisations' activities to a halt, for instance challenging the turnover of firms and member contributions of associations. It follows that, facing constrains to their incomes, interest groups would mobilise politically to secure support from government.

H4 'wealth hypothesis': Wealth-related mortality anxiety during the pandemic is likely to drive interest groups into survival-seeking inside lobbying in form of resource-extraction directed at the state.

The second form of mortality anxiety relates to *power*, understood as 'having a political impact' to sustain membership and supporters (Witjas, Hanegraaff, and Vermeulen 2020). As Gray and Lowery (1997, 28) argue, 'political influence and access to the policy process is one of the most vital resources for organisations to acquire as it contributes to an organisation's identity.' When access to insider circles is under threat, interest groups are found to displace insider lobbying efforts to outside venues with the aim of signalling to the constituency that the organisation is committed to political action and to gain legitimacy (Hanegraaff, Beyers, and De Bruycker 2016; Hanegraaff and Poletti 2019; Witjas, Hanegraaff, and Vermeulen 2020). Simulating the introduction of access barriers to inside lobbying during the COVID-19 pandemic, Junk, Crepaz, and Aizenberg (2022) experimentally demonstrate that interest groups turn to outside lobbying as a result. While the authors do not make a distinction between the strategy selection being policy or survival driven, we expect this behaviour to be linked to an organisation's mortality anxiety with regards to *power*, as our next hypothesis formulates.

H5 'power hypothesis': Power-related mortality anxiety during the pandemic is likely to drive interest groups into survival-seeking outside lobbying in form of public-oriented strategies.

The third and last form of mortality anxiety relates to *legitimacy* understood as the rationale and justification for the organisation's existence. Interest groups constantly seek to justify the appropriateness of goals, objectives, and procedures through active engagement with their supporter base (Witjas, Hanegraaff, and Vermeulen 2020). Without the support of the constituency, interest groups' legitimacy crumbles. It is therefore likely that, when an organisation's legitimacy is under threat, organisations will seek to employ strategies which engage the constituency with the aim of attracting support. This is likely to apply to the case of the COVID-19 pandemic, where interest groups reported to have 'lost touch' with their membership and support base in the absence of face-to-face interactions. For example, NGOs and citizen groups could not rely on volunteers for almost two years. Membership associations (citizen, profession or business-based) had to shift internal conferences, events and annual general meetings to an online format. We therefore expect interest groups, which perceive the loss of legitimacy as a threat to the stability of the organisation, to have engaged in other membership-oriented strategies.

H6 'legitimacy hypothesis': Legitimacy-related mortality anxiety during the pandemic is likely to drive interest groups into survival-seeking outside lobbying in form of strategies aimed at the support base.

Analysis: Lobbying Strategies for Policy Influence and Survival during the Pandemic

In this section, we test the formulated hypotheses on strategy selection to assess the influence-seeking and survival-seeking mechanisms, respectively. In each case, we first present the outcome variables to measure strategy use, and then present multivariate regression models to understand the explanatory power of different factors.

Explanatory Models of Strategies for Policy Influence

First, we explore the use of different forms of inside and outside lobbying during the pandemic. To do so, we use data from our first survey of interest group activities after the outbreak of COVID-19 (Junk et al. 2020). We capture the use of lobbying strategies through five items, which measure the frequency of political activities targeting the *media, social media, parliament, government* and *the bureaucracy* as lobbying venues (cf. Binderkrantz, Christiansen, and Pedersen 2015). We classify 'issuing press releases' and 'posting on social media about the organisation's goals, positions or political objectives' as *outside strategies*[18]. In contrast, seeking contact with 1) 'politicians in government at any level', 2) 'members of parliament' and 3) 'the bureaucracy', are grouped into *inside strategies*. These serve as our dependent variables. The answer categories take five

---

18 We assume that the routine production of press releases requires substantial internal coordination and active investment in media monitoring to guarantee effective resonance. We cannot capture more 'radical' outside strategies, given that COVID-19 has limited the possibility of large gatherings. Our dependent variable does not capture the mode of communication (which is important, see Chalmers and Shotton 2016; Huwyler and Martin 2021). However, we assume that – given national lockdowns – most lobbying communication happened via email, text, phone or video conference.

values: 'Never' (1); 'Less than once a month' (2); 'Once a month' (3); 'Once a week' (4); 'Almost on a daily basis' (5).

We test our basic assumption on the stronger prominence of outside lobbying during the pandemic by taking the difference between the average frequency of the use of inside strategies and that of outside strategies and then dividing it by the sum of both. This measures the *relative use of inside strategies over outside strategies* and indicates which strategy interest groups favoured as net of the total volume of lobbying activity (Dür and Mateo 2013, 668).

Figure 4.1 shows the distribution of frequencies (as percentages) of this measure. All frequencies to the left of the zero indicate relatively more *outside* compared to inside strategies. Everything to the right of the zero indicates more *inside* strategies relative to outside ones. In general, we observe a (somewhat) higher propensity in the use of outside strategies, but the overall distribution is quite consistent with the broader literature, which indicates that most interest groups combine the use of inside and outside strategies.

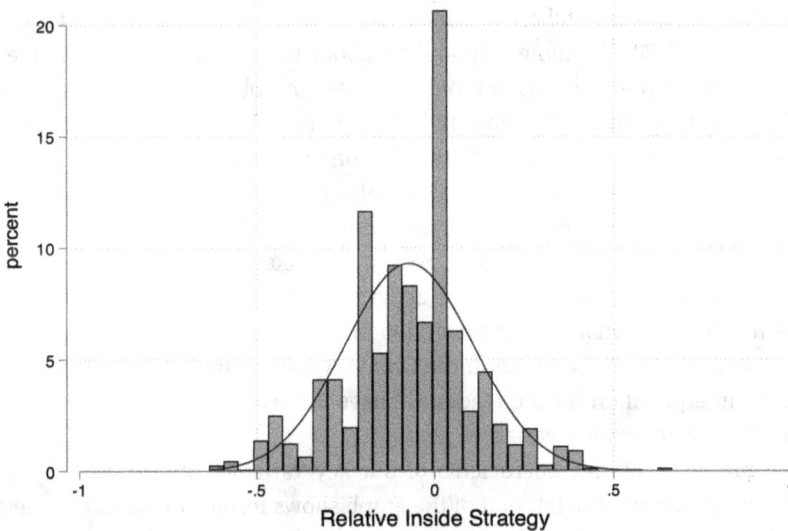

Figure 4.1: Distribution of inside strategies relative to outside strategies.

To explore the patterns in the (often simultaneous) use of both inside and outside strategies and test Hypotheses 1, 2 and 3, we conduct multivariate regression analyses. We employ five individual outcome variables capturing the use of 1) Media Strategies, 2) Social Media Strategies, 3) Government Strategies, 4) Parliament Strategies and 5) Bureaucracy Strategies, each corresponding to the survey item asking about the frequency of targeting these distinct arenas. This has the advantage of testing what drives the absolute use of these respective strategies, rather than the dichotomy of relative insider/outsider strategy use (see Figure 4.1), which might conceal that some – potentially powerful – organisations use both strategies very frequently (which would be located around the value of 0 in Figure 4.1).

To test for Hypothesis 1, we distinguish between *business groups and firms*, *profession groups and unions* and *NGOs and citizen groups*, using *business groups and firms* as reference category. We test Hypothesis 2 measuring resources for lobbying through an item that captures the number of staff working on public affairs in the organisations (in full time equivalents). This measure of human resources is an established proxy for resource endowment in lobbying (e. g. Mahoney 2008). Answers are grouped in three categories of low (<1), medium (1–4) and high (≥5). To test Hypothesis 3, we rely on a survey item that measures the extent to which an organisation, according to its own perception, was 'more or less affected by the Coronavirus crisis, compared to other stakeholders in [country]'. Answers take five values, from 'much less affected' (1) to 'much more affected' (5). For more information about these variables, see Chapter 2.

Like in the previous chapter, our analyses control for the *age* of an organisation, which captures experience in lobbying and is likely to determine strategy selection, as well as correlating with other organisation characteristics. We also control for the extent to which an organisation is an umbrella organisation, given that these tend to operate as representation *hubs* in crises circumstances (Timoneda and Vallejo Vera 2021). We include fixed effects for countries and cluster standard errors by sector of activity of the interest group. The method of estimation is ordinal logistic regression for all models. The full regression output in table form can be found in the Online Appendix to the book (Table A4.1). To ease interpretation for the reader, we have chosen to only display coefficient plots of the explanatory variables here.

Figure 4.2 plots the coefficients of our key variables on the five strategies under investigation. The left part of the graph shows results for outside strategies (media and social media), the right side shows inside strategies (government, parliament and bureaucracy). Where the confidence intervals (straight lines) of the plotted coefficients (dot in the middle) do not overlap with 0 (the vertical dotted line), we can say with high certainty that there is a significant relationship between the factor and the frequency of use of the lobbying strategy.

Remember that, according to our first Hypothesis (H1), we expected *business organisations* to be more likely to select inside strategies, and *profession groups and unions* as well as *NGOs and citizen groups* to use more outside strategies. The

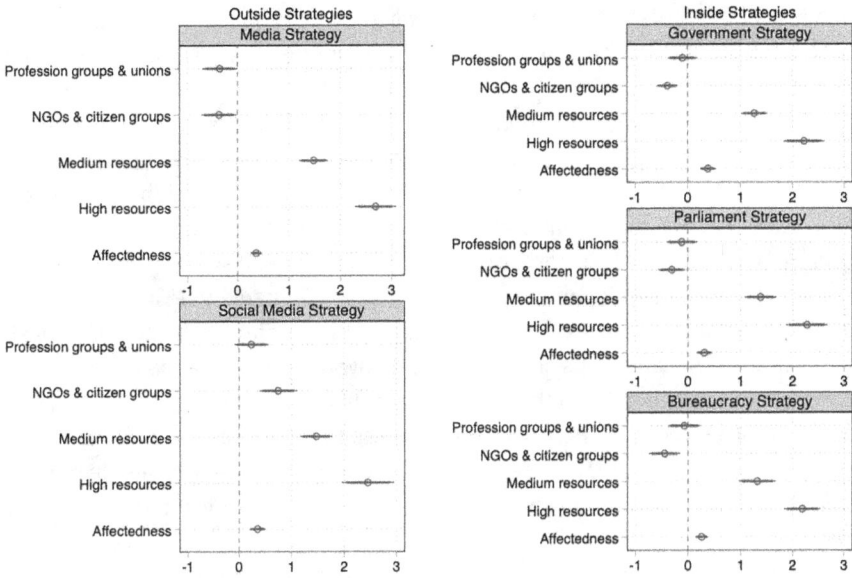

Figure 4.2: Ordered logistic regression on the use of five lobbying strategies. Coefficients and 95/90% confidence intervals.

Notes: The figure is based on five ordered logistic regressions (one for each dependent variable: media strategy; social media strategy; government strategy; parliament strategy; bureaucracy strategy). Model 1 (n=1074), Model 2 (n=1073), Model 3 (n=1072), Model 4 (n= 1071), Model 5 (n= 1071). Included controls in all these models were: organisation age, the group's potential status as an umbrella organisation, and fixed effects for the country/polity. Moreover, we clustered standard errors by sector given that strategy selection for groups within a sector is likely to be related. For results in table form see Table A4.1 in the Online Appendix. Measures of goodness of fit (pseudo R-squared) lie at 0.14 (Model 1), 0.11 (Model 2), 0.12 (Model 3), 0.10 (Model 4), 0.10 (Model 5).

coefficients presented on of the right-side in Figure 4.2 (inside strategies) are largely consistent with this expectation when *business associations and firms* and *NGOs and citizen groups* are compared (but, notably, not compared to *profession groups and unions*). Business organisations use more inside strategies (across government, parliament and bureaucracy strategy) compared to NGOs and citizen groups. Taking the bureaucracy strategy as an example (bottom-right in Figure 4.2), based on our model, the probability that business groups and firms target this venue *almost on a daily basis* is 20 percent, while this drops to 14 percent for NGOs and citizen groups (similar effect sizes are found for other inside venues).[19]

On the other hand, *NGOs and citizen groups* are more active on social media compared to business organisations. According to our models, the predicted probability for the former to use this as a platform for outside lobbying *almost on a daily basis* is 38 percent and only 23 percent for the latter. Against our expectation, however, this is not the case as far as the media strategy is concerned, which business is significantly more likely to use compared to NGOs and citizen groups. This aligns with studies of lobbying in the media which show that business associations and firms shy less and less away from the media (Thrall 2006; Aizenberg and Müller 2020) than one might think. The COVID-crisis circumstances may have produced incentives for business to be active in the media across the board by 'issuing press releases' attempting to communicate legitimate frames around government intervention in support of the economy (cf. Keller 2018).

In our second Hypothesis (H2), we expected organisations with higher available lobbying resources to use both inside and outside strategies more frequently. Results confirm this expectation. First, higher resources are significantly and substantially associated with the use of inside strategies compared to low resources. Taking the government strategy as an example, our models predict that the probability that least resourced organisations are frequent users of this strategy between a *weekly* and an *almost daily* basis is 7 and 2 percent respectively. For well-endowed organisations, on the other hand, the predicted probability of lobbying this venue with equal frequency is 35 (*weekly)* and 15 percent (*almost on a daily basis*).

Secondly, we find that organisations with high resources for lobbying are also more likely than less resourced organisations to use outside lobbying. Looking at very frequent lobbying (*almost on a daily basis*) targeting the media, the difference between organisations with low and high resources is 25 percentage points: For less resourceful groups, the predicted probability of lobbying this venue frequently (*almost on a daily basis*) is 3 percent, whereas this increases drastically to 28 percent for better-resourced organisations. This shows that it is not the case that 'poor' organisations have advantages in using outside lobbying, as some theories assumed when naming them as potential 'weapons of the weak'. This does not even hold for social media strategies, which organisations

---

19 All predicted probabilities/values are based on the main models (see Figure 4.2) when holding all other variables at means.

with high and medium resources also use significantly more frequently than groups with low resources. Furthermore, the disadvantages of less resourceful organisations in outside lobbying are not less severe than for inside lobbying (see point estimates, Figure 4.2) going against what we expected in the latter part of Hypothesis 2. Instead, 'rich' organisations seem to be well-placed to use both inside and outside strategies more frequently, presumably as complements in their strategic toolbox (cf. De Bruycker 2019).

A test of independence in the use of outside and inside strategies further underlines this point. As Figure 4.3 shows, for highly resourced organisations (on the right of the figure), the distribution of lobbying strategy use clusters in the upper-right quadrant. This means that the *combined* use of frequent inside and outside strategies occurred often for organisations with high resources during the pandemic. For the category of organisations with lower resources (on the left of Figure 4.3), observations cluster on the bottom left meaning that these organisations often have low frequencies of using both inside and outside strategies.

Finally, our third Hypothesis (H3) that higher affectedness by the pandemic increases the frequency of use of all strategies is also supported by our statistical analysis. Figure 4.2 shows that more affected groups use inside *and* outside lobbying strategies more frequently across the board. That is, they were more active in parliament, the government, the bureaucracy, the media, and on social media. Taking all venues together, most affected organisations were on average 3.4 times more likely to use the lobbying strategies under investigation *almost on a daily basis* compared to least affected groups. To illustrate, while the predicted probability of least affected groups to frequently lobby parliament is 3 percent, this percentage reaches 11 percent for most affected groups. Similar differences are predicted for other venues.

This further documents a supply-side response by interest groups to the pandemic understood as a focusing event (see Chapter 1): Not only did affected groups mobilise (Chapter 3) more intensely and timely, they also used all strategies more often than less affected groups. This suggests that in times of new pressures and high uncertainty, affected organisations decide to seek contact with multiple targets to make sure their interests are considered. Moreover, it is also likely that gatekeepers were more open to engagement with more affected organisations, which we will test in the next chapter (Chapter 5).

So far, the analysis has revealed trends in the use of policy-driven lobbying strategies during the COVID-19 pandemic related to group type, resources and affectedness. The pandemic has, however, also deeply shaken the stability of the interest group system, threatening the survival of many organisations. Before

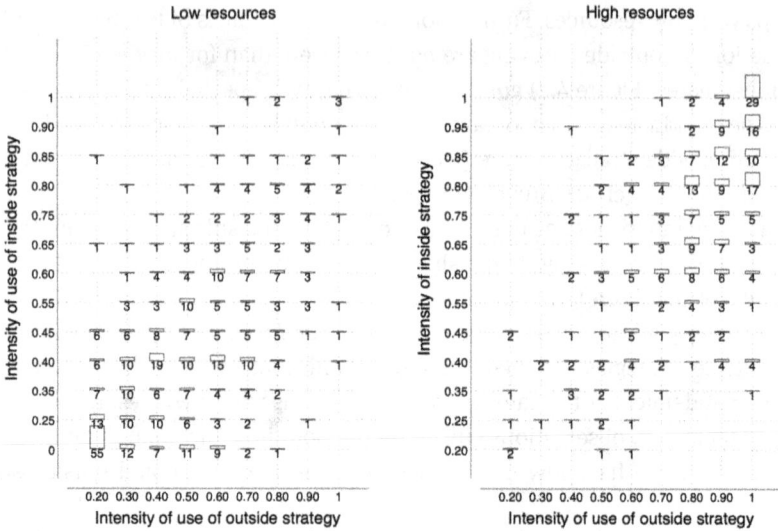

Figure 4.3: Bivariate distribution with frequency bars of the use of inside and outside strategies for interest groups with low resources (left) and high resources (right).

Note: The bars display the frequency of a bi-variate distribution of the intensity of the use of inside and outside strategies. For example, taking the left side of the graph, the lowest frequency indicates that 55 organisations have never used inside strategies (0) and used outside strategies very rarely (0.2 on a 0–1 scale).

moving on to interest group access (Chapter 5), we therefore explore the extent to which strategies were driven by mortality anxiety in the next section.

Explanatory Models of Strategies for Organisational Survival

To explore survival strategies of interest groups, we use data from our second survey (Junk et al. 2021b) of interest group activities in COVID-19 times. We operationalise the three types of survival-driven strategies as *resource-extraction strategies, public-oriented strategies* and *base-oriented strategies*. Note that the first can be seen as a form of inside strategy, whereas the latter two are forms of outside strategies, but all three have the specific aim of securing the maintenance and survival of organisations.

These three strategies were captured by three items, which measure the frequency of political activities seeking to secure organisational maintenance. The first captures the frequency of activities 'to seek public funding for organisational stability'. The second measures the frequency of activities seeking 'public and media attention for organisational stability', and the third 'activities to reach out directly to members and supporters to enhance organisational stability'. Answers to these three items could take the levels 'Never' (1), 'Only once a year' (2), 'A few times a year' (3) and 'Frequently' (4).

In line with Hypotheses 4, 5 and 6, we link these survival-orientated strategies to specific dimensions of *mortality anxiety* related to 'loss of income, funding and assets', 'loss of access to policymaking and public debate' and 'loss of supporters'. We capture these perceived threats to organisational stability with three survey items measuring mortality anxiety on a scale from 0 to 10.

Figure 4.4 shows variation in each form of *mortality anxiety* in relation to *wealth, power* and *legitimacy* (Stinchcombe 1965). All three distributions evidence a right-skewness, with 50 percent of respondents being 'not at all' or 'not worried' about organisational stability. However, 22 to 29 percent of the respondents express levels of *worry* higher than 5 about loss of income, access or supporters. We expect these higher levels of mortality anxiety to be associated with the use of resource-extraction, public- and base-oriented strategies.

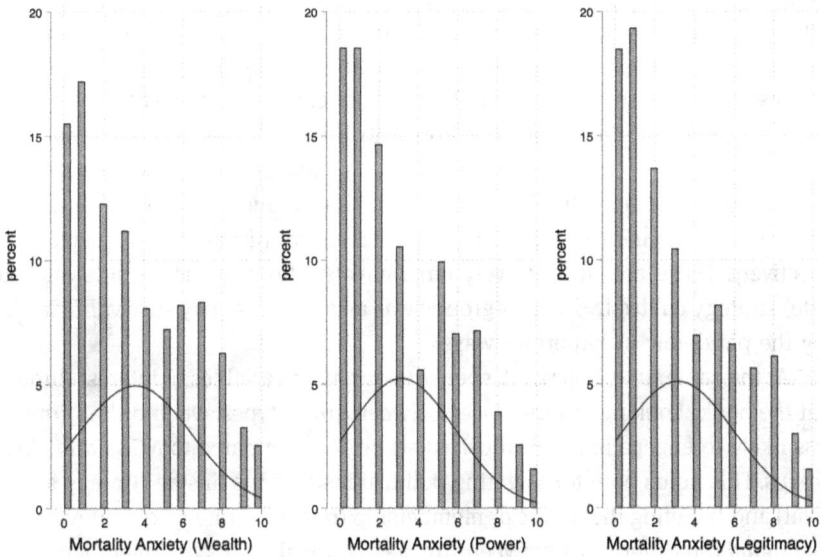

Figure 4.4: Distribution of three faces of mortality anxiety (wealth, power and legitimacy).

We test our expectations (Hypotheses 4, 5 and 6) using ordinal logistic regression with country fixed effects and clustered standard errors by sector. Like in previous analyses, we include our main predictors (group type, resources and the level of affectedness by the crisis) and control variables[20]. We expect that these should all influence the extent to which organisations engage in survival-driven strategies, and they plausibly relate to mortality anxiety. As an additional control, we include the percentage of an organisation's income coming from public funding and membership fees.

As far as group type is concerned, we disaggregate business organisations into *business associations* and *firms*. Since firms do not have members, we expect them to follow different logics of survival strategy selection compared to business associations. We set *NGOs and citizen groups* as reference category in our analysis, since the literature associates them as more active in activities of organisational maintenance (Hanegraaff, Beyers, and De Bruycker 2016).

Results are shown in Figure 4.5 based on models with the full set of controls. The figure clearly documents that our new independent variables measuring different forms of *mortality anxiety*, are a systematic predictor of the frequency of engagement in survival-driven strategies.

Perceived threats from loss of resources, access and supporters are significantly associated with the more frequent use of strategies to seek organisational stability (through public funding, access to media and public debate, and direct engagement with the supporter base). Substantially, the predicted probability of making *frequent* use of, for example, resource-extraction survival strategies increases from 6 to 36 percent from lowest to highest levels of mortality anxiety in relation to wealth. For similar changes in mortality anxiety in relation to power and legitimacy, the likelihood of making frequent use of the associated survival strategy increases from 17 to 33 percent and from 39 to 72 percent, respectively. These are substantively large effects, showing that (inside and outside) strategy choice by interest groups was also motivated by survival fears during the pandemic in important ways.

At the same time, Figure 4.5 speaks to our main variables of interest throughout the book. Looking at differences between group types, we find that *firms* are less likely to engage in survival-driven strategies, compared to *NGOs and citizen groups*. This holds both for targeting political institutions (inside strategy for survival) and targeting the public or membership (outside strategy for survival). This highlights the differences between firms as political actors and membership or-

---

20 The controls include the age of an organisation, the extent to which it is an umbrella organisation.

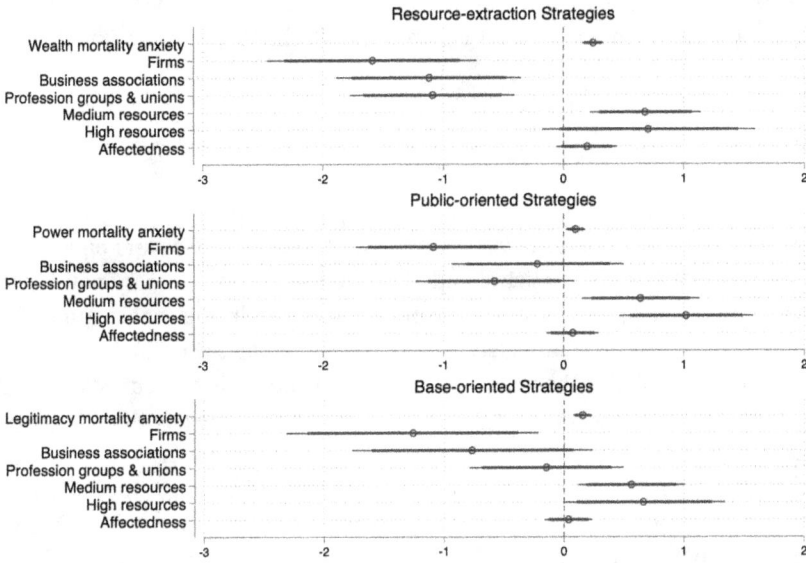

Figure 4.5: Ordered logit regressions on the use of survival-driven strategies: resource-extraction strategies (top chart), public-oriented strategies (middle), base-oriented strategies (bottom). Coefficients and 95/90% confidence intervals.

Notes: The figure is based on three ordered logistic regressions (one for each dependent variable: resource-extraction strategies, public-oriented strategies, base-oriented strategies). The full models can be accessed in Table A4.2 in the Online Appendix. Model 1 (n=414), Model 2 (n=416), Model 3 (n=412). Included controls in all these models were: organisation age, the group's potential status as an umbrella organisation, the percentage of an organisation's income coming from public funding and membership fees, and fixed effects for the country/polity. Moreover, we clustered standard errors by sector given that strategy selection for groups within a sector is likely to be related. For results in table form see Table A4.2 in the Online Appendix. Measures of goodness of fit (pseudo R-squared) lie at 0.19 (Model 1), 0.07 (Model 2), 0.08 (Model 3).

ganisations (Baroni et al. 2014; Hart 2004). Compared to NGOs and citizen groups, however, also *business associations* as well as *profession groups and unions* are found to be less likely to engage in resource-extraction strategies.

Interestingly, higher lobbying *resources* are systematically associated to more frequent use of survival-driven strategies. Like in the case of policy-driven strategies, resources empower organisations in their political actions. Affectedness, on the other hand, does not significantly impact the use of survival driven strategies. We argue, therefore that affectedness by new policy problems is theoretically distinct from mortality anxiety. While the former relates to policy disturbances and the 'logic of influence', the latter represents a perceived threat to organisational maintenance and is connected to the 'logic of survival'[21].

Chapter Summary

In this chapter, we analysed the strategic considerations of interest groups during the COVID-19 pandemic. First, we assessed the use of *inside* and *outside* strategies aimed at affecting policies, and we evaluated the explanatory power of the three main organisational characteristics considered in this book: group type, lobbying resources and affectedness by the pandemic. Our findings resonate well with the broader literature on lobbying in non-crisis circumstances, and support the hypotheses we formulated on lobbying strategies during the pandemic.

First, we show that resources are a driving force of strategy employment. We found that the use of all types of policy-oriented *inside* and *outside* strategies increases at higher levels of available lobbying resources of organisations. That is, organisations with higher staff resources used all strategic options more frequently than less resourced organisations. Moreover, we found, much in line with the literature, that lobbying resources help organisations to develop a more diverse strategic plan compared to resource-poor organisations (Pakull, Marshall, and Bernhagen 2020; De Bruycker 2019).

Second, in relation to group type, we found that business organisations were not only more actively aiming to influence inside channels, but also to target traditional media by means of press statements. Only on social media, NGOs and citizen groups were more active. While this finding is in line with earlier studies on 'the myth of the outside strategy' (Thrall 2006; also see: Tresch and Fischer 2015), we also think that the pandemic might play a role in explaining this result. As many businesses, much to their dismay, were closed due to the crisis, they were able to share personalised stories about the negative consequences of the pandemic (e.g. job loss). At the same time, their experiences had a large scope and affected many citizens (cf. Galtung and Ruge 1965), who, for instance, experienced closed shops, cancelled holidays etc. In contrast, the issues on

---

21 Also empirically, levels of correlation between our measurement of affectedness and different forms of mortality anxiety are relatively low (ranging from 0.16 to 0.27 depending on whether it is mortality anxiety in relation to wealth, power or legitimacy). This suggests that mortality anxiety does not absorb the effect of affectedness in our model. We therefore conclude that policy and other disturbances appear to explain influence-driven lobbying strategies, while mortality anxiety drives survival-driven strategies.

which many NGOs and citizen groups work, such as the environment or human rights, might have had less 'news value' (Galtung and Ruge 1965) during the crisis, which may have disincentivised these groups to try voice their interests through these channels.

Third, we document a strong effect of the *affectedness* of organisations on the use of inside and outside strategies. More affected organisations were significantly more likely to use both types of strategic options more frequently. This fits the pluralist idea that disturbances trigger political action (Truman 1951): After a focussing event, representatives of more affected societal and economic interests are incentivised to become politically active via the relevant means available. In the COVID-19 case, this holds for both inside and outside strategies. One can ask, however, whether and when other crises or focusing events give affected organisations this much media space. As Kollman (1998) implies, 'affectedness' may also need to be related to the public popularity of the position of a group, as this strongly affects the reputational consequences of going public.

In addition to the policy-oriented strategies of interest groups, we also analysed other strategic considerations. Considering the threat that the pandemic has posed to the *survival* of many organisations, we analysed whether and how levels of *mortality anxiety* drove the activity of interest groups. Our analysis clearly shows that such fears play a major role in strategy selection: organisations, which indicate to fear more for their survival, seek strategies – both in inside and outside venues – targeted at alleviating these pressures. Understanding these survival-orientated strategies is important because their use may partly come at the expense of policy-oriented strategic concerns. This might explain why NGOs and citizen groups use almost all types of *influence-seeking strategies* significantly less often than other groups: A lot of their efforts focus on *survival-seeking strategies*, which they are significantly more likely to use than all other group types. Overall, such trade-offs between the 'logic of influence' and the 'logic of survival' can lead to major imbalances in the system of interest representation, whereby weaker organisations become increasingly marginal in policy circles. In the next chapter, we assess the role of organisations in such 'insider' cycles, by looking at access to different political and media gatekeepers.

References

Adelino, M., and Dinc, I.S. (2014) 'Corporate distress and lobbying: Evidence from the Stimulus Act'. *Journal of Financial Economics* 114(2):256–72.

Aizenberg, E., and Müller, M. (2020) 'Signaling expertise through the media? Measuring the appearance of corporations in political news through a complexity lens'. *Journal of European Public Policy*, Online first.

Baroni, L., Carroll, B.J., Chalmers, A.W., Marquez, L.M.M., and Rasmussen, A. (2014) 'Defining and classifying interest groups'. *Interest Groups & Advocacy* 3(2):141–59.

Baumgartner, F.R. and Leech, B.L. (1998) *Basic interests: The importance of groups in politics and in political science*, Princeton, New Jersey: Princeton University Press.

Bennett, W.L. (1990) 'Toward a Theory of Press-State Relations in the United States'. *Journal of Communication* 40(2):103–27.

Berkhout, J. (2010) 'Political activities of interest organizations: Conflicting interests, converging strategies', Leiden: Leiden University. Available online: https://scholar lypublications.universiteitleiden.nl/access/item%3A2929778/view (accessed June 28, 2022)

Berkhout, J. (2013) 'Why interest organizations do what they do: Assessing the explanatory potential of 'exchange' approaches'. *Interest Groups & Advocacy* 2(2):227–50.

Berkhout, J., et al. (2015) 'Interest organizations across economic sectors: explaining interest group density in the European Union'. *Journal of European Public Policy* 22(4):462–80.

Beyers, J. (2004) 'Voice and access: Political practices of European interest associations'. *European Union Politics* 5(2):211–40.

Beyers, J. (2008) 'Policy Issues, Organisational Format and the Political Strategies of Interest Organisations'. *West European Politics* 31(6):1188–211.

Binderkrantz, A. (2005) 'Interest Group Strategies: Navigating between Privileged Access and Strategies of Pressure'. *Political Studies* 53(4):694–715.

Binderkrantz, A.S., Christiansen, P.M., and Pedersen, H.H. (2015) 'Interest group access to the bureaucracy, parliament, and the media'. *Governance* 28(1):95–112.

Blau, B.M., Brough, T.J., and Thomas, D.W. (2013) 'Corporate lobbying, political connections, and the bailout of banks'. *Journal of Banking & Finance* 37(8):3007–17.

Bonafont, L.C., and Iborra, I.M. (2021) 'The representation of business interests during the COVID-19 pandemic in Spain'. *Revista española de ciencia política* 57(1):21–44.

Brown, H. (2016) 'Does globalization drive interest group strategy? A cross-national study of outside lobbying and social media'. *Journal of Public Affairs* 16(3):294–302.

Chalmers, A.W., and Shotton, P.A. (2016) 'Changing the Face of Advocacy? Explaining Interest Organizations' Use of Social Media Strategies'. *Political Communication* 33(3):374–91.

Chari, R., and Bernhagen, P. (2011) 'Financial and Economic Crisis: Explaining the Sunset over the Celtic Tiger'. *Irish Political Studies* 26(4):473–88.

Chari, R.S. (2015) *Life after privatization*, Oxford: Oxford University Press.

Crepaz, M., Hanegraaff, M., and Junk, W.M. (2022) 'Is there a first mover advantage in lobbying? A comparative analysis of how the timing of lobbying affects the influence of interest groups in 10 polities'. *Comparative Political Studies*, Online First.

Crepaz, M., Hanegraaff, M., and Salgado, R.S. (2021) 'A golden key can open any door? Public funding and interest groups' access'. *West European Politics* 44(2):378–402.

De Bruycker, I. (2014) 'How Interest Groups Develop Their Lobbying Strategies', Proceedings from the Logic of Endogeneity'. Paper Prepared for the European Consortium for Political Research (ECPR) General Conference, Glasgow: Glasgow Univeristy.

De Bruycker, I. (2019) 'Lobbying: An art and a science—Five golden rules for an evidence-based lobbying strategy'. *Journal of Public Affairs* 19(4):1–4.

De Bruycker, I., and Beyers, J. (2019) 'Lobbying strategies and success: Inside and outside lobbying in European Union legislative politics'. *European Political Science Review* 11(1):57–74.

Dellmuth, L.M., and Tallberg, J. (2017) 'Advocacy Strategies in Global Governance: Inside versus Outside Lobbying'. *Political Studies* 65(3):705–23.

Dür, A., and Mateo, G. (2013) 'Gaining access or going public? Interest group strategies in five European countries'. *European Journal of Political Research* 52(5):660–86.

Dür, A. and Mateo, G. (2016) *Insiders versus Outsiders: Interest Group Politics in Multilevel Europe*, Oxford: Oxford University Press.

Eady, G., and Rasmussen, A. (2021) 'The Unequal Effects of the COVID-19 Pandemic on Political Interest Representation'. *Working paper:* https://www.annerasmussen.eu/wp-content/uploads/2021/06/EadyRasmussen050921.pdf (accessed June 28, 2022)

Galtung, J., and Ruge, M.H. (1965) 'The structure of foreign news: The presentation of the Congo, Cuba and Cyprus crises in four Norwegian newspapers'. *Journal of Peace Research* 2(1):64–90.

Gamson, W., and Wolfsfeld, G. (1993) 'Movements and Media as Interacting Systems'. *The Annals of the American Academy of Political and Social Science* 528(1): 114–125.

Grant, W. (1978) *Insider groups, outsider groups, and interest group strategies in Britain*, Warwick: University of Warwick, Department of Politics.

Gray, V., and Lowery, D. (1997) 'Life in a Niche: Mortality Anxiety Among Organized Interests in the American States'. *Political Research Quarterly* 50(1):25–47.

Gray, V., and Lowery, D. (2000) *The population ecology of interest representation: Lobbying communities in the American states*, Ann Arbor, Michigan: University of Michigan Press.

Hall, R.L. and Reynolds, M.E. (2012) 'Targeted Issue Advertising and Legislative Strategy: The Inside Ends of Outside Lobbying'. *The Journal of Politics* 74(3):888–902.

Halpin, D.R., and Thomas, H.F. (2012) 'Interest group survival: Explaining sources of mortality anxiety'. *Interest Groups & Advocacy* 1(2):215–38.

Hanegraaff, M. (2015) 'Interest Groups at Transnational Negotiation Conferences: Goals, Strategies, Interactions, and Influence'. *Global Governance: A Review of Multilateralism and International Organizations* 21(4):599–620.

Hanegraaff, M., Beyers, J., and De Bruycker, I. (2016) 'Balancing inside and outside lobbying: The political strategies of lobbyists at global diplomatic conferences'. *European Journal of Political Research* 55(3):568–88.

Hanegraaff, M., Braun, C., De Bièvre, D., and Beyers, J. (2015) 'The Domestic and Global Origins of Transnational Advocacy: Explaining Lobbying Presence During WTO Ministerial Conferences'. *Comparative Political Studies* 48(12):1591–621.

Hanegraaff, M., and Poletti, A. (2019) 'Public opinion and interest groups' concerns for organizational survival'. *European Political Science Review* 11(2):125–43.

Hart, D.M. (2004) '"Business" Is Not An Interest Group: On The Study Of Companies In American National Politics'. *Annual Review of Political Science* 7(1):47–69.

Huwyler, O. (2020) 'Interest groups in the European Union and their hiring of political consultancies'. *European Union Politics* 21(2):333–54.

Huwyler, O., and Martin, S. (2021) 'Interest group tactics and legislative behaviour: how the mode of communication matters'. *Journal of European Public Policy*, Online First.

Junk, W.M. (2016) 'Two logics of NGO advocacy: understanding inside and outside lobbying on EU environmental policies'. *Journal of European Public Policy* 23(2):236–54.

Junk, W.M., Crepaz, M., and Aizenberg, E. (2022) 'Fight or flight? How access barriers and interest disruption affect the activities of interest organizations'. *Working paper:* https://

61b80c4f-58c1-4b9d-bce6-c58106af2ef4.filesusr.com/ugd/9a0cb4_99e9221ab5864041a
   f0048ef263c2700.pdf (accessed June 28, 2022)

Junk, W.M., Crepaz, M., Hanegraaff, M., Berkhout, J., and Aizenberg, E. (2020) "InterCov
   Project: Online Survey on Interest Representation during Covid-19. Edition: June – July
   2020." https://www.wiebkejunk.com/_files/ugd/9a0cb4_eb572405723f490f8fd6e464420
   f3a33.pdf (accessed June 13, 2022).

Junk, W.M., Crepaz, M., Hanegraaff, M., Berkhout, J., and Aizenberg, E. (2021a) 'Changes in
   Interest Group Access in Times of Crisis: No Pain, No (Lobby) Gain'. *Journal of European
   Public Policy*, Online First.

Junk, W.M., Crepaz, M., Hanegraaff, M., Berkhout, J., and Aizenberg, E. (2021b) "InterCov
   Project: Online Survey on Interest Representation during Covid-19. Second Edition: July –
   August 2021." https://www.wiebkejunk.com/_files/ugd/9a0cb4_
   7d44f6c80cc84d259983d8bbdfa3a729.pdf (accessed June 13, 2022).

Junk, W.M., and Rasmussen, A. (2019) 'Framing by the Flock: Collective Issue Definition and
   Advocacy Success'. *Comparative Political Studies* 52(4):483–513.

Kastner, L. (2018) 'Business lobbying under salience – financial industry mobilization against
   the European financial transaction tax'. *Journal of European Public Policy*
   25(11):1648–66.

Keller, E. (2018) 'Noisy business politics: lobbying strategies and business influence after the
   financial crisis'. *Journal of European Public Policy* 25(3):287–306.

Klüver, H. (2010) 'Europeanization of Lobbying Activities: When National Interest Groups Spill
   Over to the European Level'. *Journal of European Integration* 32(2):175–91.

Kollman, K. (1998) *Outside lobbying: Public opinion and interest group strategies*, Princeton:
   Princeton University Press.

LaPira, T.M. (2014) 'Lobbying after 9/11: Policy Regime Emergence and Interest Group
   Mobilization'. *Policy Studies Journal* 42(2):226–51.

Lasswell, H.D. (1950) *Politics: Who Gets What, When, How*, New York: P. Smith.

Lipsky, M. (1968) 'Protest as a Political Resource'. *American Political Science Review*
   62(4):1144–58.

Lowery, D. (2007) 'Why Do Organized Interests Lobby? A Multi-Goal, Multi-Context Theory of
   Lobbying'. *Polity* 39(1):29–54.

Mahoney, C. (2008) *Brussels versus the beltway: Advocacy in the United States and the
   European Union*, Washington D.C.: Georgetown University Press.

Maloney, W.A., Jordan, G., and Andrew, M.M. (1994) 'Interest Groups and Public Policy: The
   Insider/Outsider Model Revisited'. *Journal of Public Policy* 14(1):17–38.

Muraleedharan, V., and Bryer, T.A. (2020) 'Refugee Crisis and the Role of NGO Lobbying'.
   Public Policy and Administration 19(1):22–34.

Pakull, D., Marshall, D., and Bernhagen, P. (2020) 'Shop till you drop? Venue choices of
   business and non-business interests in the European Union'. *Interest Groups &
   Advocacy* 9(4):520–40.

Rasmussen, A. and Gross, V. (2015) 'Biased access? Exploring selection to advisory
   committees'. *European Political Science Review* 7(3):343–72.

Salgado, R. (2014) 'Rebalancing EU Interest Representation? Associative Democracy and EU
   Funding of Civil Society Organizations'. *JCMS: Journal of Common Market Studies*
   52(2):337–53.

Schattschneider, E.E. (1960) *The Semisovereign People: A Realist's View of Democracy in America*, New York: Holt, Rinehart and Winston.

Schlozman, K.L., and Tierney, J.T. (1986) *Organized Interests and American Democracy*, Boston: HarperCollins Publishers.

Stinchcombe, A. (1965) 'Social structure and organizations', in J.G. March (Ed.), *Handbook of Organizations*, 142–93, Chicago: Rand McNally.

Thrall, T.A. (2006) 'The Myth of the Outside Strategy: Mass Media News Coverage of Interest Groups'. *Political Communication* 23(4):407–20.

Timoneda, J.C., and Vallejo Vera, S. (2021) 'How do shocks realign interest group lobbying in congress? Evidence from Ecuador'. *The Journal of Legislative Studies*, Online First.

Tresch, A., and Fischer, M. (2015) 'In search of political influence: Outside lobbying behaviour and media coverage of social movements, interest groups and political parties in six Western European countries'. *International Political Science Review* 36(4):355–72.

Truman, D.B. (1951) *The Governmental Process. Political Interests and Public Opinion*, New York: Alfred A. Knopf.

Van der Graaf, A., Otjes, S., and Rasmussen, A. (2016) 'Weapon of the weak? The Social Media Landscape of Interest Groups'. *European Journal of Communication* 31(2):120–35.

Victor, J.N. (2007) 'Strategic Lobbying:Demonstrating How Legislative Context Affects Interest Groups' Lobbying Tactics'. *American Politics Research* 35(6):826–45.

Walker, J.L. (1991) *Mobilizing interest groups in America: Patrons, professions, and social movements*, Ann Arbor, Michigan: University of Michigan Press.

Weiler, F., and Brändli, M. (2015) 'Inside versus outside lobbying: How the institutional framework shapes the lobbying behaviour of interest groups'. *European Journal of Political Research* 54(4):745–66.

Wilson, J.Q. (1961) 'The strategy of protest: Problems of negro civic action'. *Journal of Conflict Resolution* 5(3):291–303.

Witjas, R., Hanegraaff, M., and Vermeulen, F. (2020) 'Nothing to fear, but fear itself? Exploring the importance of mortality anxiety for interest group research'. *Interest Groups & Advocacy* 9(2):179–96.

Woll, C. (2013) 'Lobbying under Pressure: The Effect of Salience on European Union Hedge Fund Regulation'. *JCMS: Journal of Common Market Studies* 51(3):555–72.

Online Appendix

https://www.degruyter.com/document/isbn/9783110783148/html

Chapter 5
Access to Gatekeepers

Once *viral lobbying* is set in motion through successful issue mobilisation (Chapter 3) and the choice of specific strategies to advocate different interests (Chapter 4), a crucial question is whether and when active interest groups can secure actual *political access*. As we described in Chapter 1, *access* can be seen as a third step in the influence production process on a (new) set of issues – in our case policies related to the spread of COVID-19. Similarly, Binderkrantz and Pedersen (2017, 307) argue that there is 'potential in studying interest group access as a crucial step towards gaining influence' (also see: Truman 1951, 264).

One of the advantages of studying political access is that it captures whether and how interest groups actually manage to become involved in the political and media system. Halpin and Fraussen (2017, 725) define access as a situation 'where a group is granted contact with policymakers or institutions'. They add that access 'is something that not all groups have and it must in some real sense be 'won' or 'granted'. Put differently, access is a measure of whether interest groups passed a 'threshold controlled by relevant gatekeepers' (Binderkrantz and Pedersen 2017, 307). Gatekeepers here include a number of decision makers in different *arenas* or *venues* of public policy, including governments, parliaments, the bureaucracy, but also the media, as an important and exclusive forum of public policy debate (Binderkrantz, Christiansen, and Pedersen 2015; Binderkrantz, Bonafont, and Halpin 2016; Junk 2019).

Practically, such access is a first *desired outcome* for interest groups that use different lobbying strategies on an issue: Active groups compete for the time and attention of political gatekeepers both inside and outside political institutions. Securing that a group's interests receive due attention from target audiences is, in that sense, a typical lobbying goal.

At the same time, aggregate patterns in lobbying access give important insights into whether there are *biases* in the interest group system (Lowery et al. 2015; Rasmussen and Gross 2015), such as inequalities in how much attention different types of interests receive from political gatekeepers. Normatively, one can argue that the policy process should ideally give different social and economic groups similar opportunities to voice their needs and concerns. Moreover, the failure to include some societal interests in policy debates can produce inefficient policy outputs (Olson 1982) and can, for instance, lead to an upper-class bias (Schattschneider 1960) in political involvement and decision-making, where economic interests and wealthy organisations are overrepresented.

In this chapter, we therefore analyse patterns in lobbying access after the outbreak of the pandemic[22]. Existing studies suggest that political access often favours more resourceful and business interests in society (Binderkrantz, Christiansen, and Pedersen 2015; Eising 2007; Danielian and Page 1994). Our first aim is to evaluate whether this is the case at different stages of the pandemic, such as its early months, characterised by urgency and uncertainty, and the successive period of adaptation that many governments have labelled as 'living with COVID'. Secondly, we add the perspective of whether patterns in access are responsive to the underlying interests in society after a focussing event, in our case the spread of COVID-19, that has affected organisations to varying degrees (cf. Junk et al. 2021a). Finally, the interest group literature usually presents access as a combination of the *use of strategies* by interest groups, i. e. the *supply* of lobbying, and the *decisions of political gatekeepers*, i. e. their *demand* for input by lobbyists (cf. Binderkrantz and Pedersen 2017; Halpin and Fraussen 2017). Given the previous chapter has shed light on patterns in interest group strategies, we here pay special attention to the demand-driven side of access by looking at factors that explain which interest groups are more likely *to be contacted by gatekeepers* with requests to give input on Coronavirus-related policies. Since the behaviour of gatekeepers potentially varies depending on contextual factors, such as the parties that are in government or the capacities of the different political and media systems after the outbreak of the pandemic, we also assess the patterns in each of the seven countries and at the EU-level separately.

In a nutshell, three main findings stand out based on our data on political and media access at the start of the pandemic (March to June 2020) and in its later phase (June 2020 to June 2021). First, there is some evidence for a bias in favour of business organisations and other economic interest groups. Access advantages for business organisations have only been temporary and venue-specific (applying to the bureaucracy at the start of the pandemic), but gatekeeper's demand for group input has partly favoured economic groups. Second, there is strong evidence that better resourced groups had access advantages: Organisations with higher resources had more frequent access to all venues (the media, government, parliament, the bureaucracy), were more likely to be invited to comment on COVID-19 related issues by both policymakers and media gatekeepers, and were more frequently included in exclusive talks on such issues. Third, higher affectedness by the pandemic is strongly related to the frequency of access to

---

22 Our theoretical arguments build on work published elsewhere which explores *changes* in access patterns since the outbreak of COVID-19 in Europe (Junk et al. 2021a). To this, we here add further measures of the demand side of access (i. e. contact that is initiated by policymakers and journalists), as well as a more refined analysis of country-level differences.

all venues, as well as to demand-driven access in form of contact initiated by gatekeepers.

This chapter reconstructs access dynamics during the pandemic starting with a theoretical account of lobbying access dynamics after the focusing event of the spread of COVID-19. Building on classical interest group scholarship, the section presents both 'optimistic' and 'pessimistic' expectations about drivers of lobbying access during the pandemic. The following section tests such expectations and presents the results of the analyses of access patterns to key venues of public debate and policymaking in two phases of the Coronavirus pandemic (2020 and 2021). Particular attention is given to the processes which explain when gatekeepers *grant* access to interest groups. The final section summarises the results and reflects on their implications for the literature on lobbying access in general and, more specifically, for the next chapter on interest group influence on COVID-19 policy.

Lobbying Access after a Focusing Event

The existing interest group literature has pointed to both organisation-level and contextual factors that explain who gets a voice in different *venues* or *arenas* of public policy, (e.g. Beyers 2004; Binderkrantz, Christiansen, and Pedersen 2015; Chalmers 2013; Dür and Mateo 2013; Eising 2007; Danielian and Page 1994; Hanegraaff, van der Ploeg, and Berkhout 2020; Junk 2019). These studies provide evidence that access to political discussions is distributed unequally among interest groups active in a given community (cf. Baumgartner and Leech 2001; De Bruycker and Beyers 2015; Binderkrantz, Christiansen, and Pedersen 2015). A small share of groups generally receives most access, while a large share of groups is only rarely involved in the policy process (Berkhout and Lowery 2010). This finding holds across policy venues, including the media (Binderkrantz, Bonafont, and Halpin 2016), and there is evidence that the same interest groups persistently secure access across venues (Binderkrantz, Christiansen, and Pedersen 2015), potentially because they can act as central 'bridges' between venues in complex policy networks (LaPira, Thomas, and Baumgartner 2014; Ackland and Halpin 2019).

Furthermore, several studies suggest that political insiders (i.e. those that gain more regular access to policymakers and journalists), tend to be actors with higher resources, while less resourceful actors are more likely to remain political outsiders (cf. Binderkrantz, Christiansen, and Pedersen 2015; Dür and Mateo 2013; Rasmussen and Gross 2015; Maloney, Jordan, and Andrew 1994; Fraussen, Beyers, and Donas 2015). When it comes to access to *policymakers*, some studies also highlight that these interact more frequently with business actors than citizen groups (e.g. Baumgartner et al. 2009; Berkhout and Lowery 2010; Beyers 2004).

The first open question we raise against the backdrop of this literature is whether these potential biases also characterise *viral lobbying access*, i.e. access to different gatekeepers after the outbreak of the COVID-19 pandemic, as well as specifically on COVID-19 related policies. Different strands of theory on lobbying and interest groups lead to different expectations in this regard, which we can, broadly speaking, classify as a *pessimistic*, and an *optimistic* account of drivers of political access in response to a focussing event.

The *pessimistic* account builds on theories that characterise lobbying access as elitist and biased in favour of better-resourced actors. These theories would expect that, even under changing circumstances, the same economically powerful groups should enjoy systematic access benefits and be favoured by political gatekeepers. In contrast, the more *optimistic* account is rooted in pluralist theories of interest group politics, which expect that the nature and scope of the underlying interests in society drive lobbying activities, as well as the levels of political access granted by decision makers. When interest group systems are faced with a far-reaching focussing event like the pandemic, these theories would expect that highly affected interest groups lobby more (see also Chapter 3 and 4) and that gatekeepers have incentives to pay special attention to affected groups.

In the next sections, we outline these two strands of theory in more detail and with a focus on the role of political gatekeepers (i.e. the demand side), which complements the supply-side focus on mobilisation and strategies in the previous chapters.

'Pessimistic' Accounts of Biases in Political Access after a Focussing Event

Famously, Olson (1965) and Schattschneider (1960) were very critical of the ability of diverse sets of interest groups to *seek* political access, for instance due to free rider problems and upper-class biases in the ability to lobby. These arguments lead to the expectation that there are major differences at the *supply side* when it comes to seeking access after a focussing event (see also Chapter 3 and 4), especially based on the *type of organisation* and its *resources*. Like in previous chapters, we expect that business interests are best equipped to act effectively, and NGOs and citizen groups to face the largest mobilisation problems and strategy constraints. Similarly, interest groups that have higher organisational resources should be best equipped to re-align their advocacy efforts after the focussing event and *seek access*.

These advantages at the supply side might further be aggravated at the *demand* side. First, business groups and better resourced actors may be favoured by gatekeepers, because they tend to be highly professionalised (Hanegraaff, van der Ploeg, and Berkhout 2020; Heylen, Willems, and Beyers 2020). Kriesi (1996, 158) notes that organisations 'with formalised and professionalised structures tend to have easier access to public authorities, because government bureaucracies prefer to deal with organisations with working procedures similar to their own'.

Second, and perhaps most importantly, they may be in a better position to provide gatekeepers with what they want. Lobbying access is often described as an exchange relationship, where interest groups supply 'access goods' that are valued by gatekeepers (Bouwen 2004). A common assumption in exchange theories of lobbying is that political actors exchange policy-relevant information for access and influence in political arenas (see, e. g. Klüver 2013; Berkhout 2013) or a voice in the media (De Bruycker and Beyers 2015; Junk 2019). *Policy-relevant information* that organisations can provide spans several types (De Bruycker 2016; Flöthe 2019; Hall and Deardorff 2006), including political and technical information, impact assessments and research studies. These are resource-intensive to conduct and can support the work of policymakers and media gatekeepers in important ways.

Especially under new and uncertain circumstances, which arise after a far-reaching focussing event like the spread of the Coronavirus, gatekeepers face challenges when it comes to in-house resources to gather, systematise and verify information. Organisations with high levels of resources might here have special advantages because they can meet an urgent need for input and assistance in information collection. As an example, the consultancy McKinsey & Company offered free of charge support to Danish authorities to inform calculations for the 10 billion Danish Kroner's worth Crisis Fund for Danish companies in 2020. This has prompted civil society organisations to criticise the government for having given an unfair advantage to McKinsey & Company (DR 2020). Without entering into the merits of the case, this is an illustration of how informational resources can help secure a unique access position that would, otherwise, have been impossible to obtain.

Furthermore, gatekeepers arguably have incentives to favour *economic groups* (spanning business organisations, as well as associations of professionals and unions), especially in times of crisis. We expect this effect because economic downturns and high unemployment can have overwhelming effects on voters (Bloom and Price 1975), and (local) economic growth and well-being are issues that are prioritised in media debates (Andrews and Caren 2010). Different gatekeepers therefore have incentives to give access to economic groups. This is particularly evident in circumstances of *economic* crisis, where the threat of economic downturn provides incentives to gatekeepers to grant a voice to representatives of economic interests (Blau, Brough, and Thomas 2013; Adelino and Dinc 2014).

In the case of the pandemic, the economic consequences of lockdown policies were highly feared, and difficult to balance with health-related concerns. Policy design regarding the length of the lockdown, the timing of the easing of restrictions, the size of rescue packages, as well as the proportion of out-of-work benefits entailed high levels of uncertainty for policymakers. Special task-forces to evaluate crisis management and economic recovery were, therefore, created by all western governments to face unprecedented levels of uncertainty in the direction of crisis policy. This includes general task forces, such as the COVID-19 Task Force in Italy, or more specialised ones, such as the Tourism Recovery Task Force in Ireland. This anxiety about the scope and impact of crisis policies during the pandemic is likely to have increased the demand by political gatekeepers for input from economic groups (i.e. business actors, firms, trade unions and profession associations), for instance to gauge consequences of a lockdown and inform the design of economic rescue packages.

In short, based on the literature on lobbying access and gatekeeper demand in crisis situations, we expect business groups and other economic groups, as well as groups with higher resources to enjoy higher access during the COVID-19 pandemic than other groups. Moreover, we expect this to be partly driven by the demand of gatekeepers. Hypotheses 1 and 2 summarise these expectations.

H1 'group type hypothesis': Economic groups i) had higher access to political venues during the pandemic than NGOs and citizen groups, and ii) were more likely to be contacted (more often) by political gatekeepers than NGOs and citizen groups.

H2 'resources hypothesis': The more lobbying resources interest groups had, i) the more frequent was their access to political venues during the pandemic, and ii) the more likely they were to be contacted (more often) by political gatekeepers.

'Optimistic' Accounts of Inclusive Political Access after a Focussing Event

Alternatively, and perhaps more optimistically, one might argue that there are reasons to expect that access after a focussing event will favour other actors than just better resourced organisations and economic groups. When a focussing event poses new policy problems and changes the information needs of gatekeepers, as well as the preferences and concerns of interest groups, one might expect access patterns to favour those groups that are *highly affected* by these policy problems.

Quite intuitively, after an event or shock that requires policy change, gatekeepers such as policymakers and journalists should grant access to those organisations hit by the consequences of said event. In circumstances of financial and economic crises, studies have observed this for associations representing the financial and banking sector or business associations representing firms in economic distress (Blau, Brough, and Thomas 2013; Adelino and Dinc 2014; Kastner 2018; Keller 2018). Rather than evidence for a general business bias, these access advantages could also be explained by the nature of these crises.

Given the global pandemic has had far-reaching effects across many different sectors, it might arguably be seen (at the least) as a simultaneous health, economic, educational, cultural and care-taking crisis. Highly affected organisations, therefore, span many different types of groups and sectors, which had high stakes in policy. Such highly affected interest groups have reasons to *seek access* (see Chapters 3 and 4). At the same time, the input of affected groups is likely to be critical for understanding and solving the arising policy problems, so gatekeepers should have incentives *to grant them access*.

Such arguments echo pluralist theories of interest group politics. Most famously, Truman (1951, 511) argues that changes in society are a main driver for people to organise themselves. Any 'disturbance', as he calls it, 'in established relationships anywhere in society may produce new patterns of interaction aimed at restricting or eliminating the disturbance' (also see discussion by: Lowery and Brasher 2004). While such 'disturbances' are traditionally seen as drivers of the initial formation of groups, pluralist theory also applies to the activities of existing interest groups, i.e. the *supply-side* of access (see discussion in: Rasmussen, Carroll, and Lowery 2014). As we showed in Chapters 3 and 4, affectedness by a focussing event is a main driver of the decision of groups to mobilise and affects the frequency of their strategy employment. These patterns at the *supply* side are in line with pluralist theory.

The next question is, however, whether these supply-side patterns also translate into actual access of affected interests. This depends on whether there are access barriers at the *demand* side that block access even when groups are highly affected by a 'disturbance'. Pluralist theory is optimistic in the sense that it does not typically expect policymakers' attention to be (very) scarce. Salisbury (1990, 214) even holds that 'interest groups are virtually awash with access'. Still, it remains important to ask which groups manage to 'win' (most) access (Halpin and Fraussen 2017, 725).

Truman (1951, 511) arguably implies that policymakers have incentives to anticipate the effects of the disturbance on different social and economic groups by seeking to include these in the policy debate. Newer interpretations of pluralist theory (Junk et al. 2021a, 5; Rasmussen and Gross 2015, 349) assume that these incentives result in a demand-pull for input from affected interests, perhaps through the creation of new fora for interest representation (e.g Broscheid and Coen 2007). Put differently, policymakers, as well as media actors interested in 'news value' (Galtung and Ruge 1965; Binderkrantz, Bonafont, and Halpin 2016), can be expected to seek to consult groups whose interests are most affected by a focussing event.

This argument also resonates with seeing lobbying access as an exchange-relationship, subject to the value of the 'exchange goods' (Bouwen 2004), as mentioned above. While higher lobbying resources can help gather policy-relevant information, high affectedness by a focussing event might in itself mean that an interest group can offer relevant information for addressing a policy problem. In case of the COVID-19 pandemic, this could apply to associations of teachers and health care professionals, patient groups, and organisations in the tourism industry, which held policy-relevant information, irrespective of their resources.

In short, based on pluralist theories and a more optimistic interpretation of exchange theory, we expect access patterns, including the demand by political gatekeepers, to favour more affected groups after a focussing event, here the COVID-19 pandemic. We therefore formulate our next hypothesis as follows:

H3 'affectedness hypothesis': The more affected interest groups were by the pandemic i) the higher was their access to political venues, and ii) the more likely they were to be contacted (more often) by political gatekeepers.

In the next section, we test these expectations based on our cross-country survey data that allows us to assess whether lobbying access varied between different types of organisations, as well as between different venues of policymaking, different countries and/or at different stages of the pandemic.

Analysis: Lobbying Access during the Pandemic

We use data from both waves of our cross-country survey (Junk et al. 2020; Junk et al. 2021b) to speak to these expectations. We first present data on the *frequency of access* after the outbreak of the crisis (March to June 2020) and in a later phase of the pandemic (June 2020 to June 2021). As we argued earlier in this chapter, these levels of access are a product of both the *supply* of strategies by interest groups and the *demand* of gatekeepers who grant access to the group (Halpin and Fraussen 2017; Binderkrantz and Pedersen 2017). Based on our analyses of how groups *seek* access in the previous chapters, we can evaluate these access levels and infer whether practices of gatekeepers continued or changed patterns that stem from interest groups' issue mobilisation and strategy use.

In addition, the second part of our analysis is dedicated solely to the *demand side:* Here we analyse to which extent group type, resources and affectedness explain whether and how often gatekeepers reached out to an interest group and asked the organisation for input on COVID-19 related policies. Jointly, these analyses provide rich evidence on patterns in viral lobbying access, and the role of gatekeepers in granting or denying access to some interest groups. For both total access and demand-driven access, we first give a descriptive overview, and then present results from multivariate regression models.

Overview of Access Patterns

Like in the previous chapter, our empirical analyses distinguish between different *venues* in which interest groups can seek and potentially gain access to give input to public policy (cf. Binderkrantz, Christiansen, and Pedersen 2015; Binderkrantz and Pedersen 2017). Specifically, we study 'outside' access to the mainstream media and 'inside' access to governments, parliaments, and the bureaucracy. Note that for social media use, which we analysed as a lobbying strategy in the previous chapter, there is 'automatic' access, given there is usually no control by gatekeepers[23]. For this reason, social media are not included in our analyses of lobbying access. Figure 5.1 provides a descriptive overview of the frequency of access to the four venues as measured in our two waves of the survey in 2020 and 2021. Notably, the two measures vary in two respects.

First, the two measures cover different time periods and phases in the pandemic: The 2020 measure covers access in a three-months period (March 2020 to June 2020) right after the outbreak of the pandemic in Europe. As explained in Chapter 2, the survey was fielded in June 2020 shortly after many European countries had started easing lockdown restrictions after the first European wave of the virus. Arguably, this is a phase where interest groups and gatekeepers were most overwhelmed by the new policy problems connected to the virus and lockdown measures tended to be more restrictive than in successive periods. The 2021 measure, on the other hand, covers a longer period (June 2020–June

---

23 Except in rare cases, such as when Facebook and Twitter refused access to Donald Trump or other political personas.

2021), during which the intensity of the crisis varied, and both interest groups and gatekeepers have had more time to adapt to the new (and changing) reality of pandemic politics. This measure is more likely to represent interest groups' resilience to crises circumstances as well as processes of adaptation that are more likely to carry a profound impact on *viral lobbying* also after the Coronavirus pandemic.

Moreover, the two measures vary in their policy focus: The 2020 survey asked respondents to rate the frequency of access since the outbreak of the pandemic to the different political venues. This measure is '*general*' in that it did not distinguish whether the group received access on pandemic-related policies, or other policies.[24] In contrast, the 2021 survey focused on access on COVID-related issues (*viral policies:* i.e. health and safety measures, closing or opening of sectors, securing of help and economic support packages, vaccination programs) in the 12 months period described above. Other than this, the question wording was the same.

Other than this, both survey items where phrased identically and asked respondents to rate how frequently they gained access to each venue, where answer categories ranged from Never (1); Less than once a month (2); Once a month (3); Once a week (4); to Almost on a daily basis (5) [25].

As Figure 5.1 shows, both measures seem to be distributed relatively similarly, and indicate that a large share of respondents enjoyed (some) access. This is noteworthy, because it documents that intense and continuous interaction between the state and society happened during the pandemic. Nevertheless, in both measures we see a group of 'outsiders' for each venue that never attained access. Interestingly, the share of respondents that never had access is highest in the media in both waves of the survey (at 29 and 40 percent, respectively), and lowest in the bureaucracy (at 16 and 19 percent). This might tentatively suggest that media gatekeepers tended to systematically favour the same groups in their access provision – and more so than other gatekeepers in inside venues.[26] In addition, we see that the share of 'almost daily' access is highest in the bureaucracy (at 19 and 9 percent of groups) in both periods, suggesting this venue has granted most frequent access to interest groups.

---

24 However, considering the extraordinary circumstances of the first months of the crisis, we can safely assume that most groups lobbied on policy (closely) related to COVID-19 issues.

25 This is different from items we used in Chapter 4 to measure strategy use since these asked how often interest groups 'sought contact' (without guarantee of access). For exact question wording see Junk et al. (2020) and Junk et al. (2021a).

26 An alternative explanation is that bureaucratic access is less scarce than media access due to higher staff capacities in the bureaucracy.

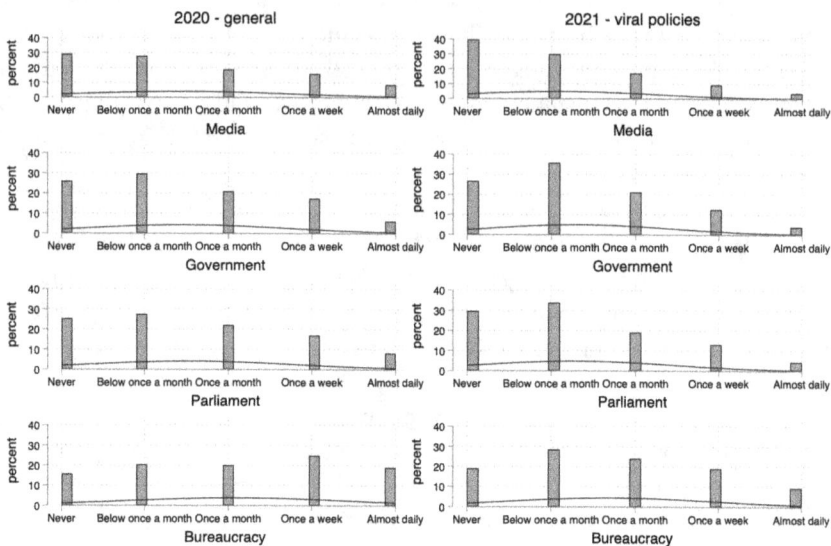

Figure 5.1: Share of groups reporting different access frequencies (in percent) to the four venues.

When comparing the 2020 and 2021 distributions, we see that access frequencies are generally lower when looking only at *viral policies* and at the longer period. This makes sense, given that gaining daily access over a year's period is harder, and given that the intensity of policy challenges caused by the pandemic varied over this period[27]. Nevertheless, the patterns look relatively alike.

Still, this distribution does not provide any insights on whether *the same (types of) organisations* gained access in these different periods. The strength of correlations between access measured in the two waves of the survey speaks to this question. It is high: spearman's rank correlation lies between 0.60 and 0.65 in the different venues for those groups that responded to both waves of the survey. This indicates that higher access early in the pandemic is strongly related to higher access later on – but by no means a perfect predictor. Similarly, correlations between access frequencies to different venues are relatively high for

---

27 Many European countries had, for example, experienced a drop in the number of cases in late 2020 before the outbreak of the much more contagious Delta variant in early 2021.

both waves of the survey, suggesting that access (to a certain extent) is cumulative (Binderkrantz et al. 2015).[28]

Next, we are interested in whether there are systematic patterns in these access levels, especially related to the expectations we started out with on the effects of group type, resources and affectedness by the pandemic. We therefore test to what extent these interest group characteristics explain the variation in access in each venue and at the different time intervals.

Explanatory Models of Access

Like in previous chapters, we distinguish between *business groups and firms, profession groups and unions,* and *NGOs and citizen groups.* In line with Hypothesis 1, we now use *NGOs and citizen groups* as reference category, in order to compare it with different types of economic groups (business organisations, profession groups and unions). We test Hypothesis 2 measuring resources for lobbying as the number of staff working on public affairs in the organisations in three categories (low (<1), medium (1–4) and high (≥5)). To test Hypothesis 3 on the effect of affectedness, we rely on the survey item that measures the extent to which an organisation, according to its own perception, was 'more or less affected by the Coronavirus crisis, compared to other stakeholders' in the polity on a 5-point scale (from (1) 'much less affected' to (5) 'much more affected'). For more details on these variables, see Chapter 2.

In addition, the following controls are included in all models: The age of an organisation, which is likely to affect existing relationships to gatekeepers, as well as plausibly being related to lobbying resources and group type. For the same reason, we control for the extent to which an organisation is an umbrella organisation. In addition, we include fixed effects for countries to take contextual differences in access into account, and cluster standard errors by sector given lobbying access for groups in the same sector is likely to be interdependent. The full regression output in table form can be found in the Online Appendix of the book (Tables A5.1 and A5.2).

Figure 5.2 plots the coefficients of interest based on a sequence of ordered logistic regressions to attend to the ordinal structure of our outcome variables (the frequency of access). Where the confidence intervals (straight lines) of the

---

28 The lowest correlation is found between access to the media and access to the bureaucracy (0.55 and 0.51 in 2020 and 2021, respectively). The highest is between access to government and parliament (0.78 and 0.71 in 2020 and 2021).

plotted coefficients (dot in the middle) do not overlap with 0 (the vertical dotted line), we can say with high certainty that there is a significant relationship between the factor and the frequency of use of the lobbying strategy. We will discuss what the figure reveals about access to the different outside and inside venues in turn.

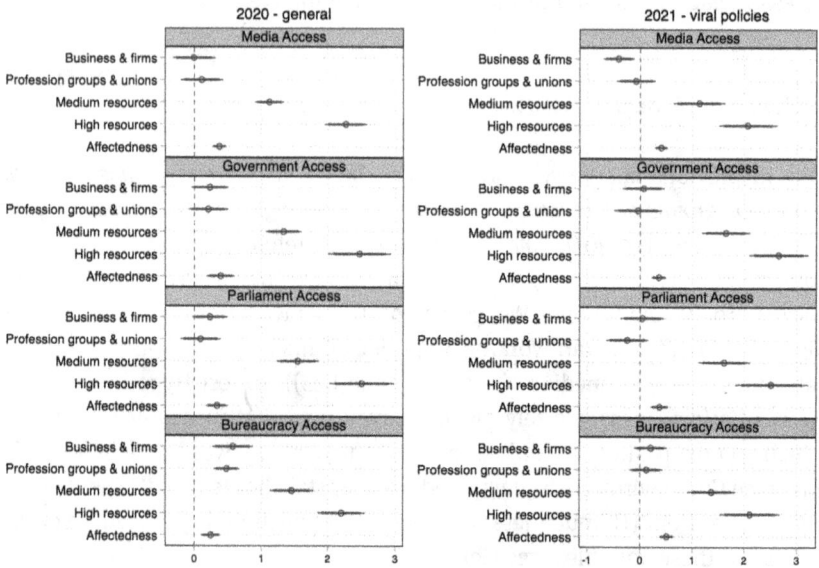

Figure 5.2: Ordered logistic regression on lobbying access to inside and outside venues for 2020 and 2021. Coefficients and 95/90% confidence intervals.

Notes: The figure is based on eight ordered logistic regressions (one for each dependent variable: media access; government access; parliament access; bureaucracy access for our 2020 and 2021 survey waves respectively). For 2020, Model 1 (n=1094), Model 2 (n=1092), Model 3 (n=1092), Model 4 (n= 1095). For 2021, Model 1 (n=637), Model 2 (n=633), Model 3 (n=636), Model 4 (n= 633). Included controls in all these models were: organisation age, the group's potential status as an umbrella organisation, and fixed effects for the country/polity. Moreover, we clustered standard errors by sector given that access for groups within a sector is likely to be related. For results in table form, see Tables A5.1 and A5.2 in the Online Appendix. Measures of goodness of fit (pseudo R-squared) lie between 0.10 and 0.13.

First, *media access* in both periods has favoured actors with medium and high resources (compared to the baseline of actors with low resources), as we expected based on the more pessimistic take on (resource exchange) theories. To illustrate the size of these effects, we calculate the predicted likelihood for different groups (not) to attain access based on these models.[29] For 2020, the predicted probability for an organisation with low resources to receive *no access* to the media venue is 45 percent. In contrast, an organisation with high resources only has an 8 percent probability to never receive media access. Conversely, organisations with low resources only have a 6 percent predicted probability to attain *weekly* access to the media, whereas this is 30 percent for organisations with high resources. Similar gaps in the likelihood that low and highly resourced organisations receive media access are present in 2021.

Second, contrary to what we also expected based on more *pessimistic* theories, differences between types of interest groups are not pronounced when it comes to outside access. Based on our data from 2020, there is no significant difference in media access between *NGOs and citizen groups* and the other types of actors. Interestingly, our data from the second wave (2021) suggests that *business associations and firms* in fact enjoyed *less* frequent access compared to NGOs and citizen groups (the baseline in these models). This difference is most evident at very high levels of access (*almost daily access*) and at no access (*never*): NGOs and citizen groups have a 27 percent predicted probability to access the media very frequently, while business groups and firms are at only 19 percent. Similarly, NGOs and citizen groups have a 35 percent predicted probability to *never* access the media, while this probability is 45 percent for business groups and firms. And this in not because business groups did not try to get into the media: in the previous chapter, we showed that business interest groups indicate to use media outside strategies more frequently than other types of actors (Figure 4.2).

Finally, higher affectedness by the pandemic is clearly related to higher access to the media. For 2020, holding other characteristics constant, our models suggest that a least affected organisation had only a 7 percent probability of accessing this venue on a *weekly* basis. In contrast, the probability is 23 percent for most affected organisations. For 2021, this substantial effect of affectedness is somewhat smaller, but still remarkable: A least affected group has only a 3 percent chance of weekly accessing the media, whereas this increases to 12 percent for highly affected groups. At the same time, these numbers suggest that access to the media has been highly competitive during the pandemic – even for highly affected groups.

With the exception of group type patterns, these findings for *outside* access to the media strongly mirror access to the other three *inside* venues: government, parliament and the bureaucracy. In all three cases, we see parallel findings when

---

29 All predicted probabilities/values are based on the main models (see Figure 5.2) when holding all other variables at means.

it comes to groups with higher and medium resources enjoying more frequent access, compared to organisations with low resources. These effects are substantial. Taking government access in 2020 as an example, the predicted probability for organisations with low resources to have *weekly* access to this venue is 6 percent but increases to 34 percent for better-resourced interest groups. At the same time, higher affectedness significantly and substantially increases access to all three inside venues. With regards to access to parliament in 2021, for example, our model predicts an 18 percent probability that most affected groups had *weekly access* to this venue, while this is only 5 percent for least affected ones. These findings concerning inside venues hold both for the 2020 and 2021 measures, meaning that they hold at the beginning *and* throughout the pandemic, as well as for general policymaking and for specific Coronavirus-related policies.

Another insight from Figure 5.2 is that differences between the venues seem limited to whether and how different types of groups enjoyed access advantages. There do not seem to be clear differences between economic groups (business groups and firms, as well as unions and profession groups) compared to non-economic groups (NGO and citizen groups) when it comes to access to parliaments and governments (in neither 2020 nor 2021). Bureaucratic access has, however, clearly favoured economic interest groups right after the outbreak of the pandemic. Nevertheless, such advantage disappears when access concerns Coronavirus-related policies in the period between June 2020 and June 2021. This could be related to the formulation and implementation of urgency legislation in the first part of the pandemic (e. g. definition of essential and not essential services, closure of economic activities and health and safety protocols for essential activities). Once defined, it may be that such access advantages disappeared, making economic interests as likely as others to access this venue.

To sum up, we find evidence for both optimistic and pessimistic accounts of lobbying access. While access is biased in the sense that better resourced groups clearly attained more access to all venues, we also see that more affected groups were granted more access across the board. Moreover, there is no consistent bias across venues in favour of some group types, and temporary advantages for economic groups in some arenas (the bureaucracy) might partly be offset by disadvantages in other venues (the media).

When comparing these patterns to the drivers of strategy use (Chapter 4), we find a high degree of consistency. Resource advantages and affectedness systematically predict the frequency of use of both inside and outside strategies to influence public policy. These then consistently translate into access to key venues of policymaking. Differences between group types in access patterns are, however, less pronounced than in the use of lobbying strategies. Chapter 4 showed that business associations and firms consistently used inside and outside strategies more frequently than NGOs and citizens groups (with the exception of social media strategies). Combined with the results in this chapter, it seems that many of the lobbying efforts by business organisations fall short of actually gaining access, given these groups do not have significantly higher access patterns compared to NGOs and citizen groups (except when it comes to access to the bureaucracy in 2020).

A potential explanation for this is that gatekeepers actively counter these biases in lobbying supply through their consultation practises. To test the role of gatekeepers in this relationship more directly, the next sections look at patterns in contact that is *initiated* by political gatekeepers, for instance when they invite interest groups to comment on legislation or news stories.

Overview of Gatekeeper Demand for Interest Group Input

In both waves of our survey, we also addressed whether groups were *contacted* by gatekeepers in relation to Coronavirus-related policies. Such attempts by gatekeepers to initiate contact with interest groups are a direct measure of their *demand* for input by interest groups.

Figure 5.3 summarises descriptively what types of interest groups in each country and at the EU level were (not) contacted by gatekeepers based on the responses to the two waves of our surveys in 2020 (left) and 2021 (right).

As in previous analyses, the 2020 measure captures the shorter timeframe after the outbreak of the pandemic (March 2020 to June 2020), while the 2021 measure captures a one-year period during the pandemic (June 2020 to June 2021). In this case, both measures address COVID-19 related policies only. These were defined in the survey as topics directly related to COVID-19 (*viral policies* i.e. health and safety measures, closing or opening of sectors, securing of help and economic support packages, vaccination programs) and also instances where another agenda is explicitly linked to COVID-19 (i.e. climate-friendly COVID-19 policies). In 2020, we only asked about governmental gatekeepers, while we added media gatekeepers in the 2021 survey.

In particular, the 2020 survey captured whether different types of government actors reached out to the interest group in the following forms: invitation to a consultation or expert meeting, contact by a civil servant (from government departments and government agencies), elected officials, or other government actors (e.g. hired specialists from the government). We treat this as a binary variable, where such contact is coded as (1), whereas we code as (0) where respondents report that government actors did not reach out to them. In 2021, we measured the frequency of contact in more detail, namely in four categories: Never (1),

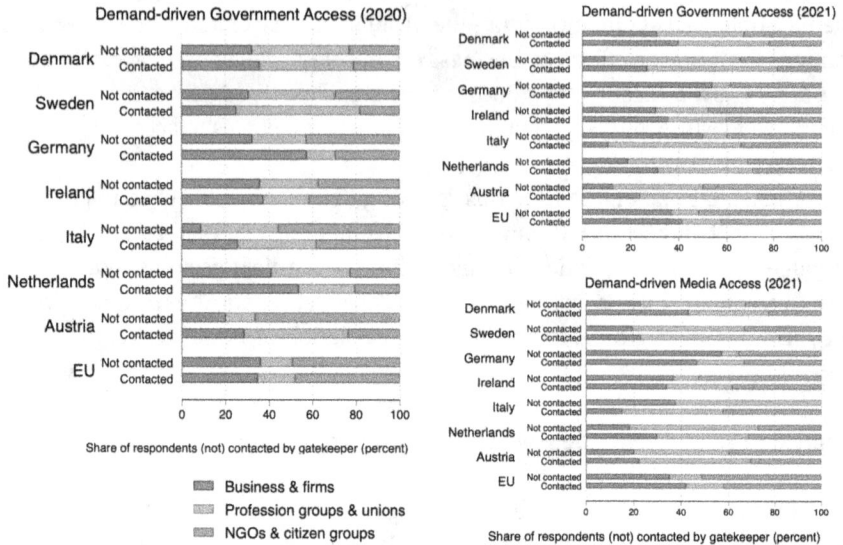

Figure 5.3: Overview of groups reporting they have (not) been contacted by gatekeepers about COVID-19-related issues

Only once (2), A few times (3), Frequently (4), and we distinguished between contact sought by policymakers and media gatekeepers. Moreover, we covered invitations to *comment* and invitations to *exclusive* discussions separately. For Figure 5.3, we transformed this into binary variables that measure whether a group was contacted by the respective gatekeeper (policymakers and media gatekeepers) in any form. In the multivariate analyses, which we present in the next section, we use the ordinal frequency of contact measures.

Given gatekeeper behaviour is likely to depend on contextual factors, such as the parties in government or the media system, we show patterns in each country and for the EU-level separately in Figure 5.3. For each country, the figure shows the share of different group types (*business groups and firms, profession groups and unions,* as well as *NGOs and citizen groups*) among respondents that *were contacted by gatekeepers,* as well as those that were *not contacted* by policymakers and/or the media. This gives a first impression of whether there are systematic group type differences in the extent to which interest groups were contacted by gatekeepers or not. Indeed, as Figure 5.3 suggests, there is country-level variation in the composition of which group types *were contacted* by gatekeepers or not.

In Denmark, Sweden, Ireland, and at EU level, for instance, the share of different group types among organisations that *were contacted by government gatekeepers* is very similar to that of groups that were *not contacted*. In case of the media (2021), however, there seem to be larger imbalances. As can be seen in the bottom-right section of the figure, in Denmark, 43 percent of the groups that reported that they were contacted by journalists were *business organisations and firms*, 34 percent were *profession groups and unions*, and 23 percent were *NGO and citizen groups*. In contrast, the share of the latter groups is considerably higher among groups that were not contacted (33 percent), while business groups and firms only account for 23 percent of the non-contacted groups. This tentatively suggests an imbalance favouring economic groups when journalists sought to speak to interest groups in Denmark. A similar trend in media access is observed also in Ireland.

We also see imbalances in government demand in some of the countries. This is evident in the Netherlands (2020 and 2021) and Germany (2020) where the share of contacted business groups and firms clearly outweighs the non-contacted ones. Still, it is important to note that some of the patterns may also be driven by the low number of responses in some of the countries, especially in the second wave of the survey (see Chapter 2 for details). Moreover, there might be confounders, that is, other factors than group type that drive the demand for access and are correlated with group type (such as lobbying resources).

Explanatory Models of Gatekeeper Demand for Interest Group Input

For that reason, it is important to probe whether there are statistically significant relationships between demand-driven access and organisational characteristics in multivariate regressions. Figure 5.4 summarises these results based on the 2020 data for both the pooled sample, which includes all countries and the EU-level, as well as the subsample of respondents in each of the eight polities. The included controls are the same as in the previous section. Given the binary outcome variable (being contacted (1) or not (0) by government actors), we here run logistic regressions.

The models summarised in Figure 5.4 bear several interesting insights. First, neither in the pooled sample, nor in most of the country samples, there is evidence that governments significantly favoured *business groups and firms* compared to *NGOs and citizen groups*. As far as business interests are concerned, Germany is the only exception, where this interest group type is significantly more likely to be contacted, compared to *NGOs and citizen groups* (the baseline in the models).

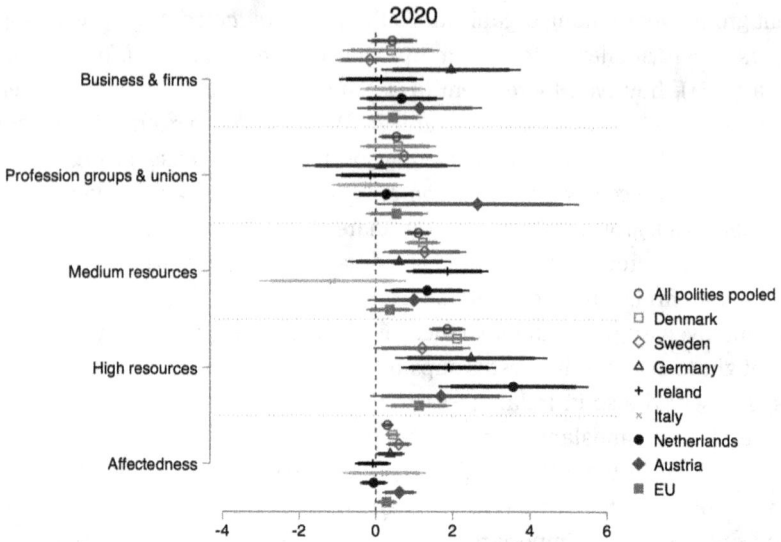

Figure 5.4: Logistic regression on demand-driven government access in 2020. Coefficients and 95/90% confidence intervals.

Notes: The figure is based on nine logistic regressions (one for each polity under investigation plus one for 'all polities pooled'. All polities pooled (n= 1,077). Denmark (n=250), Sweden (n=179), Germany (n=77), Ireland (n= 135), Italy (n= 55), Netherlands (n= 130), Austria (n= 73), EU (n= 171). Included controls in all these models were: organisation age, the group's potential status as an umbrella organisation, and fixed effects for the country/polity (in the model for 'all polities pooled' only). Moreover, we clustered standard errors by sector given that access for groups within a sector is likely to be related. For results in table form, see Table A5.3 in the Online Appendix. Measures of goodness of fit (pseudo R-squared in Table A5.3) lie between 0.07 and 0.28.

In the pooled sample, we see that *profession groups and unions* were significantly more likely to be contacted by government actors, compared to *NGOs and citizen groups* (the baseline). Yet, this relationship is not significant in the country sub-samples, except in Austria and (more weakly) in Sweden.[30]

---

30 Note that a reason for this difference between the pooled sample and individual results is likely to be the number of observations. These are lower in the country samples, which decreases modelling power and makes it less likely to find effects in the sub-samples. Moreover, it is possible that the relationship is present on average among all respondents and when controlling for

The evidence is much clearer, however, when we move to our other predictors. In the pooled sample, *medium and highly resourced* groups are significantly more likely to be contacted by government actors compared to less resourced groups (the baseline). The finding for *highly resourced* groups, in fact, holds in each of the country subsamples (weakly so in Sweden and Austria). For medium (compared to low) resourced groups the relationship is significant in most countries (exceptions are the EU-level, Italy and Germany). This gives an important verdict about patterns in government demand for input: across all countries, government gatekeepers favoured better resourced groups at the beginning of the pandemic. We interpret this as evidence that gatekeepers select organisations based on their ability to provide and communicate information, which strongly depends on their lobbying resources.

At the same time, we also find support that *more affected groups* were more likely to be contacted, meaning that gatekeepers can successfully pinpoint stakeholders in a crowded lobbying environment. This holds in the pooled analysis that takes all countries and the EU-level into account, as well as in the majority of subsample analyses. Interestingly, exceptions are Ireland, Italy and the Netherlands, where the estimated coefficient of affectedness is very close to zero. This indicates that government gatekeepers in these countries did not reach out more to affected groups at the beginning of the crisis. This might be explained by these governments' lack of capacity to do so because of the tough circumstances early in the crisis, when Italy, for instance, faced extreme challenges with a huge number of COVID-19 cases and overburdened hospitals. An alternative explanation could be that these countries' approach to policymaking has followed more standard consultation patterns, rather than adapting these based on the impacts of the pandemic. In that sense, there seems to be important variation in gatekeeper behaviour between countries. Nevertheless, in the aggregate, as well as the other polities individually (Denmark, Sweden, Germany, Austria and the EU-level), we clearly see that more affected groups were significantly more likely to be contacted.

To probe whether similar patterns hold in the later phase of the pandemic, we use more granular data from our second survey. Instead of *whether* groups were contacted by government gatekeepers, we now capture *how frequently* groups were contacted in the 12-months period (June 2020 to June 2021) under study. Answers here include four categories: 'never', 'only once', 'several times' and 'frequently'. Moreover, we capture different types of gatekeepers: pol-

---

country specific access patters (country fixed effects are included in all models) but does not hold in each country.

icymakers and journalists, and distinguish between *invitations to comment* and more *exclusive* access in form of meetings or exclusive media stories, respectively.

Figure 5.5 shows the coefficient plots of our main predictors based on ordered logistic regression models in the pooled sample (all countries plus the EU level). These findings largely confirm what is seen in Figure 5.4.

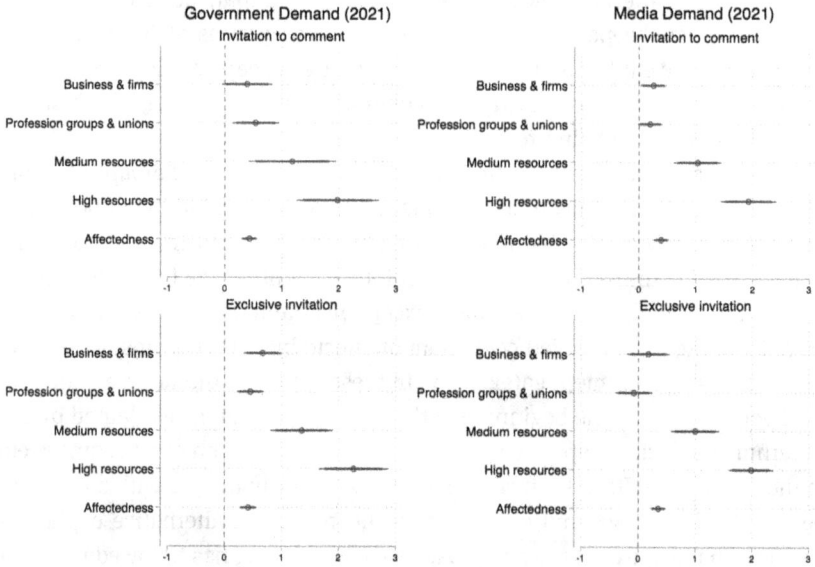

Figure 5.5: Ordered logistic regression on demand-driven government and media access in 2021. Coefficients and 95/90% confidence intervals.

Notes: The figure is based on four ordered logistic regressions (one for each dependent variable of demand-driven access). Model 1: Invitation by government to comment (n=633); Model 2: Exclusive invitation by government (n=633); Model 3: Invitation by media to comment (n=633); Model 4: Exclusive invitation by media (n= 634)). Included controls in all these models were: organisation age, the group's potential status as an umbrella organisation, and fixed effects for the country/polity. Moreover, we clustered standard errors by sector given that access for groups within a sector is likely to be related. For results in table form, see Table A5.4 in the Online Appendix. Measures of goodness of fit (pseudo R-squared in Table A5.4) lie at 0.11 (Model 1), 0.10 (Model 2), 0.10 (Model 3), 0.08 (Model 4).

Both when it comes to invitations to comment and more exclusive forms of access (meetings, exclusive newspaper stories), Figure 5.5 shows that better resourced organisations receive more frequent invitations from both policymakers and media gatekeepers. At the same time, higher affectedness is consistently associated with higher demand-driven access. In addition, Figure 5.5 gives support for our group-type expectation. Especially if we look at exclusive inside access (Figure 5.5 bottom left), we see that the two types of economic groups (*business and firms*, as well as *profession groups and unions*) receive more frequent invitations compared to *NGOs and citizen groups*. This is the highest level of insiderness as far as demand-side access is concerned. Interestingly, this also holds for invitations to comment in inside venues for *profession groups and unions* compared to *NGOs and citizen groups*.

In substantive terms, NGOs and citizens groups are predicted a 16 percent probability to be *frequently* invited to comment on policy issues by policymakers, while this compares to a predicted probability of 24 percent for profession groups and unions. The former are also less likely to be frequently invited to exclusive talks with policymakers (predicted probability equals 11 percent) while business groups and firms are more frequently invited to such talks with a 19 percent probability.

As far as the media is concerned, the advantage in favour of economic interests (namely *business and firms*) holds only for invitations to comment which represents a relatively lower level of insiderness, and the result does not hold for exclusive access. The predicted probability of being *frequently* invited to comment in the media is 23 percent for *business groups and firms* and 19 percent for *NGOs and citizen groups*. In combination with our findings on total access (Figure 5.2) this is notable: while media actors reached out significantly more often to business groups in this phase of the pandemic, this has not translated to overall access advantages for economic groups.

Jointly with our results from Chapter 4, it remains inconclusive how much gatekeeper demand *actively counters* group type biases in strategy use: on the one hand, access patterns suggest supply is filtered in this way to balance out group type differences (Figure 5.2). On the other hand, the patterns we recorded in contact *initiated* by policymakers and media gatekeepers does not provide evidence for tendencies to favour NGOs and citizen groups in order to pull them into the policy process.

Chapter Summary

Our analysis of lobbying access during the COVID-19 pandemic highlights mixed trends. As pessimistic accounts of lobbying would predict, the availability of resources for lobbying substantially constrains an organisation's ability to gain access to key venues of policymaking. This result holds across both inside (government, parliament and bureaucracy) and outside venues (the media) of policy-making. We interpreted this based on both supply- and demand side explanations. Better-resourced organisations can produce more valuable information that, conversely, gatekeepers demand from interest groups. It may also be that better-resourced organisations can use such resources to become *visible* to gatekeepers and are, therefore, more likely to be drawn into policymaking down the line. As our analysis further shows, gatekeepers were more likely to pull better-resourced organisations into the policymaking process on COVID-19 related policy-issues. This finding is robust (at least weakly significant) across all eight polities under investigation, as well as at both moments in time for which we recorded respondents' self-reported access frequencies.

Interestingly and somewhat in contrast to general expectations, our analysis does not show consistent evidence of an access bias in favour of economic groups. Looking at total access, *business associations and firms*, as well as *profession groups and unions* were found to dominate only the bureaucratic arena, while *NGOs and citizen groups* were found to have more frequent access to the media. These findings were, however, not consistent across periods of the pandemic. Economic groups, for example, had more frequent access to the bureaucracy during the early months of the pandemic, but lost such advantage in the long run. We argue that this may be driven by the specific policy issues that were discussed at the beginning of the pandemic, which required input from economic actors.

It is, however, important to underline that, when we considered access initiated by gatekeepers (*demand-driven access*), we found a more consistent advantage in favour of economic groups. According to our survey responses, policymakers (and journalists) invited *business associations and firms*, as well as *profession groups and unions* more frequently to comment on COVID-19 issues, compared to *NGOs and citizen groups*. Importantly, these groups were more frequently invited to *exclusive* discussions on COVID-19 policy with government actors, which we described as access of the highest level of *insiderness*.

Yet, there is also reason for *optimism* in our findings. More affected organisations (that is, those that felt worst hit by the pandemic) were more likely to gain frequent access to all venues of policymaking and were more frequently drawn into discussions – including exclusive ones – with policymakers and journalists. Affectedness was a significant predictor of demand-driven access in almost all polities in the analysis (exceptions were Italy, Ireland and the Netherlands). We interpret this as a form of responsiveness by the political systems under study to the effects of the pandemic on organisations, and as an attempt to integrate new organisational concerns in discussions over policy.

Overall, 'viral access', therefore, carries both positive and negative implications for the well-functioning of democratic political systems in crisis management mode: When a crisis or other focussing events hit the political system, gatekeepers seek input from interest groups, and they seem more likely to draw affected stakeholders into policymaking. Even though we found exceptions in some of the countries under study, this is a positive trend. At the same time, however, when selecting discussion partners, gatekeepers need to be careful about resource and economic biases. Our results suggest these biases are present in general access patterns and when access is initiated by gatekeepers. If inclusiveness and input legitimacy is an objective for the policy process, then gatekeepers arguably need to pay more attention to levelling the playing field for non-economic and less resourced organisations, who struggle to have their voice heard in policy debates.

Providing interest groups with access does, of course, not guarantee that their concerns will be reflected in policy outputs. In other words, access does not equal influence, although the rule of thumb is that influence is unlikely *without* access. Therefore, we keep following the influence production process and move on to the analysis of the factors which determined interest group influence in viral lobbying.

References

Ackland, R., and Halpin, D.R. (2019) 'Change or stability in the structure of interest group networks? Evidence from Scottish Public Policy Consultations'. *Journal of Public Policy* 39(2):267–94.

Adelino, M., and Dinc, I.S. (2014) 'Corporate distress and lobbying: Evidence from the Stimulus Act'. *Journal of Financial Economics* 114(2):256–72.

Andrews, K.T., and Caren, N. (2010) 'Making the News: Movement Organizations, Media Attention, and the Public Agenda'. *American Sociological Review* 75(6):841–66.

Baumgartner, F.R., Berry, J.M., Hojnacki, M., Kimball, D.C., and Leech, B.L. (2009) *Lobbying and Policy Change: Who Wins, Who Loses, and Why*, Chicago, IL: University of Chicago Press.

Baumgartner, F.R., and Leech, B.L. (2001) 'Interest Niches and Policy Bandwagons: Patterns of Interest Group Involvement in National Politics'. *The Journal of Politics* 63(4):1191–213.

Berkhout, J. (2013) 'Why interest organizations do what they do: Assessing the explanatory potential of 'exchange' approaches'. *Interest Groups & Advocacy* 2(2):227–50.

Berkhout, J., and Lowery, D. (2010) 'The changing demography of the EU interest system since 1990'. *European Union Politics* 11(3):447–61.

Beyers, J. (2004) 'Voice and access: Political practices of European interest associations'. *European Union Politics* 5(2):211–40.

Binderkrantz, A.S., Bonafont, L.C., and Halpin, D.R. (2016) 'Diversity in the News? A Study of Interest Groups in the Media in the UK, Spain and Denmark'. *British Journal of Political Science* 47(2):313–28.

Binderkrantz, A.S., Christiansen, P.M., and Pedersen, H.H. (2015) 'Interest Group Access to the Bureaucracy, Parliament, and the Media'. *Governance* 28(1):95–112.

Binderkrantz, A.S., and Pedersen, H.H. (2017) 'What is access? A discussion of the definition and measurement of interest group access'. *European Political Science* 16(4):306–21.

Blau, B.M., Brough, T.J., and Thomas, D.W. (2013) 'Corporate lobbying, political connections, and the bailout of banks'. *Journal of Banking & Finance* 37(8):3007–17.

Bloom, H.S., and Price, H.D. (1975) 'Voter Response to Short-Run Economic Conditions: The Asymmetric Effect of Prosperity and Recession'. *The American Political Science Review* 69(4):1240–54.

Bouwen, P. (2004) 'Exchanging access goods for access: A comparative study of business lobbying in the European Union institutions'. *European Journal of Political Research* 43(3):337–69.

Broscheid, A., and Coen, D. (2007) 'Lobbying activity and fora creation in the EU: empirically exploring the nature of the policy good'. *Journal of European Public Policy* 14(3):346–65.

Chalmers, A.W. (2013) 'Trading information for access: informational lobbying strategies and interest group access to the European Union'. *Journal of European Public Policy* 20(1):39–58.

Danielian, L.H., and Page, B.I. (1994) 'The heavenly chorus: Interest group voices on TV news'. *American Journal of Political Science* 38(4):1056–78.

De Bruycker, I. (2016) 'Pressure and expertise: explaining the information supply of interest groups in EU legislative lobbying'. *JCMS: Journal of Common Market Studies* 54(3):599–616.

De Bruycker, I., and Beyers, J. (2015) 'Balanced or Biased? Interest Groups and Legislative Lobbying in the European News Media'. *Political Communication* 32(3):453–74.

DR. (2020) "Finansministeriet fik gratis hjælp af McKinsey: 'Regeringen er gået i en fælde'." https://www.dr.dk/nyheder/indland/finansministeriet-fik-gratis-hjaelp-af-mckinsey-regeringen-er-gaaet-i-en-faelde (accessed June 18, 2022).

Dür, A., and Mateo, G. (2013) 'Gaining access or going public? Interest group strategies in five European countries'. *European Journal of Political Research* 52(5):660–86.

Eising, R. (2007) 'Institutional context, organizational resources and strategic choices: Explaining interest group access in the European Union'. *European Union Politics* 8(3):329–62.

Flöthe, L. (2019) 'Technocratic or democratic interest representation? How different types of information affect lobbying success'. *Interest Groups & Advocacy* 8(2):165–83.

Fraussen, B., Beyers, J., and Donas, T. (2015) 'The Expanding Core and Varying Degrees of Insiderness: Institutionalised Interest Group Access to Advisory Councils'. *Political Studies* 63(3):569–88.

Galtung, J., and Ruge, M.H. (1965) 'The structure of foreign news: The presentation of the Congo, Cuba and Cyprus crises in four Norwegian newspapers'. *Journal of Peace Research* 2(1):64–90.

Hall, R.L., and Deardorff, A.V. (2006) 'Lobbying as Legislative Subsidy'. *The American Political Science Review* 100(1):69–84.

Halpin, D., and Fraussen, B. (2017) 'Conceptualising the policy engagement of interest groups: Involvement, access and prominence'. *European Journal of Political Research* 56(3):723–32.

Hanegraaff, M., van der Ploeg, J., and Berkhout, J. (2020) 'Standing in a Crowded Room: Exploring the Relation between Interest Group System Density and Access to Policymakers'. *Political Research Quarterly* 73(1):51–64.

Heylen, F., Willems, E., and Beyers, J. (2020) 'Do Professionals Take Over? Professionalisation and Membership Influence in Civil Society Organisations'. *VOLUNTAS: International Journal of Voluntary and Nonprofit Organizations* 31(6):1226–38.

Junk, W.M. (2019) 'Representation beyond people: Lobbying access of umbrella associations to legislatures and the media'. *Governance* 32(2):313–30.

Junk, W.M., Crepaz, M., Hanegraaff, M., Berkhout, J., and Aizenberg, E. (2020) "InterCov Project: Online Survey on Interest Representation during Covid-19. Edition: June – July 2020." https://www.wiebkejunk.com/_files/ugd/9a0cb4_eb572405723f490f8fd6e464420 f3a33.pdf (accessed June 13, 2022).

Junk, W.M., Crepaz, M., Hanegraaff, M., Berkhout, J., and Aizenberg, E. (2021a) 'Changes in Interest Group Access in Times of Crisis: No Pain, No (Lobby) Gain'. *Journal of European Public Policy*, Online First.

Junk, W.M., Crepaz, M., Hanegraaff, M., Berkhout, J., and Aizenberg, E. (2021b) "InterCov Project: Online Survey on Interest Representation during Covid-19. Second Edition: July – August 2021." https://www.wiebkejunk.com/_files/ugd/9a0cb4_ 7d44f6c80cc84d259983d8bbdfa3a729.pdf (accessed June 13, 2022).

Kastner, L. (2018) 'Business lobbying under salience – financial industry mobilization against the European financial transaction tax'. *Journal of European Public Policy* 25(11):1648–66.

Keller, E. (2018) 'Noisy business politics: lobbying strategies and business influence after the financial crisis'. *Journal of European Public Policy* 25(3):287–306.

Klüver, H. (2013) *Lobbying in the European Union: interest groups, lobbying coalitions, and policy change*, Oxford: Oxford University Press.

Kriesi, H. (1996) 'The organizational structure of new social movements in a political context', in D. McAdam, J.D. McCarthy and M.N. Zald (Eds.), *Comparative Perspectives on Social Movements: Political Opportunities, Mobilizing Structures, and Cultural Framings*, 152–84, Cambridge: Cambridge University Press.

LaPira, T.M., Thomas, H.F., and Baumgartner, F.R. (2014) 'The two worlds of lobbying: Washington lobbyists in the core and on the periphery'. *Interest Groups & Advocacy* 3(3):219–45.

Lowery, D., et al. (2015) 'Images Of An Unbiased Interest System'. *Journal of European Public Policy* 22(8):1212–31.

Lowery, D., and Brasher, H. (2004) *Organized interests and American government*, New York: McGraw-Hill.

Maloney, W.A., Jordan, G., and Andrew, M.M. (1994) 'Interest Groups and Public Policy: The Insider/Outsider Model Revisited'. *Journal of Public Policy* 14(1):17–38.

Olson, M. (1965) *The Logic of Collective Action*, Cambridge: Harvard University Press.

Olson, M. (1982) *The rise and decline of nations: Economic growth, stagflation, and social rigidities*, New Haven: Yale University Press.

Rasmussen, A., Carroll, B.J., and Lowery, D. (2014) 'Representatives of the public? Public opinion and interest group activity'. *European Journal of Political Research* 53(2):250–68.

Rasmussen, A., and Gross, V. (2015) 'Biased access? Exploring selection to advisory committees'. *European Political Science Review* 7(3):343–72.

Salisbury, R.H. (1990) 'Interest Groups in Washington', in A. King (Ed.), *The New American Political System, Second Version*, Washington D.C.: The AEI Press.

Schattschneider, E.E. (1960) *The Semisovereign People: A Realist's View of Democracy in America*, New York: Holt, Rinehart and Winston.

Truman, D.B. (1951) *The Governmental Process. Political Interests and Public Opinion*, New York: Alfred A. Knopf.

Online Appendix

https://www.degruyter.com/document/isbn/9783110783148/html

Chapter 6
Lobbying Influence

As the COVID-19 pandemic developed, the disproportional political influence of some interest groups at the expense of others became a rising concern, as reflected in newspaper coverage and public discussions (Guardian 2020; FT 2020). The extensive bail-out packages provided to the flag carrier airline company Air-France-KLM, for example, attracted much criticism in the Netherlands (RTLnieuws 2020). In contrast, the Dutch cultural sector received little support, mostly because theatres, opera houses, music venues and exhibition areas were deemed non-essential and were, therefore, closed during the various national lockdowns. Moreover, many of the people working in this sector are self-employed and did not meet the criteria to be compensated (WorldEconomicForum 2022). This led to major outcries by workers in this sector, criticising the government for its lack of responsiveness to their demands and its too generous position towards big business (Parool 2020).

The question we pose in this chapter is whether such concerns were justified: were some interest groups' lobbying efforts disproportionally more influential during the COVID-19 crisis compared to others'? This question is inherently difficult to answer, because 'lobbying influence', understood as a *causal* effect of the activities of an organisation on policy outcomes, is extremely difficult to measure (see: Dür 2008; Bernhagen, Dür, and Marshall 2014; Klüver 2009; Lowery 2013; Leech 2010; Newmark and Nownes 2017). Like for political *power* in general (cf. Dahl 1957), it is extremely hard to provide empirical evidence that one actor (for instance an interest group) made another actor (for instance a legislator) do something, he or she would not otherwise have done (for instance design a rescue package).

Qualitative studies typically try to provide evidence for the causal chain leading from interest group activities to political decisions through *process tracing* (Dür 2008), which is a method that triangulates different data sources to provide plausible evidence for a connection (for empirical examples see: Dür and De Bièvre 2007; Phinney 2017; Rasmussen 2015). In contrast, the quantitative interest group literature typically works with selected *proxies* for interest group influence, which are plausible indicators for the presence of influence that do not, however, trace the causal process. One of the most frequently used proxies is *perceived influence* (Dür 2008), which builds on the influence perceptions of interest groups or policymakers (for empirical examples see: Binderkrantz and Rasmussen 2015; Heaney 2014; Junk 2020). Another common indicator is *preference attainment* (Dür 2008), which measures the extent to which policy decisions are in line with a group's goals (for empirical examples see: Dür, Bernhagen, and Marshall 2015; Klüver 2013; Junk 2019; Rasmussen, Mäder, and Reher 2018). Studies using either of these proxies build on the premise that interest group systems in which some (types of) organisations are consistently seen as more influential, or systematically see their preferences reflected in actual policies more often than others, are likely to be characterised by bias in political influence.

In this chapter, we follow this tradition and evaluate different proxies for the influence of interest groups during the COVID-19 pandemic. As in the previous chapters, we focus on *group type*, *lobbying resources* and *affectedness* as potential explanatory variables of lobbying influence, due to the supply and demand-side forces we described throughout the book (see Chapters 3–5). The contribution of this chapter lies in relating them to measures of political influence on COVID-19 related policies.

While most existing studies focus on only one measure of influence at a time, we here include three potential *proxies* for lobbying influence: 1) the *self-perceived impact* of interest groups on political decisions related to COVID-19, 2) *preference attainment* on COVID-19 related policies, and 3) *policy satisfaction* of interest groups with viral policies. Regarding the first indicator, we argue that influential organisations are likely to consider themselves able to *impact* policies by pushing policymaking into their preferred direction. The second indicator, *preference attainment*, refers to the proximity of policies with the policy positions held by interest groups on such issues (irrespective of whether lobbying is perceived to have *caused* policy to move in this preferred direction). Still, we argue that more influential organisations are more likely to see government policies closer aligned with their preferences than less influential groups do. While these two conceptions of lobbying influence are common in the interest group literature (e.g. Bernhagen, Dür, and Marshall 2014; Newmark and Nownes 2017), we add a third indicator and assess how *satisfied* organisations were with government policies. Our underlying assumption is that more influential organisations should arguably be more satisfied with government policies.

Although all three proxies for influence are likely to overlap in many instances (i.e. organisations see themselves as impactful, attain their preferences and are satisfied), we see them as conceptually and empirically distinct, which makes it fruitful to study them individually. Policy satisfaction and preference attainment, for instance, may diverge if organisations strategically adjust their preferences to what is feasible (achievable), not to what would make them entirely satisfied (Dür 2008). Moreover, interest groups may show awareness of the political or practical limitations of their preferred policy outcomes and could still be satisfied, even when their preferences remain unattained. It is, therefore, interesting to analyse all three potential proxies to understand which interest groups had higher levels of political influence.

The findings in this chapter are important for several reasons. First, they matter when evaluating pandemic politics, in particular. The COVID-19 crisis has been one of the most impactful events in decades. An analysis of patterns in (perceived) political influence, preference attainment and policy satisfaction in *viral politics* helps understand which interests policymakers prioritise(d). This provides an indication of which non-state actors had the firmest grip on the political process during this crisis. Second, a more general question is to what extent lobbying influence reflects more optimistic ('pluralist') theories of lobbying (cf. Truman 1951), or whether a narrowly set of economic and/or well-resourced groups captures political decision-making (cf. Carpenter and Moss 2013; Dal Bó 2006; Olson 1965, 1982; Schattschneider 1960). Studying lobbying influence during the pandemic as an example of a system-wide *focussing event* helps shed light on such tendencies, as well as the resilience of (subsets of) interests group systems in a crisis situation (cf. LaPira 2014). Third, those that are interested in *measuring* political influence may find our direct comparison of three potential proxies useful.

In what follows we first juxtapose three potential indicators of lobbying influence in policymaking. We hereby set out the differences and similarities between the three proxies. In the subsequent section, we extend our argument to the COVID-19 case and develop hypotheses related to the three main group characteristics, as identified in Chapter 2: levels of affectedness, lobbying resources, and group type. In the empirical section, we test our hypotheses. Here we find quite some variation across the three proxies for influence and how they are explained by resources, group type and levels of affectedness. The results provide a nuanced view regarding the influence of interest groups during the COVID-crisis, leading to several optimistic and some pessimistic interpretations, as we discuss in the conclusion.

Impact, Preference Attainment and Policy Satisfaction

Why are some interest groups more successful in influencing public policy than others? Lobbying scholars have explored this question for decades, but are still short of a simple answer (cf. Lowery 2013; Leech 2010), partly because the concept is difficult to define and measure (Dür 2008; Klüver 2009; Bernhagen, Dür, and Marshall 2014). Moreover, even when one has a clear idea of what is meant by *influence* (e.g. Dür, Marshall, and Bernhagen 2019; Klüver 2013), the messy and context-dependent nature of politics complicates the account of what drives it, because the specific situation is critical for who wins and who loses policy battles (cf. Baumgartner et al. 2009; Klüver 2011; Junk 2019). For these reasons, scholars mostly refrain from making bold statements about the general power of lobbying actors in political systems, and instead focus on specific *instances* where some interest groups are more impactful than others based on selected proxies for influence. In this chapter, we follow this logic by including three proxies when evaluating lobbying influence in context of the COVID-19 pandemic.

Our first proxy for the lobbying influence of interest groups is their *perceived policy impact.* We hereby link to the classic behavioural definition of influence stating that interest group influence refers to a situation where a policymaker takes a decision that, without the interaction with an interest group, would have turned out differently (cf. Dahl 1957). To derive such a *causal interpretation* of the effects of lobbying efforts, we rely on the perception of interest groups themselves (Dür 2008). We use the term perceived *impact* to refer to this behavioural and decision-making-oriented interpretation of influence, sometimes labelled 'decision-making lobbying success' (Binderkrantz and Pedersen 2019) or 'first face of power' (Finger 2019; Lukes 1986). The two underlying assumptions for this proxy are that, firstly, organisations only have impact when effects result from their lobbying activities aimed at specific political decisions, and, secondly, that organisations themselves are well-equipped to evaluate these effects. Lobbying impact can, in this sense, be observed as an individual trait, i.e. an organisation is (perceived to be) impactful or not and this gives an indication of who is supposedly pulling the strings in decision-making.

Our second proxy for interest group influence is *preference attainment,* meaning the degree of alignment between the goals of an interest group and actual policies. This proxy helps identify which organisations have benefitted the most from particular policy programs, in our case, during the pandemic. By approximating the distance between the preferences of organisations and actual policy outcomes, it measures which interest groups see their preferred outcomes reflected in public policy. Put differently, this measure captures the extent to which outcomes in terms of government policies are in line with demands of interest groups (e.g. Bunea 2013; Bernhagen, Dür, and Marshall 2014; Klüver 2013). While this measure does not entail assumptions about the causal reasons for attaining one's preferences, one can argue that a closer match between policies and the preferences of some interest groups compared to others suggests that political institutions have been more responsive to the needs of some organisations. Still, a key difference between preference attainment and impact is that the former does not require individual interest groups to have been politically active. Some organisations may not have lobbied (intensively) but may still see their preferences reflected in policies because, for example, structural power is at work (Dür 2008; Culpepper 2015), or because a group has been simply 'lucky' (Klüver 2013), for instance, because other actors with the same preferences have made a difference (cf. Junk and Rasmussen 2019; Mahoney and Baumgartner 2015). Rather than an individual achievement of specific lobbying organisations, preference attainment is, therefore, a broader characteristic of all groups sharing the same preferences.

Third, we analyse an additional potential proxy for the influence of interest groups, namely *policy satisfaction*. This concept is prominent in public opinion research as an indicator of the extent to which citizens are willing to accept a policy decision (Esaiasson, Gilljam, and Persson 2017). It is, however, not typically used in the interest group literature, although it might contribute fruitfully to the study of interest representation and lobbying influence. We assume that, like for citizens, it is meaningful to evaluate how satisfied interest groups are with resulting policies. While not capturing their individual impact on policies (meaning influence in a narrow, causal interpretation), satisfaction captures a broader, contextual measure of contentment with political outcomes. Satisfaction can, in this sense, be a pointer towards outcomes that do (or do not) seem fair or reasonable from the perspective of interest groups. This measure of their satisfaction with policies may, hence, consider the decision-making context and process, the positions and needs of other organisations, and other forces at play that may have impacted decision-making. Depending on such considerations, satisfaction might be high, although an organisation's preferences might not have been attained. Especially considering the state of emergency during the pandemic, which required almost all actors to accept unpleasant outcomes and compromises, we see this measure as a useful addition to more 'classic' ways of approximating lobbying influence.

In the following, we theorise how interest group characteristics relate to these three potential proxies for influence after the disruption caused by external events, in our case the COVID-19 crisis. As in previous chapters, our arguments focus on the characteristics of interest groups – their level of affectedness by the pandemic, their lobbying resources, and group type differences – which we argue are important explanatory factors for their potential lobbying influence. Like in previous chapters, these factors speak to more 'optimistic' and 'pessimistic' views of lobbying and political influence.

'Optimistic' Accounts of Affectedness as a Determinant of Influence

Our first hypothesis focuses on interest groups' level of affectedness by the pandemic. There is not much literature to build on when seeking to explain the political influence of more affected organisations in politics. As extensively discussed in this book, disturbance theory, which, in principle, links the level of affectedness by 'disturbances' experienced by societal interests to the governmental process, has not seen explicit empirical assessment as far as influence is concerned. Rather, scholars working in the tradition of Truman (1951) assume that organisations which mobilise more often and quicker compared to others will eventually be more influential (Lowery and Brasher 2004; Rasmussen, Carroll, and Lowery 2014; Hanegraaff, Berkhout, and van der Ploeg 2022).

In this book, we argue – and show empirically – that this assumption holds, because affectedness is pivotal at all stages of the influence production process: First, as we argued in Chapter 3, more affected organisations have incentives to politically mobilise (more frequently and swiftly) compared to organisations which were less affected by the pandemic. Higher affectedness also drives frequent use of all types of strategies, as we elaborate on in Chapter 4. Lobbying activity (in such various ways) is likely to make an issue more visible to policymakers (see also: De Bruycker and Beyers 2019). As we show in Chapter 5, these gatekeepers do not only react to an abundant *supply* of lobbying by more affected groups, but also actively demand input from affected groups (cf. also: Leech et al. 2005; Broscheid and Coen 2007). Put differently, they pull affected groups into the policy process, for instance to collect information about the effects of the crisis.

We expect these push- and pull-forces involving affected groups to result in higher influence on policies after the disturbance. While access can certainly not simply be equated with influence (Dür and De Bièvre 2007), researchers tend to assume that the likelihood of influence increases with more (insider) access (Binderkrantz, Christiansen, and Pedersen 2015; Danielian and Page 1994; Eising 2007). This is reasonable because policymakers should, in the first place, be more likely to 'grant' access to those interest groups that (in the eyes of policymakers) can *actually* inform policymaking (especially when policymakers themselves reach out to interest groups).

More specifically, the input of *affected* groups is likely to be relevant for solving the policy problems that policymakers face after a focussing event, like the COVID-19 pandemic. When policy-relevant information has been supplied by an affected group, this is arguably one of the most direct pathways to exerting a causal *impact* on policy, in the sense that other outcomes would have come about without the group's input (cf. Dahl 1957).

Similarly, regarding the *preferences* of more affected interest groups, these should be more likely to be attained, when groups have contributed with policy relevant information based on their own affectedness by the event. This does not only hold at an individual level, but is relevant for all like-minded groups sharing the same preferences and challenges during the pandemic. In this sense, the benefits of lobbying strategies used by some actors might spill-over to other groups with similar preferences (Egerod and Junk 2022). Such like-minded groups are sometimes called lobbying 'camps' or 'sides' promoting the same position, and existing research shows that their collective efforts are highly relevant for lobbying success (Böhler, Hanegraaff, and Schulze 2022; Klüver 2013; Junk and Rasmussen 2019; Lorenz 2020; Mahoney and Baumgartner 2015; Truijens and Hanegraaff 2021).

Finally, regarding the *policy satisfaction* of more affected groups, we expect their higher ability to voice their concerns, achieve access, and potentially enjoy impact and preference attainment to be reflected in higher levels of policy satisfaction. As we argued above, we expect policy satisfaction to be a function of the policy preferences of an organisation and the concrete policies, but weighted against an evaluation of what organisations see as reasonable or achievable in light of the broader context and other concerns. It is an interesting empirical question whether and how much this diverges from the other individual (impact) and more camp-related (preference) accounts of outcomes.

Hypothesis 1 summarises our expectations including all three proxies for influence.

H1 'affectedness hypothesis': The more affected groups were by the pandemic, i) the more (perceived) impact they had on COVID-19 related policies, ii) the higher their level of preference attainment, and iii) the higher their policy satisfaction.

'Pessimistic' Accounts of Resources and Group Type as Determinants of Influence

Again, we juxtapose these disturbance-driven and more optimistic accounts with 'elitist' expectations about resources and group type as important drivers of influence. As argued in previous chapters, Olson (1965) challenged Truman's assumptions regarding mobilisation (see Chapter 3). As articulated in his later book, Olson (1982), however, also expected lobbying influence to be substantial and, due to unequal mobilisation, to be biased in favour of *special interests*. In the long-run, he expected this to be detrimental for the quality of public policy, because the weakness of state authorities leads relatively well-staffed interest groups to be able to *de facto* control public policies in their own favour.

This argument resonates with more recent studies, as well as the concept of regulatory capture (Carpenter and Moss 2013; Dal Bó 2006), which denotes a situation where special interests (for example well-resourced industry interest) shift policy towards their own preferences and away from the public good. Based on such views, a fear would be that well-resourced organisations, as well as business groups and firms, can exert undue influence over policy outcomes.

However, existing studies have provided somewhat mixed evidence regarding whether this is the case. As far as the effect of resources is concerned, several studies, especially in the United States (US) context, follow a famous model by Grossman and Helpman (1994) and provide evidence for a relationship between money (for instance campaign contributions) and political influence (e.g. Ederington and Minier 2008; Matschke and Sherlund 2006; McKay 2018). Others have shown that lobbying expenditures systematically link to gains in tax exemption (e.g. Richter, Samphantharak, and Timmons 2009), that trade protection is granted to firms with higher assets (Egerod and Justesen 2021), or that higher available lobbying resources make an impact on decision-making more likely (Binderkrantz and Pedersen 2019; Stevens and De Bruycker 2020).

While these studies confirm that financial resources are a critical factor for lobbying influence in politics, many other studies have, perhaps surprisingly, not been able to provide conclusive evidence for this relationship. For instance, in the US context, Baumgartner et al. (2009, 203) find that for 'the most part, resources have no significant correlation with a positive policy outcome' (also see: McKay 2012). In the EU context, Klüver (2013) similarly found no association between a groups' individual lobbying resources and its lobbying success. These authors, however, provide evidence that *collective* resources by lobbyists on the same side of an issue (or in the same 'lobbying camp') are significantly related to lobbying success (also see: Mahoney and Baumgartner 2015).

Regarding potential influence advantages for business organisations, findings in the existing literature are also mixed. Several qualitative studies including different cases and policy fields suggest that business groups are more influential during legislative procedures (Rasmussen 2015; Michaelowa 1998; Michalowitz 2007). In a quantitative study of Danish and British lobbyists, Binderkrantz and Pedersen (2019) find that business groups are more successful in affecting decision-making than citizen groups. In contrast, De Bruycker and Beyers (2019) studying a wide range of issues in EU legislative politics find no difference between the (perceived) influence of business associations and NGOs. Similarly, Binderkrantz and Rasmussen (2015) find that business was not considered more influential to set the agenda of the European Commission across the

United Kingdom, Denmark and the Netherlands. And, quite surprisingly, Dür, Bernhagen, and Marshall (2015) even show that business organisations are *more likely to lose* when it comes to EU policymaking (also see: Judge and Thomson 2019).

A potential reason for these mixed findings might be that the effect of resources and group type is strongly dependent on the specific issue or political context. In addition, these mixed findings could be related to the use of different methods to measure lobbying influence, such as through process tracing, by measuring tax benefits quantitatively, comparing organisations' preferences and policy outcomes, or capturing their perceived influence. An advantage of our analysis is, in this regard, that we compare three different potential indicators for lobbying influence: perceived impact, preference attainment and policy satisfaction. While we a-priori expect all indicators of lobbying influence to be positively associated with better-resourced groups, as well as business associations and firms (based on elitist or 'pessimistic' views of lobbying), our analysis will also be able to explore whether the different measures lead to different conclusions.

Applied to 'viral lobbying' during the pandemic, we expect business organisations and groups with higher resources to have enjoyed significant supply side (see Chapters 3 and 4) and demand side advantages (see Chapter 5) throughout the influence production process, ultimately resulting in higher influence on COVID-19 related policies. Especially considering the pandemic's potential to cause a deep economic recession, we reason that governments' crisis management policies placed special focus on alleviating the pressure on economically important organisations, as well as those best able to voice their grievances thanks to higher lobbying resources (cf. Blau, Brough, and Thomas 2013, on the financial crisis). Therefore, as Hypotheses 2 and 3 summarise, we expect the levels of our three proxies for lobbying influence on viral policies to be systematically higher for groups with higher lobbying resources, as well as for business organisations.

H2 'resources hypothesis': The more resources interest groups had at their disposal, i) the more (perceived) impact they had on COVID-19 related policies, ii) the higher their level of preference attainment, and iii) the higher their policy satisfaction.

H3 'group type hypothesis': Business organisations had i) more (perceived) impact on COVID-19 related policies. ii) higher preference attainment, and iii) higher policy satisfaction, compared to NGOs and citizen groups.

Analysis: Lobbying Influence during the Pandemic

Before systematically testing our hypotheses, we provide a descriptive overview of our three dependent variables, which draw on both waves of our cross-country survey (Junk et al. 2020; Junk et al 2021).

Overview of Three Proxies for Interest Group Influence

To measure a group's perceived impact on COVID-19 related policies, we use a survey question which asked respondents to '*rate the impact of [their] organisation on political decisions related to the Coronavirus crisis*' (using a 0 – 10 scale). We asked this question in both waves of the survey (2020 and 2021). Relying on interest groups' ratings of their (own) perceived influence is a common practice in interest group surveys (e.g. Binderkrantz and Pedersen 2019; Heaney 2014; Junk 2020). Lobbyists tend to overestimate their impact somewhat (Newmark and Nownes 2017), but this seems to be consistent across group types.

The distribution of the self-perceived impact measures (2020 and 2021) is presented in Figure 6.1 (top part of the graph). On the left side, the results of the first wave covering the period between March and June 2020 are presented, and on the right are the results for the second wave covering June 2020 to June 2021. Overall, the results show much variation across organisations and the extent to which they indicate to have impacted viral policy. Many organisations do not perceive themselves as impactful, as indicated by the higher bars at the left end of the figures. Roughly half of the respondents fall into the first four answer categories, which we label as 'low impact'. Approximately 35 percent of organisations indicated to be medium to somewhat influential (categories 4 – 7). Below 15 percent indicated to have been highly influential during the pandemic (categories 8 – 10).

Notable is also that this pattern is relatively stable across the two waves. In wave 2, the reported impact by interest groups was somewhat lower than during the first wave, yet differences are marginal. Overall, the data is in line with other studies, which suggest that interest groups tend to fail in their lobbying efforts more often than not, and that there is variation across organisations (Lowery 2013). At the same time, we think that Figure 6.1 also reflects the relatively limited control interest groups had over executive-centred crisis management. Rather than a 'failure' on the part of lobbyists, one could understand this as a relative closure of government decision-making during COVID-19, also noted in COVID-related studies of parliamentary opposition (e.g. Louwerse et al. 2021; Pedersen and Borghetto 2021) and executive politics (Bolleyer and Salát 2021).

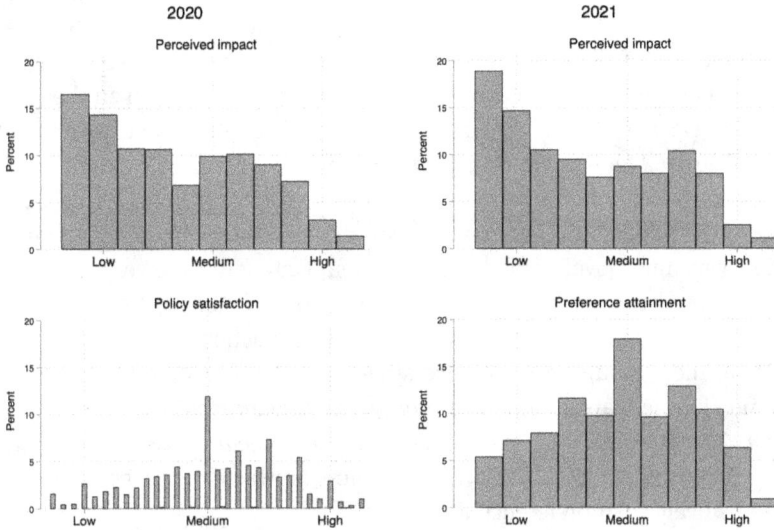

Figure 6.1: Self-reported policy impact, preference attainment and policy satisfaction in 2020 (left) and 2021 (right).

We see a somewhat different trend for our second proxy for influence: *preference attainment*. Figure 6.1 (bottom right) plots the answers to our question to what extent '*COVID-related policies in [country] were aligned with [the] organisation's goals and preferences*'. Respondents could indicate this on a scale from 0 – 10, ranging from 'to no extent' to 'the highest extent'. Note that this question was only included in the second wave of our survey and covers the period from June 2020 to June 2021. As Figure 6.1 shows, the distribution is not as right-skewed as perceived impact, and looks more similar to a normal distribution. Put differently, we see that respondents achieved higher preference attainment compared to policy impact. It is still noteworthy that very few organisations agreed to the 'highest extent' that all their preferences were attained. Overall, the figure illustrates that there is much variation across organisations when it comes to the attainment of policy preferences during the pandemic, with the majority seeing only some of their preferences attained.

Next, we plot *policy satisfaction* of interest groups with viral policies adopted by governments during the pandemic (Figure 6.1 bottom left). Respondents could indicate on a scale from 0 – 10 to what extent they agreed that decisions 1) *on health and safety measures,* and 2) *on easing restrictions had sufficiently taken into account interests of organisations like [theirs] or their members*. Moreover, we asked to what extent they agreed that 3) *economic rescue packages had addressed the needs of organisations like [theirs] or their members.* To take all these three sets of COVID-19 related policies into account, we take the mean of the three items as our dependent variable. Note that we only asked these questions in wave 1 of the survey and cover the period from March to June 2020.

As Figure 6.1 shows, we observe quite some variation in the extent to which organisations were, in this sense, satisfied with government policies in the early phase of the pandemic. Most observations are stacked in the middle, which indicates a medium level of policy satisfaction. Only few were very dissatisfied, and only few were very satisfied, with the majority (almost 58 percent) falling in the middle categories (satisfaction ≥ 4 and satisfaction < 8). This is relatively similar to the measure of preference attainment: Mean values, standard deviation and skewness are comparable (*policy satisfaction: mean = 5.3, standard deviation: 2.2, skewness: -0.3; preference attainment: mean = 4.8, standard deviation: 2.6, skewness: -0.1*). If anything, policy satisfaction has been evaluated more positively than preference attainment.

Overall, this indicates that interest groups were moderate in their evaluation of policy (dis)satisfaction, as well as in their assessment of preference attainment regarding COVID-19 related policies (although to a slightly lesser extent)[31]. In contrast, ratings of perceived impact are on average lower (*mean = 3.7 (2020) and mean = 3.6 (2021)* on a 0 – 10 scale). The patterns in Figures 6.1 tentatively indicate that there are differences between our three proxies of lobbying influence. This fits the argument we started out with. As we reasoned in the beginning, *perceived impact* is centred on the effects of individual lobbying efforts in a causal link evaluated by the respondent. *Preference attainment,* instead, can also be due chance, free-riding or structural power dynamics. Finally, *policy satisfaction* adds a contextual evaluation regarding the sufficient inclusiveness of the process and policy decisions. In the next section, we test our hypotheses on these three dependent variables.

Explanatory Models of Lobbying Influence

We now test our hypotheses by means of a series of regressions. Like in previous chapters, our independent variables are the level of affectedness, resources, and group type. Affectedness is measured through a survey item that captures the extent to which an organisation, according to its own perception, was '*more or less*

---

31 Note, however, that we measure this at two different points in time.

affected by the Coronavirus crisis, compared to other stakeholders in [country]?. Answers take 5 values, from 'much less affected' (1) to 'much more affected' (5). Lobbying resources are captured by a question that asks about the number of staff working on public affairs in the organisation (in full time equivalents). Answers are grouped in three categories of low (<1), medium (1–4) and high (≥5). Finally, organisations are grouped into three interest group categories: *business groups and firms, profession groups and unions,* as well as *NGOs and citizen groups.* We use *business groups and firms* as reference category in our analyses. For more information about these variables, see Chapter 2.

In addition, we control for the *age* of an organisation, which captures experience in lobbying and is likely to relate to both influence and other organisational characteristics, such as resources. We also control for whether an organisation is an umbrella organisation, given that these representation hubs might be more influential. The analyses also include fixed effects for countries/polity and clustered standard errors by sector of activity of the interest groups.

The results, based on four ordinary least squares (OLS) regressions, are presented in Figure 6.2 in form of coefficient plots, whereas table-form results can be found in the Online Appendix (Table A6.1). Where the confidence intervals (straight lines) of the plotted coefficients (dot in the middle) do not overlap with 0 (the vertical dotted line), we can say with high certainty that there is a significant relationship between the factor and the respective proxy for influence. The figure depicts the measures from 2020 on the left (perceived impact and policy satisfaction), and 2021 on the right (perceived impact and preference attainment). The first insight from the Figure 6.2 is that the evaluation of patterns in influence varies depending on which proxy is used.

Starting with *perceived impact,* which we measured in both 2020 and 2021, we see clear support for our 'affectedness hypothesis' (Hypothesis 1). *More affected organisations* saw themselves as more impactful compared to *less affected organisations* across both survey waves. To illustrate, our 2020 model predicts that the perceived impact of least affected groups on COVID-19 related policies equals 2.4 on a 0 to 10 scale[32]. This reaches 4.8 for most affected interest groups. The size of this effect is very similar when based on our 2021 model of perceived impact.

At the same time, patterns in perceived impact support our resource and group type hypotheses (Hypotheses 2 and 3): Better resourced organisations and business organisations saw themselves as more influential, compared to re-

---

32 All predicted values are based on the main models (see Figure 6.2) when holding all other variables at means.

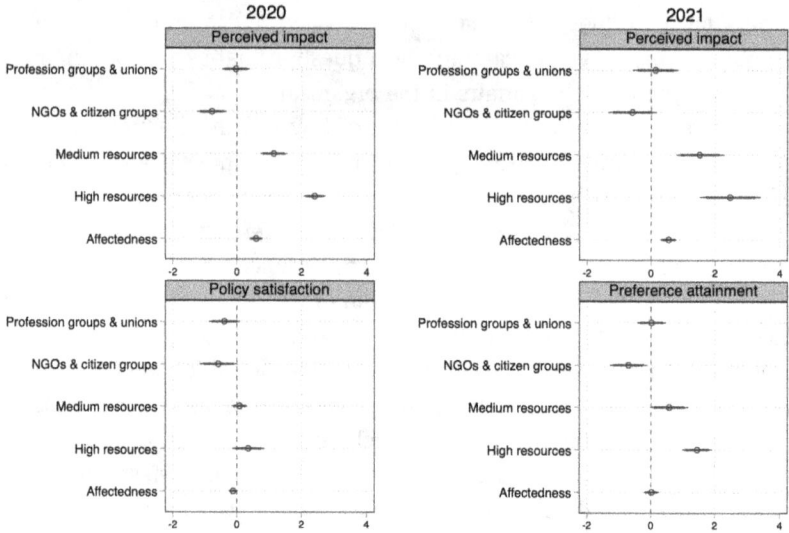

Figure 6.2: Ordinary least squares regression on three proxies for the influence of interest groups during the COVID-19 crisis (2020 left; 2021 right). Coefficients and 95/90% confidence intervals.

Notes: The figure is based on four ordinary least squares regressions, one for each proxy for influence. For 2020: perceived impact (n=1081) and policy satisfaction (n=1059); for 2021: perceived impact (n=625) and preference attainment (n= 596). Included controls in all these models were: organisation age, the group's potential status as an umbrella organisation, and fixed effects for the country/polity. Moreover, we clustered standard errors by sector given that influence of groups within a sector is likely to be related. For results in table form, see Table A6.1 the Online Appendix. Measures of goodness of fit (R-squared in Table A6.1) lie at 0.27 (Model 1), 0.07 (Model 2), 0.20 (Model 3), 0.09 (Model 4).

source poor organisations, and NGOs and citizen groups, respectively. Again, the findings are consistent across both waves (left and right side of Figure 6.2). More specifically, *better-resourced organisations* see themselves almost twice as impactful compared to *less resourceful ones*. Our model for 2020 estimates the perceived impact of groups with high resources at 5.1 points on a 0 to 10 scale, while this is 2.7 for groups with low resources. Again, substantially similar effects are predicted based on the 2021 model.

Group type differences exist but are less pronounced. Our 2020 model predicts a perceived impact score for *business groups and firms* of 4, while this is 3.2 for *NGOs and citizen groups*. This difference is statistically significant. For

2021, this difference is only slightly smaller but does not reach conventional levels of statistical significance.

When looking at our second proxy of influence, *preference attainment* (2021), results look different compared to perceived impact in at least one important regard: *affected organisations* did not see their preferences more attained compared to organisations which were less affected by the crisis. This means that there is no support for Hypothesis 1 based on this proxy. A potential explanation for this could be that due to the collective nature of lobbying (Klüver 2013; Junk and Rasmussen 2019; Lorenz 2020; Mahoney and Baumgartner 2015), whereby high lobbying involvement and (perceived) impact of the most affected organisations leads to broader benefits that also spill-over to less affected (and less individually impactful) groups. For example, the lobbying efforts of the highly affected travel and tourism industry for sizable economic rescue packages that reflect their preferences may have 'spilled-over' to other sectors by raising expectations for government spending and support, also in more moderately affected sectors such as retail. Put differently, the active lobbying impact of affected groups does not seem to make all affected groups significantly better off than less affected groups.

Regarding Hypotheses 2 and 3, however, the results support the previous conclusions. High resources (compared to low) and being a business organisation (compared to an NGO or citizen group) are associated with significantly higher levels of preference attainment in viral politics. Our model estimates a score of 4.3 on a 0 to 10 scale of preference attainment for *less resourceful organisations*, compared to 5.8 for *better-resourced* ones. Comparing group types, *NGO and citizen group*'s level of preference attainment is estimated at 4.4. In contrast, *business groups and firms* reach a significantly higher level of preference attainment at 5.1 on the same scale. This might suggest that resourceful organisations and business groups, indeed, lobby for more concentrated interests, as Olson (1965/1982) assumed. If the benefits of such lobbying efforts spill-over to like-minded groups (cf. Egerod and Junk 2022), then this seems to benefit the attainment of preferences for other resourceful organisations and business groups, rather than a broader set of interest groups. From a normative perspective this is worrisome, as it indicates that policy outcomes favour some organisations disproportionately, hence confirming an elitist reading of interest group politics.

The results based on the third proxy, *policy satisfaction* (2020), add to this picture. However, they show that group type differences in policy satisfaction are less pronounced than based on perceived impact and preference attainment. Moreover, we observe no significant differences in levels of policy satisfaction among groups with higher and lower levels of resources. In other words, there is no support for Hypotheses 2 (resources) and 3 (group type). This might indicate that disadvantaged organisations in terms of policy impact and preference attainment (i.e. less resourceful groups and NGOs), *accepted* policies as sufficient or adequate, at least to the same extent of business groups and resourceful organisations. This could be related to the severity of the crisis. Arguably, the health crisis and severe risk of economic turmoil were so pressing for governments and society in general that these interest groups may have moderated their expectations and were, therefore, willing to accept compromises[33]. Anecdotal evidence supports this interpretation (see also Chapter 7). That is, some NGOs we encountered stopped their advocacy efforts, as they understood that these were not a priority given the crisis at hand.

With regards to the levels of *affectedness* by the pandemic, the finding based on *policy satisfaction* is surprising. Against our general expectation (Hypothesis 1), we see in Figure 6.1 that more affected groups were *less* satisfied with policies adopted by the government during the crisis (although only at a weak level of statistical significance). To illustrate, mean levels of policy satisfaction are estimated to lie at 5.5 for *least affected groups* and at 5.1 for *most affected groups*. Again, this difference is only weakly significant and relatively small in substantive terms. Nevertheless, this complements our previous findings in interesting ways. While affected groups felt more impactful on COVID-19 policy, they did not see their preferences more likely to be attained than less affected groups. This, in turn, might explain their lower level of satisfaction with policy outcomes.

This result also points to an important reservation regarding our more optimistic findings: Despite the efforts of gatekeepers to alleviate the concerns of highly affected organisations (Chapter 5), affected groups were still extremely hard-hit by the pressures and circumstances caused by the pandemic. As an example, one can imagine highly affected organisations in the education sector, such as associations of teachers and parents. Representatives of the sector may have felt *impactful* and may have attained some of their *preferences* in the passage of policies, such as on health and safety measures, financial support and priority in the re-opening of schools after lockdown periods. At the same time, they were presumably still relatively dissatisfied with government policies, given the continued presence of major challenges and grievances in the running and the implementation of school programs during the pandemic. In that sense, our analysis suggests that after a focussing event (in our case the pandemic), af-

---

33 An alternative explanation could be that NGOs and citizen groups have generally lower expectations of policy impact and preference attainment, because they perceive themselves as lobbying outsiders compared to other groups (such as economic groups).

fected groups might enjoy increased attention and achieve higher lobbying impact, but still remain worse off than less affected societal groups.

Chapter Summary

In this chapter, we analysed the final stage of the influence production process: the influence of interest groups on policymaking. We relied on two common indicators for lobbying influence in the literature: *perceived impact* and *preference attainment*. In addition, we introduced a new potential proxy for lobbying influence in a polity, namely *policy satisfaction*. We argue that this adds relevant insights regarding the distribution of lobbying influence, because it contains a broader reflection by interest groups whereby their own preferences are weighted against the broader societal and economic context. Whenever analyses of lobbying influence are meant to speak to the broader question of biases in political decision-making, this can be an important addition. Not only is it relevant to ask which groups see themselves as influential and attain their preferences, but also whether satisfaction or grievances are distributed unequally among groups. After a focussing event like the global pandemic, it might be that more impactful groups still have relatively low policy satisfaction. At the same time, some of the factors which drive impact and preference attainment, such as group type differences, might disappear when policy satisfaction is considered. Our results speak to the case of COVID-19 and show that impact, preference attainment and policy satisfaction seem to tap into different perceptions expressed by organisations during this crisis. It is plausible this difference also holds outside of the specific crisis circumstances.

Methodologically, our results therefore highlight that these three measures potentially capture different aspects of interest group influence in the political arena. While there was certainly overlap between some findings, no pair of proxies led to the same conclusions regarding our three hypotheses on affectedness, resources and group type. This indicates that the three proxies of influence are related, but that the choice of indicator has far-reaching consequences for the results.

This means that, substantively, our findings on patterns in lobbying influence in viral politics are mixed. Regarding *perceived impact,* which we see as the best measure of *individual* and *behavioural* lobbying influence of organisations (based on their causal interpretation of their own lobbying efforts), we observed optimistic and pessimistic trends. The good news is that more affected organisations saw themselves as more influential compared to less affected groups. This is good news from a pluralist perspective, as it highlights that governments were not only consulting relatively strong organisations, but also seem to have taken the input provided by relatively more affected organisations into account. At the same time, well-staffed interest groups, as well as business organisations were also relative winners as they had a higher perceived policy impact compared resource-poor organisations, as well as NGOs and citizen groups, respectively. Jointly, these findings fit the view of elite pluralism, as coined by Coen (1998), where the system is responsive to a broad set of actors, but still consistently favours relatively powerful groups active in the system (see also: Eising 2007).

For *preference attainment,* we observed similar trends only when it comes to resources and group type. That is, while better-resourced groups and business organisations experienced significantly higher levels of preference attainment, this was not the case for more affected organisations. Our reasoning for this is that the collective nature of lobbying in camps, which promote similar preferences (Klüver 2013; Mahoney and Baumgartner 2015; Junk and Rasmussen 2019), means that the (individual) *impact* of some actors spills over to other like-minded organisations (Egerod and Junk 2022). In other words, the impact of an organisation may be more diffuse, benefitting the attainment of preferences for other (more and less) affected organisations. Who benefits, in this sense, from the lobbying efforts of others, is therefore an important question to ask when evaluating lobbying influence in a political system. We showed that the higher impact of affected groups does not systematically help all affected groups to achieve higher levels of preference attainment.

Finally, for *policy satisfaction* we observed both interesting variation as well as relevant null-findings. Both resources and group type did not matter for policy satisfaction. This is interesting considering the former significant findings for preference attainment and impact. This may suggest that less resourced organisations, as well as NGOs and citizen groups, who were less impactful and attained lower levels of their preferences in policy outcomes, still found government policies sufficiently balanced, perhaps because they had lower expectations of attaining their preferences and goals given the severity of the crisis.

With this diverse view of lobbying influence, we reached the end of the influence production process, covering issue mobilisation (Chapter 3), strategy selection (Chapter 4), access (Chapter 5) and, finally, influence (this Chapter). In the concluding chapter of this book, we tie the most important findings together and highlight what we have learned from studying *viral lobbying.* Before this, however, we first substantiate our quantitative analysis of the influence production process with qualitative nuances, derived from focus group interviews with selected interest groups. Most importantly, we assess how the conjunctures we made in this book in relation to resources and affectedness fit in with the experiences of interest groups. This qualitative evidence also sheds more light on the mechanisms that may explain our findings. In the next chapter, we therefore let practitioners narrate and share how COVID-19 has changed lobbying for them.

References

Baumgartner, F.R., Berry, J.M., Hojnacki, M., Kimball, D.C., and Leech, B.L. (2009) *Lobbying and Policy Change: Who Wins, Who Loses, and Why*, Chicago, IL: University of Chicago Press.

Bernhagen, P., Dür, A., and Marshall, D. (2014) 'Measuring lobbying success spatially'. *Interest Groups & Advocacy* 3(2):202–18.

Binderkrantz, A.S., Christiansen, P.M., and Pedersen, H.H. (2015) 'Interest Group Access to the Bureaucracy, Parliament, and the Media'. *Governance* 28(1):95–112.

Binderkrantz, A.S., and Pedersen, H.H. (2019) 'The lobbying success of citizen and economic groups in Denmark and the UK'. *Acta Politica* 54(1):75–103.

Binderkrantz, A.S., and Rasmussen, A. (2015) 'Comparing the domestic and the EU lobbying context: perceived agenda-setting influence in the multi-level system of the European Union'. *Journal of European Public Policy* 22(4):552–69.

Blau, B.M., Brough, T.J., and Thomas, D.W. (2013) 'Corporate lobbying, political connections, and the bailout of banks'. *Journal of Banking & Finance* 37(8):3007–17.

Bolleyer, N., and Salát, O. (2021) 'Parliaments in times of crisis: COVID-19, populism and executive dominance'. *West European Politics* 44(5–6):1103–28.

Broscheid, A., and Coen, D. (2007) 'Lobbying activity and fora creation in the EU: empirically exploring the nature of the policy good'. *Journal of European Public Policy* 14(3):346–65.

Bunea, A. (2013) 'Issues, preferences and ties: determinants of interest groups' preference attainment in the EU environmental policy'. *Journal of European Public Policy* 20(4):552–70.

Böhler, H., Hanegraaff, M., and Schulze, K. (2022) 'Does climate advocacy matter? The importance of competing interest groups for national climate policies'. *Climate Policy*, Online First.

Carpenter, D., and Moss, D.A. (2013) *Preventing regulatory capture: Special interest influence and how to limit it*, Cambridge: Cambridge University Press.

Coen, D. (1998) 'The European Business Interest and the Nation State: Large-firm Lobbying in the European Union and Member States'. *Journal of Public Policy* 18(1):75–100.

Culpepper, P.D. (2015) 'Structural power and political science in the post-crisis era'. *Business and Politics* 17(3):391–409.

Dahl, R.A. (1957) 'The concept of power'. *Behavioral Science* 2(3):201–15.

Dal Bó, E. (2006) 'Regulatory Capture: A Review'. *Oxford Review of Economic Policy* 22(2):203–25.

Danielian, L.H., and Page, B.I. (1994) 'The heavenly chorus: Interest group voices on TV news'. *American Journal of Political Science* 38(4):1056–78.

De Bruycker, I., and Beyers, J. (2019) 'Lobbying strategies and success: Inside and outside lobbying in European Union legislative politics'. *European Political Science Review* 11(1):57–74.

Dür, A. (2008) 'Measuring interest group influence in the EU: A note on methodology'. *European Union Politics* 9(4):559–76.

Dür, A., Bernhagen, P., and Marshall, D. (2015) 'Interest Group Success in the European Union: When (and Why) Does Business Lose?'. *Comparative Political Studies* 48(8):951–83.

Dür, A., and De Bièvre, D. (2007) 'Inclusion without Influence? NGOs in European Trade Policy'. *Journal of Public Policy* 27(1):79–101.

Dür, A., Marshall, D., and Bernhagen, P. (2019) *The political influence of business in the European Union*, Ann Arbor, Michigan: University of Michigan Press.

Ederington, J., and Minier, J. (2008) 'Reconsidering the empirical evidence on the Grossman-Helpman model of endogenous protection'. *Canadian Journal of Economics/Revue Canadienne d'Économique* 41(2):501–16.

Egerod, B.C.K., and Junk, W.M. (2022) 'Competitive lobbying in the influence production process and the use of spatial econometrics in lobbying research '. *Public Choice*, Online First.

Egerod, B.C.K., and Justesen, M. (2021) 'Asset Specificity, Corporate Protection and Trade Policy: Firm-Level Evidence from Antidumping Petitions in Nineteen Jurisdictions'. *British Journal of Political Science*, Online first.

Eising, R. (2007) 'The access of business interests to EU institutions: towards élite pluralism?'. *Journal of European Public Policy* 14(3):384–403.

Esaiasson, P., Gilljam, M., and Persson, M. (2017) 'Responsiveness Beyond Policy Satisfaction: Does It Matter to Citizens?'. *Comparative Political Studies* 50(6):739–65.

Finger, L.K. (2019) 'Interest Group Influence and the Two Faces of Power'. *American Politics Research* 47(4):852–86.

FT. (2020) "Companies jostle for aid in coronavirus lobbying frenzy." https://www.ft.com/content/08ae8086-6259-475b-9b38-97fe0eb5c47e (accessed June 11, 2022).

Grossman, G.M., and Helpman, E. (1994) 'Protection for sale'. *The American Economic Review* 84(4):833–50.

Guardian. (2020) "Labour criticises lobbyist's involvement in Covid strategy calls." https://www.theguardian.com/politics/2020/nov/15/labour-criticises-lobbyists-involvement-in-covid-strategy-calls (accessed June 11, 2022).

Hanegraaff, M., Berkhout, J., and van der Ploeg, J. (2022) 'Exploring the proportionality of representation in interest group mobilization and political access: the case of the Netherlands'. *Acta Politica* 57(2):254–76.

Heaney, M. (2014) 'Multiplex networks and interest group influence reputation: An exponential random graph model'. *Social Networks* 36(1):66–81.

Judge, A., and Thomson, R. (2019) 'The responsiveness of legislative actors to stakeholders' demands in the European Union'. *Journal of European Public Policy* 26(5):676–95.

Junk, W.M. (2019) 'When Diversity Works: The Effects of Coalition Composition on the Success of Lobbying Coalitions'. *American Journal of Political Science* 63(3): 660–74.

Junk, W.M. (2020) 'Co-operation as Currency: How Active Coalitions Affect Lobbying Success'. *Journal of European Public Policy* 27(6):873–92.

Junk, W.M., and Rasmussen, A. (2019) 'Framing by the Flock: Collective Issue Definition and Advocacy Success'. *Comparative Political Studies* 52(4):483–513.

Junk, W.M., Crepaz, M., Hanegraaff, M., Berkhout, J., and Aizenberg, E. (2020) "InterCov Project: Online Survey on Interest Representation during Covid-19. Edition: June – July 2020." https://www.wiebkejunk.com/_files/ugd/9a0cb4_eb572405723f490f8fd6e464420 f3a33.pdf (accessed June 13, 2022).

Junk, W.M., Crepaz, M., Hanegraaff, M., Berkhout, J., and Aizenberg, E. (2021) "InterCov Project: Online Survey on Interest Representation during Covid-19. Second Edition: July – August 2021." https://www.wiebkejunk.com/_files/ugd/9a0cb4_ 7d44f6c80cc84d259983d8bbdfa3a729.pdf (accessed June 13, 2022).

Klüver, H. (2009) 'Measuring Interest Group Influence Using Quantitative Text Analysis'. *European Union Politics* 10(4):535–49.

Klüver, H. (2011) 'The contextual nature of lobbying: Explaining lobbying success in the European Union'. *European Union Politics* 12(4):483–506.

Klüver, H. (2013) *Lobbying in the European Union: interest groups, lobbying coalitions, and policy change*, Oxford: Oxford University Press.

LaPira, T.M. (2014) 'Lobbying after 9/11: Policy Regime Emergence and Interest Group Mobilization'. *Policy Studies Journal* 42(2):226–51.

Leech, B.L. (2010) 'Lobbying and Influence', in L.S. Maisel, J.M. Berry, G.C. Edwards and B.L. Leech (Eds.), *The Oxford Handbook of American Political Parties and Interest Groups*, 534–52, Oxford: Oxford University Press.

Leech, B.L., Baumgartner, F.R., La Pira, T.M., and Semanko, N.A. (2005) 'Drawing Lobbyists to Washington: Government Activity and the Demand for Advocacy'. *Political Research Quarterly* 58(1):19–30.

Lorenz, G.M. (2020) 'Prioritized Interests: Diverse Lobbying Coalitions and Congressional Committee Agenda Setting'. *The Journal of Politics* 82(1):225–40.

Louwerse, T., Sieberer, U., Tuttnauer, O., and Andeweg, R.B. (2021) 'Opposition in times of crisis: COVID-19 in parliamentary debates'. *West European Politics* 44(5–6):1025–51.

Lowery, D. (2013) 'Lobbying influence: Meaning, measurement and missing'. *Interest Groups & Advocacy* 2(1):1–26.

Lowery, D., and Brasher, H. (2004) *Organized interests and American government*, New York: McGraw-Hill.

Lukes, S. (1986) *Power*, New York: New York Univeristy Press.

Mahoney, C., and Baumgartner, F.R. (2015) 'Partners in Advocacy: Lobbyists and Government Officials in Washington'. *The Journal of Politics* 77(1):202–15.

Matschke, X., and Sherlund, S.M. (2006) 'Do Labor Issues Matter in the Determination of U.S. Trade Policy? An Empirical Reevaluation'. *American Economic Review* 96(1):405–21.

McKay, A. (2012) 'Buying Policy? The Effects of Lobbyists' Resources on Their Policy Success'. *Political Research Quarterly* 65(4):908–23.

McKay, A.M. (2018) 'Fundraising for Favors? Linking Lobbyist-Hosted Fundraisers to Legislative Benefits'. *Political Research Quarterly* 71(4):869–80.

Michaelowa, A. (1998) 'Impact of interest groups on EU climate policy'. *European Environment* 8(5):152–60.

Michalowitz, I. (2007) 'What determines influence? Assessing conditions for decision-making influence of interest groups in the EU'. *Journal of European Public Policy* 14(1):132–51.

Newmark, A.J., and Nownes, A.J. (2017) 'It's all relative: Perceptions of interest group influence'. *Interest Groups & Advocacy* 6(1):66–90.

Olson, M. (1965) *The Logic of Collective Action*, Cambridge: Harvard University Press.

Olson, M. (1982) *The rise and decline of nations: Economic growth, stagflation, and social rigidities*, New Haven: Yale University Press.

Parool. (2020) "Storm van kritiek op cultuurminister: 'Zonder kunstenaars geen kunst'." https://www.parool.nl/nederland/storm-van-kritiek-op-cultuurminister-zonder-kun stenaars-geen-kunst~b69f07944/?referrer=https%3A%2F%2Fwww.google.com%2F (accessed June 20, 2022).

Pedersen, H.H., and Borghetto, E. (2021) 'Fighting COVID-19 on Democratic Terms. Parliamentary Functioning in Italy and Denmark during the Pandemic'. *Representation* 57(4):401–18.

Phinney, R. (2017) *Strange Bedfellows: Interest Group Coalitions, Diverse Partners, and Influence in American Social Policy*, Cambridge: Cambridge University Press.

Rasmussen, A., Carroll, B.J., and Lowery, D. (2014) 'Representatives of the public? Public opinion and interest group activity'. *European Journal of Political Research* 53(2):250–68.

Rasmussen, A., Mäder, L.K., and Reher, S. (2018) 'With a Little Help From The People? The Role of Public Opinion in Advocacy Success'. *Comparative Political Studies* 51(2):139–64.

Rasmussen, M.K. (2015) 'The Battle for Influence: The Politics of Business Lobbying in the European Parliament'. *JCMS: Journal of Common Market Studies* 53(2):365–82.

Richter, B.K., Samphantharak, K., and Timmons, J.F. (2009) 'Lobbying and Taxes'. *American Journal of Political Science* 53(4):893–909.

RTLnieuws. (2020) "Woedende reacties op steunpakket KLM: 'te mager', 'stupéfait', 'illegaal." Available at: https://www.rtlnieuws.nl/economie/bedrijven/artikel/5167932/reacties-op-steunpakket-hoekstra-voor-klm-nederland (accessed June 28, 2022)

Schattschneider, E.E. (1960) *The Semisovereign People: A Realist's View of Democracy in America*, New York: Holt, Rinehart and Winston.

Stevens, F., and De Bruycker, I. (2020) 'Influence, affluence and media salience: Economic resources and lobbying influence in the European Union'. *European Union Politics* 21(4):728–50.

Truijens, D., and Hanegraaff, M. (2021) 'The two faces of conflict: how internal and external conflict affect interest group influence'. *Journal of European Public Policy* 28(12):1909–31.

Truman, D.B. (1951) *The Governmental Process. Political Interests and Public Opinion*, New York: Alfred A. Knopf.

WorldEconomicForum. (2022) "COVID-19 hit the creative industries particularly hard. How can they be supported in future?". https://www.weforum.org/agenda/2022/02/creatives-job-losses-covid-employment/ (accessed June 20, 2022).

Online Appendix

https://www.degruyter.com/document/isbn/9783110783148/html

Chapter 7
Interest Groups' Experiences with Lobbying during the Pandemic

The previous chapters of this book relied on two cross-national surveys among interest representatives to analyse lobbying processes after the start of the COVID-19 pandemic. With a focus on interest groups' issue mobilisation (Chapter 3), the use of strategies (Chapter 4), access to venues of political decision-making and public debate (Chapter 5), and, ultimately, influence on government policies (Chapter 6), the chapters analysed pattern in *viral lobbying* quantitatively. The results portray a mixed picture of lobbying during the pandemic. On the one hand, they highlight an optimistic account of the role of interest groups in modern democratic societies. Quite consistently, we found that more affected organisations, meaning groups which needed political support the most during the pandemic, were able to politically mobilise (intensely and quickly), used a broad range of influence-seeking strategies more frequently, gained frequent access to policymakers and journalists, and saw themselves as more influential in government decision-making on virial policies, compared to less affected groups. On the other hand, we found similarly consistent advantages for groups with higher lobbying resources, as well as business organisations compared to NGOs and citizen groups, throughout the stages of the influence production process.

Ultimately, these broad patterns arise from the daily activities of the people active in interest group politics. Their considerations and activities jointly create the mechanisms through which the observed patterns come about. For this reason, their experiences are of great importance when the aim is to assess these mechanisms. Additionally, they help identify potential alternative explanations that our quantitative analyses might have overlooked. In this chapter, we therefore focus on the experience of professionals that lead and work for interest groups. We draw on a rich series of qualitative interviews covering approximately 50 interest group leaders. More specifically, we rely on twelve focus group interviews with four interest group representatives each to get insights into their *experiences* with seeking (and gaining) lobbying influence during the crisis.

The aim of the chapter is to provide illustrative examples of challenges and opportunities that arose when interest groups lobbied during the pandemic. By qualitatively analysing the perspectives of organisations on their lobbying practices (cf. Leech 2014), we hope to lift the lid on the lobbying processes during the crisis, especially with regards to the impact of *resources* and *affectedness* on viral lobbying. While the previous chapters provided an aggregate and statistical account of trends in the influence production process, this chapter complements the analysis with narratives offered by organisations as to what, in their view, characterised viral lobbying practices. Jointly, we think these accounts will help readers gain a more lively, concrete and nuanced view of viral lobbying.

Our focus group interviews with 50 interest group leaders were distributed equally across three countries: Denmark, Ireland, and the Netherlands. We decided to focus on these countries given our high level of familiarity with their interest group systems, as well as their comparability in terms of size and the practices in policymaking. Importantly, the selection of focus group participants was identical in all three countries and included different types of interest groups (NGOs, business associations, profession organisations and labour unions), as well as different policy fields of activity (such as health and social policy, education, development policy, retail/trade, environment). This selection ensured that a diverse set of interest groups were included in the focus groups, which were designed to give groups the opportunity to share their lobbying experiences, successes and failures during the Coronavirus crisis with each other.

At the same time, our composition of focus groups oversampled organisations from the *health sector* in order to cover this key area during the health crisis adequately. Additionally, we oversampled *NGOs* to improve the level of comparability of the experiences shared by interest group representatives (see for more details: Berkhout et al. 2021). Therefore, this chapter is less suited to compare the experiences of different group types, such as comparing business organisations to NGOs. That said, given that nearly 40% of our focus group participants represented business associations, profession associations or labour unions[34], we still include rich accounts of their perspectives in this chapter, without, however, putting analytical focus on group type differences.

In what follows, we first briefly introduce focus groups as a research method in interest group research. Second, we discuss key insights, which we gathered from the rich qualitative data related to the lobbying practices of organisations during the pandemic. Several main patterns stand out based on these interviews, which help reinforce and nuance our quantitative findings: First, the interviews shed light on how the use of *resources* impacts the influence production process. More precisely, we discuss evidence that shows that resources improve an interest group's ability to maintain long-term contacts and provide information to gatekeepers. In addition, the interview material added that, as a potential coun-

---

[34] We decided not to include individual firms in the focus groups, given the other group types were expected to have more in common, for instance when discussing membership activities during the crisis.

terforce to these tendencies, *viral policies* allocated new resources to selected (new) organisations. Second, the focus groups helped reflect on the *nature of affectedness*, which simultaneously affects the ability to provide valuable information in an 'upwards'-way to gatekeepers, as well as 'downwards', to affected (member) groups. Furthermore, interviewees indicate that some groups experienced actual cascades of attention, and that affectedness by COVID-19 also played a role in the organisations' strategic framing of issues. Finally, the focus group interviews added important perspectives on the role of *solidarity* during the crisis, which meant that some groups down-prioritised their own causes – or even held back points of criticism – in light of more pressing medical, societal and economic challenges.

Focus Groups as Opportunities for Sharing Experiences

As we argued in Chapter 1, the COVID-19 pandemic has been an unexpected and highly impactful focussing event, which hit organisations as a major shock to which they had to adapt. In order to learn about whether, how, and to what effect lobbying practices adapted to this shock, we conducted twelve focus group interviews with four interest group representatives each. Focus groups are interviews taking place in small groups where the moderator takes a less intrusive role compared to a classical interview (Cyr 2019). This provided a setting for *actual experience sharing* between organisations, all of which were at the time impacted by the pandemic (in different ways and to a varying degree). We held the focus group interviews online in the spring of 2021, that is, approximately one year after the first wave of the virus in Europe.

The main content and communicated goal of the interviews was to exchange 'best practices' during the ongoing COVID-19 pandemic. Organisations were easily recruited to participate with a recruitment rate after first contact of approximately 70 percent. In the interviews, group representatives tended to interact frequently with each other and shared detailed information about their experiences. As moderators, we could witness the dynamics that unfolded between group representatives with regards to the willingness of sharing advocacy knowledge with different organisations (see: Berkhout et al. 2021, which also provide further details on our focus group design)[35]. In addition, the focus

---

[35] The focus group interviews lasted for 45 to 60 minutes. We moderated our focus groups based on the same interview guide in all countries. For details on the focus group composition and interview guide, consult the book's Online Appendix (Chapter 7).

group interviews provided rich informational content when it comes to which lobbying practices worked well for interest groups during the pandemic.

In this chapter, we use transcriptions and *verbatims* from the interviews. In particular, we analysed the parts of the transcribed meetings where participants reflected on their experiences with lobbying, their success and failures during the pandemic, and assess how the shared experiences help reflect on our findings regarding the importance of *resources* and *affectedness* for viral lobbying. First, we summarise how these shared experiences speak to the importance of resources. Next, we describe accounts that revolve around the role of more affected interests and organisations. Finally, we add a third account that arose from the interviews and has partly been missing in the quantitative findings: the role of solidarity and community in lobbying during the pandemic.

Resources and Viral Lobbying

A main finding from Chapters 3, 4, 5 and 6 was that better-resourced groups (and business groups and firms) enjoyed advantages throughout the influence production process. The focus groups provide some interesting insights into the potential reasons for this finding in terms of 1) the ability of resourceful groups to provide *information*, and 2) the tendency of well-endowed organisations to benefit from previous ties with policymakers and *insiderness* in policy networks. At the same time, the interviews illustrate that, 3) in reaction to the crisis, large inflows of *new resources* were distributed to some organisations, changing the lobbying landscape. In the following subsections, we present selected examples of *verbatims* from the interviews that illustrate these tendencies.

Resources and Information Provision

A common observation throughout the focus groups was that public authorities tended to be overwhelmed by the complexity and severity of the crisis and lacked the necessary knowledge and information to respond to different societal and economic needs and, therefore, to develop effective policies. Interest groups with the capacity to collect, select and supply relevant information were thus in a good position to secure lobbying advantages.

One respondent representing an NGO in the health sector observed that the health authorities *"first had to build everything up (...) they did not know what they should answer to questions, because they did not know the answers"*. A respondent working for an organisation in the same sector added to this logic:

"*Politicians do not have time to delve into all issues by themselves. They look for input on the issues that dominate the agenda. The moment you can give them something relevant, something which they can use to profile themselves... then that is very good. In this case, it is easy to get a member of parliament to listen to you*". Being able to supply meaningful policy input requires an adequately staffed organisation, even when the policy doors are wide open. One respondent from a volunteer-run organisation representing parents pointed to the implications of this requirement: "*In terms of organisation, it is difficult and I have to do many activities without [financial] compensation. We are at the point where we need to professionalise [to be able to meet the information demands of policy makers]*".

A major benefit for well-resourced organisations with higher numbers of staff working on lobbying and public affairs was that they were better positioned to respond to policymakers' needs and fill this informational vacuum. This observation resonates well with existing interest group literature, which emphasises the link between (human or monetary) resources and information, which is a key exchange good in lobbying (e. g. Bernhagen 2013; Chalmers 2013; De Bruycker 2016; Flöthe 2019; Hanegraaff and De Bruycker 2020; Klüver 2012).

Resources and Insiderness

At the same time, the respondents in our focus group interviews suggested that some groups enjoyed special advantages in lobbying, because they already enjoyed close ties to political gatekeepers before the crisis. The nurturing of such long-term contacts takes substantial investment in organisational staff. Informational exchanges were particularly beneficial for interest groups with prior ties to civil servants and politicians. As existing literature suggests, these tend to be better-resourced (or economic) organisations (cf. Dür and Mateo 2016; Fraussen, Beyers, and Donas 2015; Fraussen and Beyers 2016).

Evidence from the focus group interviews illustrates this point, for instance, with the contrast between the following statements made by two NGOs working in the health sector. The first is a large and professionalised organisation and indicates that it was not difficult to access policymakers during the crisis: "*Together with [other organisation] we have had structural meetings with the Ministry of Health – long before Corona. And yes, our contacts with the Ministry are tight.*" In contrast, the second NGO, who lacked these ties, explained why they could not get access to the policymaking process: "*We could not get any contact with civil servants and politicians. Again, we were at the end of the line. There are umbrella organisations (...) who talk to them. This is a big problem, because these (...) are controlled by patient organisations with paid staff. These are all in the same build-ing or are closely located, they lunch together, it's a network where volunteer organ-isations cannot enter."*

Across focus group interviews, and irrespective of the sector of activity, we found evidence for the importance of previous networks for securing access and influence on government policies during the pandemic. Such networks exist to the extent that organisations have the resources to build and sustain them. A representative of a union, for instance, shared that their organisation *"had the advantage of being used to it"*, that is a close cooperation with relevant ministries. *"We knew each other really well in advance, and had all the secret, pri-vate phone numbers of everyone, so we could talk with each other"*, the respond-ent said. An NGO in the health sector that did not have previous strong ties, frus-trated with lack of access, commented: *"All the listed numbers are for offices that are empty, and not everyone redirected their phones, so if you don't have a list of personal contacts, you're very much restricted to email and emails are not appro-priate for everything"*.

Even organisations without previous ties, but that managed to access policy-making during the pandemic seem to have faced difficulties to connect to deci-sion makers, especially given that physical meetings were so rare (if not entirely absent). As a representative of a profession association active in the health sector with only few years of experience in the job put it: *"Those with a lot of experience and a big network have noticed this less, but (...) political interest representation has been hard, because one only had these (online) meetings, which are easy to set up, but lack the real and informal aspects"*.

In short, the focus group interviews suggest that previous contacts were im-portant, not least given the online format of lobbying during the pandemic. It seems that organisations which had existing ties to politicians were clearly in the drivers' seat of viral lobbying; and we know from previous research that such insider organisations tend to be better resourced groups (Crepaz, Hane-graaff, and Salgado 2021; Dür and Mateo 2016; Rasmussen and Gross 2015). In addition to the advantages when it comes to collecting and communicating in-formation, this might be a second mechanism that explains our central finding on resources.

At the same time, however, the focus group interviews pointed to a blind spot of our analysis of resources: It hardly took *new* resources into account that were allocated after the outbreak of the pandemic.

New Resource Provision during the Pandemic

Several of our focus group respondents also highlighted that the pandemic had changed the rules of the game, because large amounts of new resources were made available to interest groups to tackle the challenges posed by the pandemic. This opened new doors for otherwise more peripheral interest groups. An NGO in the health sector, for instance, shared that it *"had never before been invited to so many meetings, so in that sense (they) came much closer (to decision-making)"*. At the same time, the organisation was able to secure money through different channels for some of its (new) activities.

Two other organisations, the first an NGO in the health sector, the second a membership association in the sport and culture sector said that *"there was really, really a lot of money spitted out"* and there was *"a level of funding to distribute that would be way above anything that [they] had had before"*. Both observations signal that it had been much harder to secure financial support before the pandemic. As another respondent representing a health-related NGO put it: *"Before this, we could come with ideas regarding some (problem) that should be solved, which almost did not cost anything, compared to the astronomical amounts, that are sent out into society now"*.

Interestingly, some respondents suggested that this funding was not always exclusively Coronavirus-project related, but also structural in nature. An NGO working on poverty relief, for example, noted a *"breakthrough in structural funding due to the Corona crisis"*. In contrast, a couple of other NGOs without an explicit pandemic-related cause noted that government support programs overlooked them. An NGO working on (international) human rights noted that 2020 was *"the year of rejected subsidy proposals"*. And a patient NGO told us that they could not apply for usual subsidies for (self-help) meetings, because they could not organise these meetings.

It is interesting to ask how the allocation of such new resources during the pandemic fits in with our findings. Notably, our focus group interviews suggest that especially groups in the health and social sector enjoyed new inflows of resources to fund their activities, such as channelling information to their members, as well as to decision makers. Assumedly, these are organisations and constituencies that were *highly affected* by the pandemic, which means that policymakers might partly have tried to counter resource shortages for affected organisations. In the next section, we reflect more on what the evidence from the focus group meetings suggests when it comes to the effects of affectedness on viral lobbying.

Affectedness and Viral Lobbying

The experiences shared in the focus group interviews also provided insights that speak to our other finding, namely that higher affectedness by the pandemic entailed advantages throughout the influence production process. The focus group responses highlighted especially 1) the role of affected organisations in information provision, 2) demand-side forces whereby gatekeepers pull in (some) affected organisations into public policy, leading to cascades of attention, which also include the new funding inflows discussed previously. Moreover, the material from the focus groups illustrates that 3) the importance given by policymakers to the levels of affectedness by the pandemic led some interest groups to *reframe* issues in terms of COVID-19 in order to gain access to policymaking and influence. We now discuss these insights in turn.

Affectedness and Information

Notably, the importance of information in viral lobbying not only favoured the inclusion of better-resourced organisations, but also more affected groups. As a respondent representing an NGO in the health sector put it: *"The government was simply dependent on that [we were] out there and could support and contribute by passing information on to the people that were affected"*. Several affected organisations conveyed in the interviews how they played an important role in processing, channelling and legitimising information to and for their members in this way. As another NGO in the health sector explained: *"[We showed the health authorities] in relationship to the Corona situation, that we acted reasonably and, in many ways, saved their asses, if I am to use an ugly term, because their communication has been miserable in many contexts (...). We had to translate, interpret and present it"*.

At the same time, other affected interest groups experienced a clear demand for their input on 'expert panels'. A leader of a health-related association of professionals, for example, shared that *"in relationship to interest representation one can say that people became fond of 'experts' again [...] and we thought it is great that we can cover that"*. As an NGO active in the health sector declared, the prominence of *expertise* also incentivised organisations to allocate resources to internal research: *"We were constantly trying to keep up with the research and trying to keep up with what policy was, and the constantly evolving situation"*.

Like well-resourced organisations, it seems that affected groups were equipped to meet the information demands of policymakers. They contributed with information 'upwards' by seeking access to political and media gatekeepers. In addition, they seem to have had an advantage when it came to ensuring that information was processed and passed on 'downwards' to affected constituents, such as vulnerable patients, health professionals and other stakeholders. In some cases, the role of these organisations as key information providers (both upwards and downwards) meant they were extremely busy, located in the 'eye of the storm', so to speak.

Affectedness and Cascades of Attention

There was ample evidence in the interviews that affected organisations in sectors such as health, social policy and education experienced heightened and at times extreme levels of attention. For example, an organisation, which represents parents in the education sector and whose members were highly affected by the crisis, highlighted how they became much more active as a result of it: *"There is much more attention to our issues and we have much more work. Our say in debates has become much larger and we get more subsidies. [...] And we didn't even have to work hard for it. I'm asked for [input in] many different discussions and events on a diversity of issues. Totally awesome"*. Similarly, an NGO in the health and social sector emphasised major changes in the relationship with politicians: *"We have more effective meetings, we have more frequent meetings, and our role has changed. So now we almost have a form of sparring partner-like function, where we can sit and play ball around these topics and say what are the real solutions, rather than before, where we came in with the hat in hand and presented a message and a problem"*.

Another NGO in the education sector shared how the heightened attention for their input spanned all (inside and outside) venues: *"The whole thing opened a channel for increased influence and increased networking, both with ministries, ministers and politicians"*. At the same time, as the respondent added, the organisation also wrote *"articles or Facebook-posts and had some completely crazy numbers of reads and users on some of [their] online media"*. In other words, also *"in relationship to media coverage [they] received huge access"*.

Put differently, some organisations were in the *"eye of the storm"*, as another respondent from a business organisation in the health sector argued. Based on the focus group evidence, it seems that these organisations tended to represent interests that were highly affected by the pandemic, which resonates with our quantitative findings.

Affectedness, Issue-Linkage and Framing

An additional perspective that was raised in the focus group interviews was that the tendency to focus on affected interests crowded out other political issues, which according to one respondent *"came to a standstill"*. As a representative of an NGO in the health sector explained to us, *"for a period of time during the pandemic nothing was allowed to be discussed during Parliament time and speaking time except for COVID related issues"* and that, in order to be heard, questions needed to be addressed to the Minister of Health instead of other ministers. This also meant that organisations had incentives to link other issues to COVID-19, meaning that they (re-)framed them in ways that were related to the pandemic. As an NGO in the health sector explained: *"There were some other agendas, that we already had difficulties [in raising], and then this did not get easier with Corona. But, well, easier in the way that as long as we talked 'Corona', then there was an open window"*. Another NGO in the health sector stated that organisations in their sector quickly realised that *"everything they were dealing with was COVID-related"*. Interest groups therefore regularly reframed issues using COVID as *'lever'* to *'get in'*, as NGOs in the health sector put it.

As a representative from a business group in the agricultural sector shared: *"If one has had success with defining one's tasks as critical for society, then it was easier to get some of the problems solved, which confronted one's members. [...] If one can talk oneself into an agenda that one contributes to the greater good, [...] then one can solve some of the problems one confronts."* Another business group in the same sector stressed that the particular circumstances of the COVID-19 pandemic opened up new possibilities: There were *"certain policies [...] that were annoying us for years and that we were told couldn't be changed under any circumstances. [Then] Covid hit and overnight the policies were changed"*.

In short, the COVID-19 crisis pushed interest groups, which were less affected by the crisis to the periphery of the political system. Some were able link their concerns to COVID-related policies, but this could only reasonably be done by a limited set of actors. The evidence from the focus groups complements our findings in Chapters 4, 5, and 6 by showing that *strategies* by less affected groups also included *framing* the COVID-19 dimension of their causes. This is likely to have affected their *access* and *influence* beyond the patterns we traced in the quantitative analysis. In addition to this, the focus groups highlighted normative and community-based considerations in strategy choice that add in important ways to our previous chapters.

Solidarity, Appropriateness and Viral Lobbying

Another reoccurring theme in the interviews was the role of civil society and potential self-restraint of organisations. Indeed, several group representatives reflected on the limited importance of their own agenda during the COVID-19 crisis. An NGO in the education sector, for instance, stressed that part of their strategy was *"an acceptance of, that all health-related issues have priority over everything else"*. A spokesperson for an organisation in the financial sector said that their focus was *"completely political, and that (they were) standing a little bit at the end of the line [...], because there [were] many things that regulate themselves"*. Other interest groups also indicated to have purposely taken a step back considering that some organisations were much more affected by the crisis. This was also illustrated by an NGO in the health sector, that indicated that, when the pandemic started, it *"understood that the focus should be on Corona. You want this problem to be solved first"*. As the respondent added: *"We realised that if we pushed for our message, we would not be going in the right direction, but gain much resentment"*. It is impossible to say to what extent such decisions were motivated by solidarity (cf. Halpin 2006), a logic of appropriateness (March and Olsen 2004), or the result of a rational calculation of the likely benefits from (not) lobbying.

In any case, the considerations nicely connect to our findings in Chapter 6 related to policy satisfaction, where organisations judge policies also based on contextual factors. Organisations, such as the above-quoted NGOs, which did not have much influence during the crisis, seemingly understood *why* governments acted the way they did. They understood that COVID-related issues had priority, and even took a deliberate step back from lobbying activity. Similarly, policy satisfaction, as we argued in Chapter 6, can exceed particularistic demands and weigh them against the general situation. In this sense, 'losers' in the interest group community (less affected groups, resource-poor organisations, and, to some degree NGOs) may, in some situations *understand* why governments take decisions which do not favour them. This might be why the lack of influence does not always translate into dissatisfaction, which is an important conclusion from our analysis in Chapter 6.

Furthermore, some respondents of our focus groups voiced that even when they were dissatisfied and critical of government policy, they were unsure how much public criticism would be appropriate during the pandemic. *"Could we allow ourselves [to criticise]? Well, we felt there was the urgent need to show that [...] the (government) strategy, [...] has been right and has been good"*. These examples shed light on how group representatives restrained from lobbying and potentially demonstrated an orientation towards the common good by taking responsibility for supporting government policies in these unprecedented times.

Chapter Summary

Through qualitative accounts of the experiences of lobbying practitioners, this chapter added a number of nuances to the quantitative findings presented in this book. In the spring of 2021, we conducted a series of focus group interviews with approximately 50 representatives of interest groups in Denmark, Ireland and the Netherlands. Their narratives point to some of the potential mechanisms that link *lobbying resources* and *affectedness* to successes and failures in lobbying during the pandemic.

Specifically, our analysis revealed at least three ways in which resources mattered. First, they were linked to an interest group's ability to meet decision makers' informational demands. The focus groups revealed that interest groups were very aware of the information-needs of decision makers. With this in mind, some of the participants declared to have spent resources on researching and producing much-needed information. Second, resources appeared to matter in building ties to decision makers *before* the pandemic. Such ties were relevant for access *during* the pandemic. In other words, who was already an 'insider', had an easier time maintaining access during the pandemic (see also: Junk et al. 2021). Third, we noticed an aspect, which potentially countered these tendencies: The *new* resources distributed by governments in the form of crisis-related funding and rescue packages. These arguably helped to level the playing field for some organisations, which would otherwise have been at the periphery of the interest group system. Additionally, some of these organisations were surprised to experience that it was substantially easier to secure funding during the pandemic compared to normal circumstances.

Our qualitative analysis also substantiated our findings on the effect of affectedness. Again, we identify three trends: First, affectedness by the pandemic appeared to be related to a dual role in information transmission: 'upwards' to policymakers, and 'downwards' to affected constituencies. Second, some affected organisations perceived themselves as situated in the 'eye of the storm' and received 'cascades of attention', which provided them with improved visibility and voice, but also put them under strain in terms of workload. Third, the interviews revealed that interest groups often reframed or linked issues to COVID-policy, as a means to gain increased attention.

Overall, this qualitative evidence from the focus groups helps understand how resources and affectedness empowered issue mobilisation, strategy use, access and influence. In line with other findings discussed in this book, better-resourced and affected organisations were the 'winners' of viral lobbying. At the same time, however, the COVID-19 circumstances offered new opportunities for less prominent interest groups. For example, new sources of income helped organisations conduct activities during the pandemic that would otherwise have been difficult to conduct. Moreover, COVID-19 offered the opportunity to reframe issues or link them to the pandemic in a way to pursue otherwise difficult policy change.

Finally, the focus groups offered a perspective that our statistical analyses of the influence production process in previous chapters could not capture. In some of the interviews, interest groups declared to have down-prioritised their lobbying activity or criticism of government policy in recognition that public health needed to be a key priority during the crisis. This points towards an aspect of lobbying that is usually absent in the interest group literature. Interest group representatives might consider the contextual importance of their own causes relative to the overall circumstances and the public good and decide whether to take political action based on an evaluation of what seems appropriate in the given situation. While this may be more unusual in normal circumstances, we believe it to be a plausible course of action in times of crises. This offers an alternative reading of *viral lobbying*, even though it remains difficult to say whether groups were motivated by solidarity with others, or by a rational and strategic calculation because they believed that lobbying against the public good could backfire. One way or the other, forces pulling organisations towards *self-restraint in lobbying* might be a fruitful avenue of future research, both in crisis circumstances and beyond.

This brings us to the end of the empirical chapters. We have provided a wide range of evidence, both quantitative and qualitative, about the role and impact of interest groups during the COVID-19 pandemic. In the final chapter, we tie the different strands of evidence together, reflect on their implications and point to other avenues for future research.

References

Berkhout, J., Crepaz, M., Hanegraaff, M., and Junk, W.M. (2021) 'A focus on focus groups: Assessing interest group learning by means of the focus group method'. *Paper presented at the ECPR General Conference, Online Event, 30 August–3 September, 2021.*

Bernhagen, P. (2013) 'When do politicians listen to lobbyists (and who benefits when they do)?'. *European Journal of Political Research* 52(1):20–43.

Chalmers, A.W. (2013) 'Trading information for access: informational lobbying strategies and interest group access to the European Union'. *Journal of European Public Policy* 20(1):39–58.

Crepaz, M., Hanegraaff, M., and Salgado, R.S. (2021) 'A golden key can open any door? Public funding and interest groups' access'. *West European Politics* 44(2):378–402.

Cyr, J. (2019) *Focus groups for the social science researcher*, Cambridge: Cambridge University Press.

De Bruycker, I. (2016) 'Pressure and Expertise: Explaining the Information Supply of Interest Groups in EU Legislative Lobbying'. *JCMS: Journal of Common Market Studies* 54(3):599–616.

Dür, A., and Mateo, G. (2016) *Insiders versus Outsiders: Interest Group Politics in Multilevel Europe*, Oxford: Oxford University Press.

Flöthe, L. (2019) 'Technocratic or democratic interest representation? How different types of information affect lobbying success'. *Interest Groups & Advocacy* 8(2):165–183.

Fraussen, B., and Beyers, J. (2016) 'Who's in and who's out?: Explaining access to policymakers in Belgium'. *Acta Politica* 51(2):214–36.

Fraussen, B., Beyers, J., and Donas, T. (2015) 'The Expanding Core and Varying Degrees of Insiderness: Institutionalised Interest Group Access to Advisory Councils'. *Political Studies* 63(3):569–88.

Halpin, D.R. (2006) 'The Participatory and Democratic Potential and practice of Interest Groups: between Solidarity and Representation'. *Public Administration* 84(4):919–40.

Hanegraaff, M., and De Bruycker, I. (2020) 'Informational demand across the globe: toward a comparative understanding of information exchange'. *European Political Science Review* 12(4):525–43.

Junk, W.M., Crepaz, M., Hanegraaff, M., Berkhout, J., and Aizenberg, E. (2021) 'Changes in Interest Group Access in Times of Crisis: No Pain, No (Lobby) Gain'. *Journal of European Public Policy*, Online First.

Klüver, H. (2012) 'Informational Lobbying in the European Union: The Effect of Organisational Characteristics'. *West European Politics* 35(3):491–510.

Leech, B.L. (2014) *Lobbyists at work*, New York: Apress.

March, J.G., and Olsen, J.P. (2004) 'The logic of appropriateness'. Arena Working Papers WP 04/09. Arena, Centre for European Studies: University of Oslo. Available at: https://www.researchgate.net/profile/Johan-Olsen/publication/5014575_The_Logic_of_Appropriateness/links/55d2f0c808aec1b0429f03e4/The-Logic-of-Appropriateness.pdf (accessed June 28, 2022)

Rasmussen, A., and Gross, V. (2015) 'Biased access? Exploring selection to advisory committees'. *European Political Science Review* 7(3):343–72.

Online Appendix

https://www.degruyter.com/document/isbn/9783110783148/html

Chapter 8
Trends and Biases in Viral Lobbying and their Implications

The spread of the Coronavirus in Europe in early 2020 set a chain of events in motion that led to a set of policies nobody could have imagined. Freedom of movement was restricted in unprecedented ways with, for example, curfews and both national and international travel restrictions. Cultural, educational and retail activities were put on hold to stop the virus from spreading. At the same time, governments made enormous economic rescue packages available to protect businesses and employees from the negative repercussions of these safety measures. In addition to national recovery packages in Europe, the EU devised its 'largest stimulus package ever' (Commission 2021) as a response to the pandemic: a total of 1.8 trillion Euros in the EU's 2021–2027 long-term budget were allocated to rebuild a post-COVID-19 Europe.

All these decisions had massive effects on the lives and activities of different social and economic groups. One of the key ways for such interests to express their concerns and needs during the pandemic was through political activity taking the form of *viral lobbying*, which we defined as all organised attempts to influence public debates or policies during the COVID-19 pandemic (see Chapter 1).

Under the extreme strain of this crisis, a myriad of interest groups competed for attention and support to represent different interests and voice the concerns of affected sections of the population. To illustrate, the organisation Eurochild, which is a network of organisations and individuals working with and for children in Europe, tried to draw attention to the fact that the 'COVID-19 pandemic has exacerbated existing problems of social inequality, with [...] school closures creating a wider educational divide, impacting children's life chances, and their physical and mental health' (Eurochild 2020). Eurochild and its members, therefore, called for 'recovery plans that take children's needs into account' (ibid). At the same time, the European Tourism Sector pleaded through the European Tourism Manifesto for 'urgent supportive measures to reduce the devastating impact of COVID-19' (HOTREC 2020). The organisation pointed out that millions of jobs were 'currently at stake, while many small and medium enterprises (SMEs) risk closing their business'. So, the organisation argued that 'support for tourism must be a priority in the crisis response, recovery plans and actions of affected economies' (ibid). These examples constitute just two of the extensive lobbying efforts interest groups advanced during the pandemic, of which many did not even make the newspapers.

In this book, we analysed quantitatively what characterised such *viral lobbying* efforts at different stages of the *influence production process*. Specifically, we looked at the *mobilisation* of interest groups after the outbreak of the pandemic (Chapter 3), the *strategies* used by groups seeking to influence and secure their survival (Chapter 4), their *access* to policymakers and the media (Chapter 5), and, ultimately, their *influence* on COVID-19-related policies (Chapter 6). Moreover, we reflected on our quantitative findings based on the diverse experiences shared with us by lobbying practitioners in three countries (Chapter 7).

Throughout the chapters, we were interested in evaluating whether there is support for what we labelled more *optimistic* or *pessimistic accounts* of lobbying in times of crisis. More pessimistic views of lobbying (Olson 1965, 1982; Schattschneider 1960) would expect systematic advantages for business groups and better-resourced organisations throughout the influence production process. In contrast, more optimistic accounts would assume that lobbying reflects the underlying changes and needs that exist at the societal level (Truman 1951). In times of COVID-19, that would have meant that groups that were highly affected by the pandemic should have been drawn into political activity, should have enjoyed the attention of subsequently better-informed gatekeepers and exerted a constructive influence on resulting policy choices.

To test these accounts, we traced the explanatory power of three main factors throughout all phases of the influence production process: *resources*, *group type* and the *level of affectedness* by the pandemic. In each chapter, we employed several alternative measures of the outcome variable of interest, each of which captures a different aspect of the stages of the influence production process. In this way, we captured differences in degree and type of *issue mobilisation*, *strategies*, *access* and *influence*, as well as variation over time throughout the pandemic.

Our analysis of viral lobbying in eight European polities is based on two waves of a cross-country survey (Junk et al. 2020; Junk et al. 2021b), which we conducted at different stages of the pandemic (see Chapter 2 for details) and complemented with qualitative focus group interviews (see Chapter 7). The findings of these endeavours show that the glass is both half-full and half-empty when it comes to the explanatory power and associated normative evaluation of our three factors (*resources*, *group type* and the level of *affectedness*), as we will summarise in the following sections.

Evidence for 'Pessimistic' Views of Viral Lobbying

We find strong evidence that better *resourced,* i.e. better staffed, groups enjoyed advantages at each step of the influence production process. They were more likely to mobilise after the outbreak of the pandemic, and they did so faster and more intensely than less resourced organisations (Chapter 3). Better-resourced organisations were able to use all types of inside and outside strategies more frequently than less resourceful groups (Chapter 4), accessed venues of decision-making and public debate more frequently and were even contacted more frequently by political gatekeepers themselves (Chapter 5). In that sense, both the supply-side of lobbying (i.e. the strategies of groups) and the demand-side (i.e. the behaviour of political decision makers) favoured better-resourced groups during the pandemic. Reaching the final stage of the influence production process, we found that better resourced groups also saw themselves as more impactful on the passage of COVID-19-related policies and attained their policy preferences to a higher degree than less resourceful organisations (Chapter 6). Tracing this mechanism in focus group interviews, we conclude that such resource advantages in the influence production process most likely relate to an interest group's improved ability to provide useful information to gatekeepers and being recognised as insider by politicians and journalists themselves (Chapter 7).

Thus, the verdict based on our analyses at different stages of the lobbying process and different points in time (2020 and 2021) is clear: during the COVID-19 pandemic, low lobbying resources (measured as low staff capacities for policy work and public affairs) were a clear hindrance for interest representation. Against the backdrop of existing research this finding is remarkable, because, in general, the effects of resources on lobbying success have been inconclusive (see for instance: Baumgartner et al. 2009, 190–214; Mahoney 2007; Klüver 2011), or identified as being contingent on contextual factors (Dür and Mateo 2014; Stevens and De Bruycker 2020). In contrast, our findings are unambiguous: at all stages of the influence production process, organisations with higher lobbying resources enjoyed advantages. This finding arguably supports a *pessimistic* view of lobbying in contemporary democracies and suggest that there are 'elitist' tendencies in lobbying, as Olson (1965) and Schattschneider (1960) warned.

An important follow up question is how (unequally) these resources are distributed between interest groups in the European polities we studied. Our findings would be more worrying if lobbying resources were available only to organisations representing narrow interests. As shown in Chapter 2, however, the distribution of resources among organisations is fairly even (at least in our data), between the three categories, as well as across the three group types we investigated. This is (at least) a first indication that different types of organisations are able to attract (member and government) resources, and this includes also organisations that represent broadly shared societal views (also see Chapter 7 for a discussion of the distribution of new resources during the pandemic). That said, resource advantages are still a problem in interest group communities and they do bias lobbying. Governments should therefore be aware of their potential impact on the policymaking process (Crepaz and Hanegraaff 2020; Mahoney 2008; Salgado 2014).

Our findings regarding the effects of *group type* also speak to the more pessimistic interpretations of *viral lobbying*. We find evidence for biases in favour of business organisations or other economic groups, yet these are not as consistent throughout all stages of the influence production or alternative measures of our outcome variables. There is evidence that NGOs and citizen groups were disadvantaged compared to business organisations in several instances: they mobilised at a slower pace and less intensely (Chapter 3); they used *inside* strategies less often (Chapter 4); compared to trade unions and profession groups, NGOs and citizen groups were also clearly contacted less often by political gatekeepers both in the early and later phases of the pandemic (Chapter 5); finally, they reached lower levels of perceived impact and preference attainment compared to business groups (Chapter 6). Nevertheless, it needs to be stressed that our analyses provide a nuanced picture regarding both advantages and disadvantages for different group types. We found, for instance, that NGOs and citizens were *more* involved than business organisations in the use of social media strategies. This is adds to other research, which shows that different interest group types enjoy advantages in different venues of public policy (Binderkrantz, Christiansen, and Pedersen 2015), while evidence for the effect of group type is mixed (e.g. Beyers 2004; Binderkrantz and Pedersen 2019; Eising 2007; Dür, Bernhagen, and Marshall 2015; Rasmussen and Carroll 2013).

Figure 8.1 summarises our findings that document biases based on resources and group type at different stages of the influence production process.

Evidence for 'Optimistic' Views of Viral Lobbying

At the same time, our analyses, also provide evidence for a more optimistic view of lobbying, a (half) full glass, so to speak: They show that lobbying at all stages of the influence process was responsive to the changes in societal interests after the outbreak of the pandemic. We see the pandemic as an example of an 'actual' *focusing event* (see Chapter 1) triggering interest groups to lobby (i.e. a supply side response) and gatekeepers to consult relevant groups (i.e. at the demand

Evidence for 'pessimistic' lobbying theories stressing biases in influence production

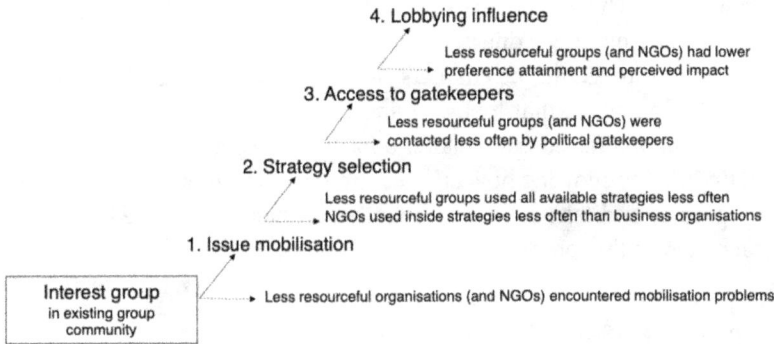

4. Lobbying influence

Less resourceful groups (and NGOs) had lower
preference attainment and perceived impact

3. Access to gatekeepers

Less resourceful groups (and NGOs) were
contacted less often by political gatekeepers

2. Strategy selection

Less resourceful groups used all available strategies less often
NGOs used inside strategies less often than business organisations

1. Issue mobilisation

Interest group
in existing group
community

Less resourceful organisations (and NGOs) encountered mobilisation problems

Figure 8.1: Problems in the lobbying process: Summary of the effects of resources and group type.

side) to inform new policies. More specifically, we found that organisations that were more *affected* by the pandemic were more likely to mobilise and did so at a higher pace and more intensely (Chapter 3). They also used all types of influence-seeking strategies more frequently (Chapter 4), accessed policymaking and public debate more frequently *and* were also contacted more frequently by policymakers themselves during the early months of the pandemic, and by both political and media gatekeepers one year into the crisis (Chapter 5). Finally, more affected organisations registered higher levels of perceived impact on COVID-19 related policies both in the first months of the pandemic and one year later (Chapter 6). As documented in our focus group interviews, such advantages have likely been associated with the affected groups' ability to act as transmission belts between government and affected constituencies, providing an 'upwards' and 'downwards' channel for the flow of information (Chapter 7). Thanks to this role, affected groups received 'cascades of attention', which have sometimes put them under intensive strain and workload.

Interestingly, however, more affected organisations were neither more likely to attain their policy preferences compared to less affected organisations, nor were they more satisfied with policy outcomes (Chapter 6). This might suggest that policies after a focussing event attend to affected groups to compensate for negative impacts, but do not necessarily *favour* affected groups in a way to fully compensate their losses, compared to the less affected actors. Moreover, the implications of *viral politics* may have been so broad that the benefits of policy outcomes also spilled over to less affected groups, even if these took a step back from lobbying to leave room for stakeholders lobbying on urgent crisis-related issues (Chapter 7). At the same time, groups had the option to *reframe* their agendas in terms of COVID-19 to have a voice in policymaking (Chapter 7), which nuances our finding on affectedness.

Still, our evidence throughout the chapters clearly documents, based on the case of the COVID-19 pandemic, that lobbying and gatekeeper practices help ensure the representation of affected groups after a focussing event. Figure 8.2 summarises these findings by showing how affected groups move through the influence production process and take more prominent roles than less affected organisations at each step of this process.

Evidence for 'optimistic' lobbying theories stressing responsiveness to the focussing event

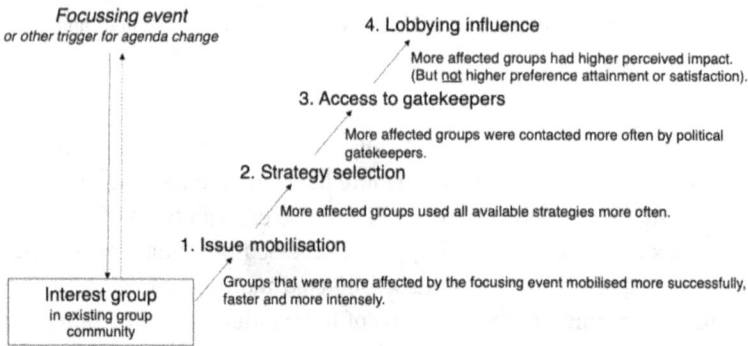

Figure 8.2: Responsiveness in the lobbying process: Summary of the effects of affectedness.

Our analyses throughout the chapters here attended to both the supply-side of lobbying (mobilisation and strategy use), and the demand-side (patterns in gatekeeper contact), as well as their combination (access and influence). Notably, our results show that the political system was more responsive to affected organisations throughout the entire influence production process; and this was a function of both supply-side and demand-side practices during the pandemic.

We see this focus on affectedness of interest groups by a focussing event as an important addition to a *normative* evaluation of the role of interest groups. As we argued throughout the book, we consider it important that interest effectively signal changes in society or plausible implications of policy initiatives to political gatekeepers, who, in turn, consult these groups to inform policy reactions. That is, *responsiveness* of affected parts of the group system to a focussing event, as well as policymakers' *responsiveness* to these affected groups is impor-

tant for the groups themselves, as well as for the quality of public policy outcomes in terms of the information weighted, the likely support and effectiveness
in the realisation of policy objectives (see also: Lindblom 1968).

Implications beyond the Pandemic

To sum up, our analyses entail both good and bad news about lobbying during
the COVID-19 pandemic. The bad news first: The lack of lobbying resources was a
clear hindrance for interest representation at all stages of the lobbying process.
Not only did less resourced groups lobby less, but the practices of gatekeepers
also disfavoured them – instead of supporting them by pulling them into the political process, which would arguably be desirable. The good news, however, is
that both groups and gatekeepers managed well when it comes to ensuring
that more affected interests received a voice in politics.

One can further ask: what do these patterns in 'viral lobbying' tell us about
interest group politics in more general terms? Some may argue: 'not a great deal'
given the pandemic was such an exceptional and unique situation. We disagree.
There is evidence of a high degree of continuity with non-crisis circumstances,
even though COVID-19 gave rise to unprecedented political situations. Bonafont
and Iborra (2021, 21), for instance, show that the COVID-19 pandemic 'did not
alter business groups' position in the policymaking process' in Spain. Eady
and Rasmussen (2021) suggest that the pandemic has not drastically changed
biases in lobbying at the EU-level, and Junk et al. (2021a) show that access to
different gatekeepers in nine European countries and at the EU-level has remained constant for approximately 60 percent of interest groups after the pandemic broke out.

To put it in the words of Fraussen et al. (2020), the COVID-19 pandemic
seems to have brought out 'the good, bad, and the ugly' in lobbying, in the
sense that it exemplified good and bad tendencies in lobbying that also exist
in non-crisis times. This is also how we interpret our findings: the patterns we
documented throughout the book – advantages for better-resourced organisations, as well as a responsiveness to affected groups – are general trends in interest group politics, and what we observed here is likely to characterise other
lobbying situations.

Policy Implications of our Findings

This book can inform a number of practical lessons for decision makers interested in fostering more equality in lobbying access and influence both in crisis and normal circumstances. As we document throughout Chapters 3 and 4, less resourced groups are less likely to engage in political action and use inside and outside lobbying strategies less frequently. If their voice ought to be included equally in policymaking, then demand-side forces are needed to identify them and pull them into the process (see Chapter 5). There are different ways how this can be achieved.

First, policymakers can use consultation instruments, which proactively invite interest representatives to participate in the policy process. These instruments are on the rise in European policymaking (Bunea 2013; Bunea and Thomson 2015; Binderkrantz, Blom-Hansen, and Senninger 2021; Fraussen, Albareda, and Braun 2020; Klüver 2012). However, while consultations offer an open platform of participation, their effectiveness in terms of meaningful consultation and impact remains contested (Fraussen, Albareda, and Braun 2020; Braun and Busuioc 2020).

Second, policymakers can specifically seek to pull less active and disadvantaged interest groups into the policy process. The challenge in this case is that it is difficult to identify such interest groups. Laws to improve lobbying transparency, such as lobbying registers, can help policymakers and journalists to map the interest group population, making it easier to document and correct biases in interest representation (Chari et al. 2020; Crepaz 2020; Fraussen and Braun 2018; Năstase and Muurmans 2020).

An alternative or complementary intervention targets the resource differences themselves. It is common practice that NGOs partly rely on government support to fund their activities. At the same time, research shows that better-resourced organisations and well-represented groups have better chances of obtaining grants (Crepaz and Hanegraaff 2020; Persson and Edholm 2018). Our results suggest that equitable grant allocation practices can play an important role in ensuring that groups can participate in policy processes also in crisis circumstances. Conversely, limitations to the extent to which funding can be used for advocacy and political action may undermine the ability of 'weaker' organised interests to mobilise and diversify the use of strategies of political action (Chavesc, Stephens, and Galaskiewicz 2004; Mosley 2012; Neumayr, Schneider, and Meyer 2013; Leech 2006). With the purpose of empowering political participation, public donors could allocate some funding towards projects that aim at improving advocacy efforts and lobbying for organisations under a certain threshold of political activity.

In a long-term perspective, a combination of measures can be fruitful to level the playing field when it comes to the involvement of less resourced actors. At the same time, with such measures in place, interest group communities could find themselves better prepared when new crises hit political systems in the future. In crises circumstances, having an attentive eye on marginal and less resourced organisations is arguably especially important. When urgency drives decision-making, it is normal for policymakers to select and listen to groups that are well-adapted to give efficient and information-rich consultation input. However, such practice can bias policy outputs, especially in situations where political outsiders could also contribute with important perspectives for solving new policy problems.

By the same token, our findings imply that interest groups should strategically invest in advocacy and public affairs capacities, if they wish to have a say in policymaking. Our results show that lobbying resources correlate with issue mobilisation, a broad use of lobbying strategies, but also access and influence. This may be because lobbying becomes more professionalised when conducted by designated public affairs staff, but may also relate to the fact that higher numbers of lobbying staff help interest groups become visible and 'get noticed' by policymakers and journalists. When organisations receive new funding, it can therefore pay off to use parts of the newly acquired resources to empower lobbying capacity, including information gathering on new policy problems and their effects on members (see Chapter 7).

At the same time, any attempts to improve policy or lobbying practices based on our study need to take into account that all findings are *contextual*. An important caveat for our results is that they do not necessarily hold across all *policy issues*. A key finding in existing lobbying research is that the characteristics of a policy issue, such as its complexity, the level of conflict and its salience, are an important explanatory factor for lobbying patterns and success (Klüver 2011; Junk 2016; Rasmussen, Mäder, and Reher 2018; Junk 2019). While our results draw a picture across policy issues related to COVID-19, nuances at the issue level should be taken into account.

Implications of Context Conditions

The COVID-19 pandemic is an example of a *highly salient* issue where many interest groups jumped on the 'bandwagon' (Baumgartner and Leech 2001; Halpin 2011) and became active on COVID-19 related policies. We would argue that our findings are likely to travel to other issues that are characterised by such high salience. When a policy issue dominates media headlines, at least for a period of time (cf. Downs' issue attention cycles (1972)), there is a good chance that affected organisations will mobilise into the policymaking process and will be further pulled into decision-making by political gatekeepers. As we argued in Chapter 1, *viral lobbying* can even be interpreted to denote the situation where a highly salient issue attracts high levels of lobbying activity (i.e. 'goes viral'), and our results are likely to be informative in such contexts.

When it comes to less salient issues, however, where only a handful of interest groups mobilise and there is little or no media attention, the rules of the lobbying game are likely to be quite different. As Schattschneider (1960, 20) put it, the 'outcome of the political game depends on the scale on which it is played': when salience and conflict is low, both interest groups and political gatekeepers are likely to have different incentives than on salient issues. This is likely to affect the entire influence production process, as some existing studies also document by showing that patterns in lobbying success vary on more and less salient issues (Junk 2019; Klüver 2011; Rasmussen, Mäder, and Reher 2018).

How our findings travel to less salient issues is therefore an open question and should be tested in future research. Arguably, *more salient* issues, such as the COVID-19 pandemic, are *most likely cases* for finding an impact of affectedness. That is, without the pressure of public and media attention, affected interest groups arguably have lower incentives and opportunities to mobilise intensely, given their members, stakeholders and potential influence targets are likely to pay less attention to their activities. At the same time, on issues with low salience, gatekeepers are less likely to fear being penalised in terms of decreasing public support or electoral consequences for a lack of responsiveness to affected interests. In Hacker and Pierson's (2014) words, they may operate in the 'electoral blindspot' and can cater more to moneyed interests even against broader public interests, without the fear of electoral punishment. On highly salient issues, in contrast, incentives to mobilise and consult affected groups should be higher. These types of issue-specific hypotheses have increasingly been the focus of recent studies of interest group politics (e.g. Hanegraaff and Berkhout 2019; Junk 2016; Klüver 2011), but the particular interrelation between affectedness, salience, and, plausibly, group type surely merits attention in future research.

Innovations and Avenues for Future Research

We hope that our analyses are useful for future researchers and practitioners that seek to design studies to evaluate the effects of lobbying. We first reflect on the distinct ways in which we measured outcomes and subsequently identify promising avenues for future research related to the key explanatory factors studied.

Novel Measures of Lobbying Outcomes

To start, throughout the chapters, we exemplify the diverse ways in which we can capture steps in the influence production process as outcome variables. Table 8.1 summarises the diverse measures we employed throughout the book for these important outcomes of interest. As the table shows, our measures include both more common operationalisations, as well as additional operationalisations that have not often been used before. We hope that our focus on pace (Chapter 3), survival-seeking strategies (Chapter 4), demand-driven access (Chapter 5), and policy satisfaction of interest groups (Chapter 6) adds new nuances to the study of interest group politics and its effects.

Table 8.1: Overview of dependent variables to operationalise stages in the influence production process.

	Mobilisation	Strategies	Access	Influence
More common operationalisations	Issue mobilisation (*binary*) Mobilisation intensity (*count or frequency of activity*)	Influence-seeking inside strategies: government, parliament, bureaucracy (*frequency of use*) Influence-seeking outside strategy: media and social media (*frequency of use*)	Inside access: government, parliament, bureaucracy (*frequency of access*) Outside access: media (*frequency of access*)	Perceived impact (*level of impact of policy decisions*) Preference attainment (*extent to which policies reflected preferences*)
Additional (newer) operationalisations	Mobilisation pace (*early or later time intervals*)	Survival-seeking inside and outside strategies: resource-extraction, public-oriented and base-oriented strategies (*frequency of use*)	Demand-driven access: contact initiated by inside and outside gatekeepers (*binary or frequency of contact*)	Policy satisfaction (*level of satisfaction*)

Notably, we relied exclusively on survey data in two waves or our cross-country survey to capture different facets of these important concepts (see Chapter 2). Future research could further develop these (new) operationalisations, potentially adding other data sources, such as (automated) coding of websites or social media content, newspaper articles, consultation responses and policy documents (Aizenberg and Binderkrantz 2021; Bunea and Ibenskas 2015; Dwidar 2022; Grimmer and Stewart 2013; Klüver 2009), for instance, with a focus on timing (Crepaz, Hanegraaff, and Junk 2022). Interviews with lobbyists and gatekeepers could also provide additional data needed to account for the motivations behind particular activities and the effects of the contextual factors (Baumgartner et al. 2009; Beyers et al. 2014; Leech 2002; Statsch and Berkhout 2020). In this book, we used focus group interviews (Cyr 2019), which we see as a fruitful research strategy to investigate interest group experiences and interactions (cf. Berkhout et al. 2021). In twelve online focus groups with approximately 50 participants, we were able to collect rich qualitative data on how interest representatives perceived the role of resource constrains and affectedness during the pandemic (see Chapter 7). We argue that this method, which is rarely used in political science, has high potential when participants are interest group representatives.

Substantively, there are a number of open questions connected to these newer operationalisations that we have presented in the book: How and when does mobilising early lead to first mover advantages in lobbying (see also: Crepaz, Hanegraaff, and Junk 2022)? How do survival-seeking and influence-seeking strategies complement or compromise each other? To what extent are the decisions by gatekeepers to contact interest groups dependent on interpersonal relationships and/or on institutionalised party-interest group connections (see: Allern et al. 2021)? And, is it a broader trend that policy satisfaction varies so little between different types of actors as it did during the pandemic? In addition to raising these questions, our findings on the three main explanatory factors may fruitfully inform future studies.

Future Research Directions based on our Findings

We have several future research suggestions deriving from our findings on *resources*, *group type* and *affectedness*, respectively. As noted, we found staff resources to be an important explanatory factor in all stages of the influence production process. At the same time, more work is needed to assess the actual normative implications of this finding; both in terms of 'bias' in interest representation and the instrumental value of interest representation for public policy.

In studies of US lobbying and campaign finance, lobbying power and 'money' is typically assumed to be highly unequally distributed and there are fears of 'regulatory capture' (Carpenter and Moss 2013; Dal Bó 2006) by moneyed interests that shift policy away from the public interest and towards special (industry) interests. When this is the case, an effect of resources on lobbying influence is a strong indicator of representational 'bias' in politics, and a clear substantiation of pessimistic views on interest representation. However, it remains an open question whether and when well-resourced organisations systematically lobby to counter public interests.

As Flöthe and Rasmussen (2019) show, for example, firms and business associations often lobby for positions that enjoy the support of a sizable share of the public. Similar patterns might hold for well-resourced organisations, some of which use their resources to advocate for highly popular positions. Further empirical studies are needed to assess how and when staff resources help or hinder constituent representation and congruence between public policy and citizen interests. By extension, these studies could speak to the difficult question of whether well-staffed organisations instrumentally improve the quality of the public policy outcomes (e.g. Anderson 1977; Lindblom 1968).

As regards *group type*, throughout the conceptual sections of the chapters, we pointed to arguments that suggest that some of the effects noted are plausibly different for business organisations compared to other interest groups. At the same time, existing studies suggest that the effect of group type on lobbying strategies and influence depends on other organisation and issue characteristics (e.g. Dür and Mateo 2013; Dür, Bernhagen, and Marshall 2015). However, we did not study such potential interactions and their implications after a focussing event. As discussed above and in Chapter 1, our focus on the COVID-19 pandemic means that we studied a set of highly salient issues after a (quite unprecedented) focussing event. More generally speaking, however, such events or crisis circumstances might affect different types of groups in distinct ways, for instance providing a platform for public advocacy for some and triggering public withdrawal for others. While each event or crisis has its unique characteristics, we see strong merit in studies comparing interest representation during a broad variety of events or crises, to uncover such potential patterns.

We know that that events trigger policy processes in unexpected ways (e.g. Birkland 1997) and that party politics is (partially) event-driven (e.g. van der Brug and Berkhout 2015), but we have limited conceptual or empirical understanding of the types of events that trigger particular interest group activities (but see: LaPira 2014). At minimum, an 'event-measure' could be included in issue-level research designs, such as done by Mahoney (2008), where she found meaningful differences in the likelihood of policy change following events such as the Enron scandal in 2001, the 9/11 terrorist attack in New York, and the 2004 Madrid metro bombings. More elaborately, future studies could compare interest representation following a larger number of events and unpack the political implications of distinct event-characteristics on the stages of influence production and different types of interest groups.

Finally, our analysis of the effect of *affectedness* could be expanded in the future. In the earlier chapters of the book, we conceptually embed affectedness as a supply-side effect arising from socio-political disturbances, whereas the later chapters emphasise the demand-side needs of policymakers in search of information to design well-targeted public policies. These conceptual arguments align with the research questions posed in the different chapters, but we do not test them as empirically distinct forms of affectedness – which they potentially are. Future studies could develop such more precise *types of affectedness* (see also: Junk et al. 2021a), such as 'social affectedness' versus 'policy affectedness'. This could help to disentangle supply- and demand-side mechanisms further and advance our understanding of the role of affected organisations in the policy process.

We hope that our analyses of *viral lobbying* in this book can inform such future research. And, most importantly, we hope they have helped practitioners, students and scholars interested in this pandemic to understand the ability of interest groups to contribute to *viral politics* by voicing the needs and concerns of different social and economic groups.

References

Aizenberg, E., and Binderkrantz, A.S. (2021) 'Computational approaches to mapping interest group representation: a test and discussion of different methods'. *Interest Groups & Advocacy* 10(2):181–92.

Allern, E.H., et al. (2021) 'Conceptualizing and measuring party-interest group relationships'. *Party Politics* 27(6):1254–67.

Anderson, C.W. (1977) 'Political design and the representation of interests'. *Comparative Political Studies* 10(1):127–52.

Baumgartner, F.R., Berry, J.M., Hojnacki, M., Kimball, D.C., and Leech, B.L. (2009) *Lobbying and Policy Change: Who Wins, Who Loses, and Why*, Chicago, IL: University of Chicago Press.

Baumgartner, F.R., and Leech, B.L. (2001) 'Interest Niches and Policy Bandwagons: Patterns of Interest Group Involvement in National Politics'. *The Journal of Politics* 63(4):1191–213.

Berkhout, J., Crepaz, M., Hanegraaff, M., and Junk, W.M. (2021) 'A focus on focus groups: Assessing interest group learning by means of the focus group method'. *Paper presented at the ECPR General Conference, Online Event, 30 August–3 September, 2021.*

Beyers, J. (2004) 'Voice and access: Political practices of European interest associations'. *European Union Politics* 5(2):211–40.

Beyers, J., Braun, C., Marshall, D., and De Bruycker, I. (2014) 'Let's talk! On the practice and method of interviewing policy experts'. *Interest Groups & Advocacy* 3(2):174–87.

Binderkrantz, A.S., Blom-Hansen, J., and Senninger, R. (2021) 'Countering bias? The EU Commission's consultation with interest groups'. *Journal of European Public Policy* 28(4):469–88.

Binderkrantz, A.S., Christiansen, P.M., and Pedersen, H.H. (2015) 'Interest Group Access to the Bureaucracy, Parliament, and the Media'. *Governance* 28(1):95–112.

Binderkrantz, A.S., and Pedersen, H.H. (2019) 'The lobbying success of citizen and economic groups in Denmark and the UK'. *Acta Politica* 54(1):75–103.

Birkland, T.A. (1997) *After disaster: Agenda setting, public policy, and focusing events*, Washington D.C.: Georgetown University Press.

Bonafont, L.C., and Iborra, I.M. (2021) 'The representation of business interests during the COVID-19 pandemic in Spain'. *Revista española de ciencia política* 57(1):21–44.

Braun, C., and Busuioc, M. (2020) 'Stakeholder engagement as a conduit for regulatory legitimacy?'. *Journal of European Public Policy* 27(11):1599–611.

Bunea, A. (2013) 'Issues, preferences and ties: determinants of interest groups' preference attainment in the EU environmental policy'. *Journal of European Public Policy* 20(4):552–70.

Bunea, A., and Ibenskas, R. (2015) 'Quantitative text analysis and the study of EU lobbying and interest groups'. *European Union Politics* 16(3):429–55.

Bunea, A., and Thomson, R. (2015) 'Consultations with Interest Groups and the Empowerment of Executives: Evidence from the European Union'. *Governance* 28(4):517–31.

Carpenter, D., and Moss, D.A. (2013) *Preventing regulatory capture: Special interest influence and how to limit it*, Cambridge: Cambridge University Press.

Chari, R., Hogan, J., Murphy, G., and Crepaz, M. (2020) *Regulating lobbying: a global comparison* (2nd edn.), Manchester: Manchester University Press.

Chavesc, M., Stephens, L., and Galaskiewicz, J. (2004) 'Does Government Funding Suppress Nonprofits' Political Activity?'. *American Sociological Review* 69(2):292–316.

Commission (2021) "The 2021–2027 EU budget – What's new?". https://ec.europa.eu/info/strategy/eu-budget/long-term-eu-budget/2021-2027/whats-new_en (accessed June 23, 2022).

Crepaz, M. (2020) 'To inform, strategise, collaborate, or compete: what use do lobbyists make of lobby registers?'. *European Political Science Review* 12(3):347–69.

Crepaz, M., and Hanegraaff, M. (2020) 'The funding of interest groups in the EU: are the rich getting richer?'. *Journal of European Public Policy* 27(1):102–21.

Crepaz, M., Hanegraaff, M., and Junk, W.M. (2022) 'Is there a first mover advantage in lobbying? A comparative analysis of how the timing of lobbying affects the influence of interest groups in 10 polities'. *Comparative Political Studies*, Online First.

Cyr, J. (2019) *Focus groups for the social science researcher*, Cambridge: Cambridge University Press.

Dal Bó, E. (2006) 'Regulatory Capture: A Review'. *Oxford Review of Economic Policy* 22(2):203–25.

Downs, A. (1972) 'Up and Down with Ecology: The Issue Attention Cycle', in D.L. Protess and M. McCombs (Eds.), *Agenda Setting: Readings on Media, Public Opinion and Policymaking*, 38–50, London: Routledge.

Dwidar, M.A. (2022) 'Coalitional Lobbying and Intersectional Representation in American Rulemaking'. *American Political Science Review* 116(1):301–21.

Dür, A., Bernhagen, P., and Marshall, D. (2015) 'Interest Group Success in the European Union: When (and Why) Does Business Lose?'. *Comparative Political Studies* 48(8):951–83.

Dür, A., and Mateo, G. (2013) 'Gaining access or going public? Interest group strategies in five European countries'. *European Journal of Political Research* 52(5):660–86.

Dür, A., and Mateo, G. (2014) 'The Europeanization of interest groups: Group type, resources and policy area'. *European Union Politics* 15(4):572–94.

Eady, G., and Rasmussen, A. (2021) 'The Unequal Effects of the COVID-19 Pandemic on Political Interest Representation'. *Working paper* available at: https://www.anner asmussen.eu/wp-content/uploads/2021/06/EadyRasmussen050921.pdf (accessed June 28, 2022)

Eising, R. (2007) 'Institutional context, organizational resources and strategic choices: Explaining interest group access in the European Union'. *European Union Politics* 8(3):329–62.

Eurochild (2020) "Growing up in lockdown: Europe's children in the age of COVID-19." https://www.eurochild.org/resource/growing-up-in-lockdown-europes-children-in-the-age-of-covid-19/ (accessed June 23, 2022).

Flöthe, L., and Rasmussen, A. (2019) 'Public voices in the heavenly chorus? Group type bias and opinion representation'. *Journal of European Public Policy* 26(6):824–42.

Fraussen, B., Albareda, A., and Braun, C. (2020) 'Conceptualizing consultation approaches: identifying combinations of consultation tools and analyzing their implications for stakeholder diversity'. *Policy sciences* 53(3):473–93.

Fraussen, B., Albareda, A., Braun, C., Muller, M., and Sullivan, E. (2020) 'Blog Parts I-III: Lobbying in times of (Corona)-Crisis: the Good, the Bad and the Ugly', in Leiden University, available at: https://www.universiteitleiden.nl/en/news/2020/06/lobbying-in-times-of-corona-crisis-the-good-the-bad-and-the-ugly-i (accessed June 28, 2022)

Fraussen, B., and Braun, C. (2018) '"De Lobby'aan Banden'? Over het ongelijk speelveld en de regulering van belangenvertegenwoordiging'. *Tijdschrift voor Toezicht* 9(4):103–13.

Grimmer, J., and Stewart, B.M. (2013) 'Text as Data: The Promise and Pitfalls of Automatic Content Analysis Methods for Political Texts'. *Political Analysis* 21(3):267–97.

Hacker, J.S., and Pierson, P. (2014) 'After the "Master Theory": Downs, Schattschneider, and the Rebirth of Policy-Focused Analysis'. *Perspectives on politics* 12(3):643–62.

Halpin, D. (2011) 'Explaining Policy Bandwagons: Organized Interest Mobilization and Cascades of Attention'. *Governance* 24(2):205–30.

Hanegraaff, M., and Berkhout, J. (2019) 'More business as usual? Explaining business bias across issues and institutions in the European Union'. *Journal of European Public Policy* 26(6):843–62.

HOTREC. (2020) "European Tourism Sector Demands Urgent Supportive Measures To Reduce Devastating Impact Of Covid-19." https://www.hotrec.eu/european-tourism-sector-demands-urgent-supportive-measures-to-reduce-devastating-impact-of-covid-19/ (accessed June 23, 2022).

Junk, W.M. (2016) 'Two logics of NGO advocacy: understanding inside and outside lobbying on EU environmental policies'. *Journal of European Public Policy* 23(2):236–54.

Junk, W.M. (2019) 'When Diversity Works: The Effects of Coalition Composition on the Success of Lobbying Coalitions'. *American Journal of Political Science* 63(3): 660–74.

Junk, W.M., Crepaz, M., Hanegraaff, M., Berkhout, J., and Aizenberg, E. (2020) "InterCov Project: Online Survey on Interest Representation during Covid-19. Edition: June – July 2020." https://www.wiebkejunk.com/_files/ugd/9a0cb4_eb572405723f490f8fd6e464420 f3a33.pdf (accessed June 13, 2022).

Junk, W.M., Crepaz, M., Hanegraaff, M., Berkhout, J., and Aizenberg, E. (2021a) 'Changes in Interest Group Access in Times of Crisis: No Pain, No (Lobby) Gain'. *Journal of European Public Policy*, Online First.

Junk, W.M., Crepaz, M., Hanegraaff, M., Berkhout, J., and Aizenberg, E. (2021b) "InterCov Project: Online Survey on Interest Representation during Covid-19. Second Edition: July – August 2021." https://www.wiebkejunk.com/_files/ugd/9a0cb4_ 7d44f6c80cc84d259983d8bbdfa3a729.pdf (accessed June 13, 2022).

Klüver, H. (2009) 'Measuring Interest Group Influence Using Quantitative Text Analysis'. *European Union Politics* 10(4):535–49.

Klüver, H. (2011) 'The contextual nature of lobbying: Explaining lobbying success in the European Union'. *European Union Politics* 12(4):483–506.

Klüver, H. (2012) 'Informational Lobbying in the European Union: The Effect of Organisational Characteristics'. *West European Politics* 35(3):491–510.

LaPira, T.M. (2014) 'Lobbying after 9/11: Policy Regime Emergence and Interest Group Mobilization'. *Policy Studies Journal* 42(2):226–51.

Leech, B.L. (2002) 'Asking Questions: Techniques for Semistructured Interviews'. *PS: Political Science & Politics* 35(4):665–8.

Leech, B.L. (2006) 'Funding Faction or Buying Silence? Grants, Contracts, and Interest Group Lobbying Behavior'. *Policy Studies Journal* 34(1):17–35.

Lindblom, C.E. (1968) *The policy-making process*, Hoboken, New Jersey: Prentice-Hall.

Mahoney, C. (2007) 'Lobbying Success in the United States and the European Union'. *Journal of Public Policy* 27(1):35–56.

Mahoney, C. (2008) *Brussels versus the beltway: Advocacy in the United States and the European Union*, Washington D.C.: Georgetown University Press.

Mosley, J.E. (2012) 'Keeping the Lights On: How Government Funding Concerns Drive the Advocacy Agendas of Nonprofit Homeless Service Providers'. *Journal of Public Administration Research and Theory* 22(4):841–66.

Năstase, A., and Muurmans, C. (2020) 'Regulating lobbying activities in the European Union: A voluntary club perspective'. *Regulation & Governance* 14(2):238–55.

Neumayr, M., Schneider, U., and Meyer, M. (2013) 'Public Funding and Its Impact on Nonprofit Advocacy'. *Nonprofit and Voluntary Sector Quarterly* 44(2):297–318.

Olson, M. (1965) *The Logic of Collective Action*, Cambridge: Harvard University Press.

Olson, M. (1982) *The rise and decline of nations: Economic growth, stagflation, and social rigidities*, New Haven: Yale University Press.

Persson, T., and Edholm, K. (2018) 'Assessing the Effects of European Union Funding of Civil Society Organizations: Money for Nothing?'. *JCMS: Journal of Common Market Studies* 56(3):559–75.

Rasmussen, A., and Carroll, B.J. (2013) 'Determinants of Upper-Class Dominance in the Heavenly Chorus: Lessons from European Union Online Consultations'. *British Journal of Political Science* 44(2):445–59.

Rasmussen, A., Mäder, L.K., and Reher, S. (2018) 'With a Little Help From The People? The Role of Public Opinion in Advocacy Success'. *Comparative Political Studies* 51(2):139 – 64.

Salgado, R. (2014) 'Rebalancing EU Interest Representation? Associative Democracy and EU Funding of Civil Society Organizations'. *JCMS: Journal of Common Market Studies* 52(2):337 – 53.

Schattschneider, E.E. (1960) *The Semisovereign People: A Realist's View of Democracy in America*, New York: Holt, Rinehart and Winston.

Statsch, P., and Berkhout, J. (2020) 'Lobbying and policy conflict: explaining interest groups' promiscuous relationships to political parties'. *Interest Groups & Advocacy* 9(1):1 – 20.

Stevens, F., and De Bruycker, I. (2020) 'Influence, affluence and media salience: Economic resources and lobbying influence in the European Union'. *European Union Politics* 21(4):728 – 50.

Truman, D.B. (1951) *The Governmental Process. Political Interests and Public Opinion*, New York: Alfred A. Knopf.

van der Brug, W., and Berkhout, J. (2015) 'The Effect of Associative Issue Ownership on Parties' Presence in the News Media'. *West European Politics* 38(4):869 – 87.

Online Appendix

https://www.degruyter.com/document/isbn/9783110783148/html

www.ingramcontent.com/pod-product-compliance
Lightning Source LLC
Chambersburg PA
CBHW052009270326
41929CB00015B/2852